Enterprise
Project
Governance

Enterprise Project Governance

A Guide to the Successful
Management of Projects Across
the Organization

Paul C. Dinsmore
Luiz Rocha

⊹AMACOM

American Management Association
New York • Atlanta • Brussels • Chicago • Mexico City • San Francisco
Shanghai • Tokyo • Toronto • Washington, D. C.

Bulk discounts available. For details visit:
www.amacombooks.org/go/specialsales
Or contact special sales:
Phone: 800-250-5308
Email: specialsls@amanet.org
View all the AMACOM titles at: www.amacombooks.org

This publication is designed to provide accurate and authoritative information in regard to the subject matter covered. It is sold with the understanding that the publisher is not engaged in rendering legal, accounting, or other professional service. If legal advice or other expert assistance is required, the services of a competent professional person should be sought.

"PMI" and the PMI logo are service and trademarks of the Project Management Institute, Inc. which are registered in the United States of America and other nations; "PMP" and the PMP logo are certification marks of the Project Management Institute, Inc. which are registered in the United States of America and other nations; "PMBOK", "PM Network", and "PMI Today" are trademarks of the Project Management Institute, Inc. which are registered in the United States of America and other nations; ". . . building professionalism in project management . . ." is a trade and service mark of the Project Management Institute, Inc. which is registered in the United States of America and other nations; and the Project Management Journal logo is a trademark of the Project Management Institute, Inc.

PMI did not participate in the development of this publication and has not reviewed the content for accuracy. PMI does not endorse or otherwise sponsor this publication and makes no warranty, guarantee, or representation, expressed or implied, as to its accuracy or content. PMI does not have any financial interest in this publication, and has not contributed any financial resources.

Additionally, PMI makes no warranty, guarantee, or representation, express or implied, that the successful completion of any activity or program, or the use of any product or publication, designed to prepare candidates for the PMP* Certification Examination, will result in the completion or satisfaction of any PMP* Certification eligibility requirement or standard.

Library of Congress Cataloging-in-Publication Data
Dinsmore, Paul C.
Enterprise project governance : a guide to the successful management
    of projects across the organization / Paul C. Dinsmore and Luiz
    Rocha.
        p. cm.
        Includes bibliographical references and index.
        ISBN-13: 978-0-8144-1746-1
        ISBN-10: 8144-0-1746-9
1. Project management. 2. Strategic planning. I. Rocha, Luiz. II. Title.
    HD69.P75D568 2012
    658.4'04--dc23
                                                    2011034981

About AMA

American Management Association (www.amanet.org) is a world leader in talent development, advancing the skills of individuals to drive business success. Our mission is to support the goals of individuals and organizations through a complete range of products and services, including classroom and virtual seminars, webcasts, webinars, podcasts, conferences, corporate and government solutions, business books and research. AMA's approach to improving performance combines experiential learning—learning through doing—with opportunities for ongoing professional growth at every step of one's career journey.

Printing number
10   9   8   7   6   5   4   3   2   1

Contents

Foreword

Can an organization ever achieve full maturity in its ability to consistently deliver successful programs and projects? Can an enterprise ever achieve perfection or near perfection in the planning and management of all its projects? These are not theoretical questions. What CEO does not want to maximize profits (or mission success), while reducing risks and maintaining the approval and support of key stakeholders, especially customers, investors, and shareholders? What C-level executive does not want her or his programs and projects to be completed successfully, ahead of schedule or under budget, by knowledgeable, experienced, and capable project managers? So are real maturity and near perfection for project-oriented organizations possible? Absolutely not! Not without effective governance.

Over the last two decades, we have seen the project management field grow from a set of applications and methods for managing large individual projects to a wide range of knowledge, skills, and technologies for managing multiple projects, programs, and portfolios of programs and projects. In his classic 1998 book, *Winning in Business with Enterprise Project Management*, Paul Dinsmore captured the important global trend of the 1990s, the organizing and managing of multiple projects within organizations with consistent enterprise-wide processes, systems, and techniques in order to increase efficiency and profitability.

Enterprise Project Management, or EPM as it came to be known, gave rise to the project management office (PMO), now globally recognized as a best practice for EPM and project-oriented organizations. These led in turn to a much greater focus on the investment and return on investment in professional project management education, training, qualifications, systems development, and process improvements. Many organizations failed in their attempts to implement successful EPM and PMOs, but many others succeeded, especially those with strong executive support, customer orientation, and global competition.

During the first decade of the twenty-first century, the role and importance of programs and projects in many organizations, industries, and economies increased dramatically. This has led in turn to first the awareness and then to the sometimes painful understanding that the success of many programs and projects can dictate the success or failure of the entire organization. The need to align programs and projects with organizational strategies and missions became obvious. The project portfolio management (PPM) approach was born and was rapidly embraced by industry and project management service and technology suppliers. In the last few years, the subject of organizational project management maturity has risen in visibility and importance, as enterprise-wide efficiency and performance in project-based organizations and industries have clearly been linked to the maturity of people and processes—all in the context of international project management standards and best practices.

These trends, of course, have been reflected and supported by project management professional organizations—AIPM (Australia), APM (United Kingdom), IPMA (European, now global), and PMI (based in the United States, but with 350,000 members worldwide)—with standards, certifications, courses, publications, and services. At the same time, a very robust marketplace for PPM software, consultants, and solution providers has also emerged. In fact, we have seen the project management professional field itself grow to embrace program and portfolio management and all of the issues and needs associated with those broader enterprise-wide topics.

But increased knowledge, qualifications, processes, skills, and experience are not enough. As the dot.com bubble of the late 1990s, then the corporate failures and associated scandals such as Enron and Société Générale a few years later, dramatically displayed, someone must be looking out for the stakeholders—the shareholders, investors, employees, and general public, in many cases. As corporate governance was overhauled in America and Europe by both governmental and industry regulators, the issue of governance of projects and project-oriented organizations was raised. Who was monitoring ethical behavior, executive and managerial competence, organizational risks, customer feedback, organizational maturity, and other important factors that can affect project, program, and organizational performance on behalf of the stakeholders?

As pointed out by the authors in Chapter 1, professional leaders in the United Kingdom recognized the need for the governance of project management early, with several important guides and several books published on the topic. Now, with *Enterprise Project Governance*, Paul Dinsmore and Luiz Rocha have created a framework for more organizations around the world to both understand the topic and implement critical governance processes and structures. This is an exciting development. Independent oversight and the use of outside program and project management experts have been favorite topics of mine, addressed in several editorial articles in recent years. And I personally favor the board-level governance option. But the authors have thoroughly researched the subject and have presented a wide range of important and useful steps that can be taken to improve enterprise performance.

Outstanding project performance is great. Project management maturity is a wonderful goal. Continuous improvement is important. But wouldn't you also like to have someone checking the facts, looking at enterprise-wide issues, and identifying organizational risks, issues, and opportunities—especially in a global economy?

David L. Pells, PMI Fellow
Hon. Fellow APM (UK), PMA (India), SOVNET (Russia)
Managing Editor, *PM World Today* eJournal

Preface

This book evolved as part of a natural process. Some of our previous works were aimed at the basics of project management (*AMA Handbook of Project Management*[1]) and the people side of projects (*Human Factors in Project Management*[2]). A broader view of the world of projects was presented in *Winning in Business with Enterprise Project Management*[3] and was later complemented by *Creating the Project Office*[4] and *Right Projects Done Right.*[5] Through our research and writings, the transformation of project management from a single-project focus to a full-scale organizational view became initially evident beginning in the 1990s and increasingly so in the early twenty-first century. That's what brought us to elaborate the Enterprise Project Governance view, which provides a holistic framework for connecting all project-related components within an organization.

Enterprise Project Governance (EPG) is the outgrowth of the evolution of a profession known as project management. Scarcely recognized decades ago, project management expanded from a collection of techniques for controlling schedule, cost, and quality for single projects to embrace multiple projects including portfolios, programs, project offices, and issues of organizational governance.

Enterprise Project Governance encompasses an in-depth view into the broader organizational panorama of project management, representing the overarching umbrella under which the rest of the project components reside. We chose to focus on the governance side of projects because it represents an organizational frontier for boosting benefits in organizations. Although research has been done and publications exist on related topics, organizations still struggle with finding effective ways to govern the multiplicity of projects needed to survive and prosper in increasingly challenging times.

The book aims to show that governance issues affect the classic components of project management, including portfolios, stakeholders, programs, and support structures. The book's scope includes all project-related factors in an organization and shows how a top-down governance structure is fundamental to ensure beneficial and healthy projects.

Target Audiences

The audiences for the book are as follows:

Board Members. Understanding the relationship between corporate governance and Enterprise Project Governance is fundamental for members of the board. Although board members generally focus on issues of auditing, compliance, risk, top management performance, and internal board affairs, a knowledge of EPG sheds fresh light on how the board can influence the implementation of strategic projects.

CEO. Chief executive officers are charged with making things happen in organizations, which inevitably involves provoking change. Beneficial change takes place when a well-honed portfolio of projects is managed artfully across the organization. EPG offers the structure to ensure that those project benefits are reaped.

Other C-Level Executives. In general, all C-level executives are involved in the implementation of strategic projects to some degree. Chief project officer, chief risk officer, chief information officer, chief knowledge officer, chief financial officer, and chief operations officer are examples.

PMO Managers. Managers of PMOs, ranging from project management offices, to portfolio management offices, to program management offices, stand to gain by perceiving the power of installing the umbrella of EPG to buttress the sundry components for managing a broad portfolio of projects successfully.

Middle Management. For managers and executives who find themselves in the flight path between corporate strategies and the implementation of multiple projects, the EPG concepts help put into context the need for governance-level policies related to projects, thus helping managers deal with the multitude of projects that make up their daily fare.

Project Professionals. Managers and other project players often face the challenge of managing projects in an organization that is not prepared to provide adequate support. This book can be used as a guide for middle management and professionals, and concepts from the book can be channeled to upper management.

Academics and Consultants. Academics can tap the book, both as a research source and as recommended reading in business schools as a new twist in management based on solid technical principles. Consultants who are trying to convince clients to gear up for a more project-oriented world can draw from the documented sources given to support proposals and recommendations to clients.

How to Read This Book

Although everybody can read it for getting up-to-date on an important management trend, the book can be used as a framework for change in companies that are moving toward a more project-based organization. Other than the conventional cover-to-cover approach, which follows a theory-to-practice logic, other ways to read this book are available for the busy person who is looking for specifics. This means using the index to zero in on particular topics of interest. In addition, here are common areas of interest and the related chapters:

- For executives interested in governance issues and how to integrate EPG into corporate governance policies, see Chapters 1, 2, 3, 6, 9, and 13.
- For professionals challenged with managing multiple projects effectively, see Chapters 1, 2, 4, 5, 8, 9, and 12.
- For those seeking the basics of project management, the recommended sequence is Chapters 1, 2, 5, and 9.

- For those who are initiated in project management but who are unfamiliar with the principles of EPG, the path is Chapters 1, 2, 4, 5, 8, and 9.

Understanding the full scope of Enterprise Project Governance is essential for people who deal with projects, whether the view is from the board room, the executive suite, the project management office, the project war room, or the project trenches. All pieces of the project world are interconnected. Thus a holistic view helps all parties across the enterprise work toward systematically completing quality projects on time, within budget, and to the clients' and users' satisfaction. This across-the-board synergy, under the banner of EPG, makes a major contribution toward surpassing company goals.

Paul C. Dinsmore and Luiz Rocha

Acknowledgments

We received timely, efficient and good-natured support from the Dinsmore Associates staff based in Rio de Janeiro. The marketing group, including Vanda Souza, Virgínia Mayrinck, Camillo Penna, along with Beto Almeida and his graphics personnel, was exceptionally supportive and patient in finalizing the exhibits.

Thanks also go to Walther Krause, ex-president of the Rio de Janeiro chapter of the Project Management Institute (PMI), for reviewing some of the texts, as well as to Gustavo Horbach of Braskem, who gave us access to available information. Pedro Ribeiro, board member of PMI's Educational Foundation, also deserves credit for suggesting that Enterprise Project Governance would be a timely theme for a new book. We are also grateful to experienced consultant Alberto Mutti, who offered pertinent comments with respect to mega projects and alliancing. And finally, our special thanks go to executive assistant Cristiane Souza for her joyful dedication in helping organize and expedite the manuscript material.

Paul C. Dinsmore and Luiz Rocha

CHAPTER

1

Introduction to Enterprise Project Governance

Evolution affects everything—including projects and how projects are managed. Projects have existed since the beginning of humankind. Egypt's Cheops, Leonardo da Vinci, and John F. Kennedy are some of the icons that have initiated or influenced the evolution of projects and their management. From its simplest form of running a single project, such as building a shelter from storms, to dealing with multiple and complex initiatives in ever-changing environments, such as high-tech space exploration, project management has broadened to a state of organizational entanglement that requires a rock-solid set of policies, structure, guidelines, and procedures. And the complexity is necessary if project managers are going to wrangle the plethora of projects that often butt heads at a stampede pace to achieve their desired goals.

Project management began from the intuitive logic of ancient architects and grew through successive stages of development that include these factors:

- Single projects

- Methodologies
- Software
- Multiple projects
- Programs
- Project portfolios
- Project management office
- Issues of governance

Thus the field of managing projects shows an ever broadening scope—from ad hoc, single-project approaches to a complex, all-encompassing view of portfolios, programs, and projects. This evolution peaks at the level of *Enterprise Project Governance* (EPG), the umbrella of policies and criteria that comprise the laws for the sundry components that make up the world of projects.

In real life, scenarios of governance in project management vary from free-flowing laissez-faire to formalized corporate PMO oversight. The typical ways project management is handled in organizations are:

1. *Laissez Faire* (whatever will be will be). Projects are carried out as required using intuitive approaches or methodologies that vary from one project to another. Nobody knows how many projects are underway in the company or the status of all the projects.

2. *Departmental* (territorial). Each department or area develops methodology and practice appropriate for that department. No cross-fertilization exists with other departments.

3. *PMOs, Project Management Offices* (one or several). Some companies have multiple PMOs, either at different levels or in different regions. They are sometimes connected, but they often operate independently.

4. *Corporate-Level PMO* (top-down oversight). Here, a chief project officer, a corporate project management office, or a strategic project management office cares for the implementation of strategic projects and for the overall project management practice in the company, including project portfolio management.

EPG goes a step further, proposing an all-encompassing approach to the management of projects across an enterprise, involving all players, including board members, CEO, other C-level executives, portfolio managers, PMO managers, and project managers. This book focuses on this overriding issue of Enterprise Project Governance and shows how the components of projects fit under its protective umbrella. The essence of EPG is explained in the answers to the following questions.

What is EPG anyway? Enterprise Project Governance is a framework residing under the umbrella of top management and corporate governance. It is aimed at ensuring the alignment of the corporate portfolio and its programs and projects with overall strategy, and that actions are proactively taken to confirm that everything stays on track ultimately to create value for the organization.

Why implement EPG? Enterprise Project Governance is designed to meet an urgent need: to find a way to deal intelligently and efficiently with the numerous projects and programs demanded by the marketplace, evolving technology, company stakeholders, regulatory agencies, and the quest to innovate. All of this is to be done with limited resources and at record-making speed. EPG presents an orderly and effective organizational approach for dealing with these critical issues.

Who are EPG stakeholders? Enterprise Project Governance stakeholders include initiators, change agents, and affected parties. An initiator might be a board member, the CEO, the CIO, other C-level executive, or an influential middle manager. Once the seeds are planted, active participation is required from change agents such as corporate PMO players, PMO members, IT (information technology) participants, and HR agents. The parties benefited include organizational stakeholders who need projects performed effectively and the professionals who deal directly or indirectly with projects.

When is it right to implement EPG? The conventional approach to deciding the right time is to do a size-up of the situation, using internal or external resources. A quick project management maturity assessment is helpful to understand the depth of knowledge and competency available in the organization. Answers to these questions also help evaluate the right time frame: What are the short-, mid-, and long-term benefits? Is the organization's culture ready, or is more change management required first? Is the right leadership prepared to take on the task?

Where should EPG be implemented? Implementation of Enterprise Project Governance is facilitated in a fertile setting and surrounded by influential stakeholders. Let's say a specific business unit has major challenges in implementing its projects and strong awareness among its executives. That is a good place to implement EPG. A ripe spot for initiating EPG is where a high-level champion of the cause resides and when a solid need for structuring projects exists.

How do you go about implementing EPG? Enterprise Project Governance can be implemented on sundry ways. How to proceed depends on such factors as the actual need, the existing culture, the presence of a champion, and a feasible plan for making the implementation. Initiative for promoting the EPG concept may start at different levels, such as with the board, CEO and executive team, or middle management, or at the professional level in a bottom-up approach. This book is aimed at providing examples and cases of what works and what doesn't work in managing multiple projects and major strategic projects across an enterprise. The relationships between the components of EPG and the suggestions on how to implement EPG are shown in the list of abridged chapters at the end of this chapter.

Is a comprehensive EPG approach needed to achieve effective project management across the enterprise? Even though an orchestrated program under the EPG label stands the best chance of generating effective results on a timely basis, formal EPG is in reality an evolutionary approach involving different initiatives depending on each organizational setting.

A number of reasons justify using incremental approaches to upgrade the overall effectiveness of project management across the enterprise. Some of these are:

- Minimal awareness in the organization about the impact that project management at all levels has on overall results.
- A lack of a project management culture, including trained professionals and managers.

- Insufficient sponsorship to champion the cause.
- A lack of expertise in change management techniques.

When the scenario isn't yet favorable for a formal program, partial initiatives are appropriate, such as:

1. Intensifying training programs in the basics of project management.
2. Stimulating the use of project management techniques across the enterprise in all areas including engineering, IT, R&D, new product development, marketing, and HR.
3. Creating awareness at the executive level through the literature, benchmarking, and conferences.
4. Identifying potential sponsors for a broader program.
5. Stimulating the implementation and development of PMOs.

With these measures in place, an organization will be on its way to producing highly successful projects of all types across the enterprise.

When the scenarios are favorable, however, a comprehensive EPG program offers an accelerated, holistic, and integrated way to guarantee optimal project performance and boost overall organization results.

EPG and Corporate Governance

EPG evolved in part due to the cascading changes that affected overall corporate governance beginning in the 1990s. Pressures from the marketplace, governments, and regulatory agencies placed a disconcerting spotlight on company boards to ensure that decisions and corresponding actions are fully traceable from the top down. Because a major part of organizational survival depends on new projects, EPG adds a measure of traceability and corresponding accountability to the basics of corporate governance.

The increasing focus on corporate governance can be traced to the stock market collapse of the late 1980s, which precipitated numerous corporate failures through the early 1990s. The concept started becoming more visible in 1999 when the Organization for Economic Co-operation and Development

(OECD) released its *Principles of Corporate Governance.*[1] Since then, over 35 codes or statements of principles on corporate governance have been issued in OECD countries.

In 2001 and 2002, high-profile corporate failures plagued major institutions. In the United States, Enron, WorldCom, Xerox, AOL Time Warner, Tyco, and Arthur Andersen were in deep trouble. In Europe, the same happened with Ahold, Bertelsmann, Vivendi, SK Corporation, Elf-Aquitaine, Londis, and Parmalat. The scandals in the United States led to the refinement of existing corporate governance aimed at protecting investors by improving the accuracy and reliability of corporate disclosures. The Sarbanes-Oxley Act of 2002[2] (SOX) is legislation enacted in response to protect shareholders and the general public from accounting errors and fraudulent practices in the enterprise. In the United Kingdom, in 2003, the Higgs Report[3] zeroed in on the same critical issues.

Corporate governance emerged from the shadows of boardrooms and is in common use, not just in companies but also in the public sector, charities, and universities. The phrase has become shorthand for the way an organization is run and is classically composed of committees charged with responsibility for regulatory compliance, auditing, business risk, hiring and firing the CEO, and the administration of the board of directors' activities. The demand of shareholders and other stakeholders for good governance is strong and continuing. The evolution of corporate governance was prompted by cycles of scandals, followed by reactive corporate reforms and government regulations intended to improve the practice. Investors, unions, government, and assorted pressure groups are increasingly likely to condemn businesses that fail to follow the rules of good practice.

Corporate governance also serves to enhance organizational performance by establishing and maintaining a corporate culture that motivates directors, managers, and entrepreneurs to maximize project-based and operational efficiency, thereby ensuring returns on investment and long-term productivity growth. To that end, boards may also include additional committees for topics like research, ethics, and portfolios. Other high-priority themes, such as strategic projects, special events, and programs, may be included in board-level committees, but generally these are delegated to the organization under the guidance of the CEO.

Currently, there is no evidence of a universal set of corporate governance principles applicable to all countries and their organizations. However, corporate governance guidelines produced by OECD encourage the application of good corporate governance as a precondition for international loans to governments for financial sector and other structural reforms, as well as equity investment and bank loans to large companies. Although the pressure is currently on listed companies to make transparent their corporate governance principles, this requirement is likely to be extended not only to all listed companies, but also to other privately and publicly owned companies and organizations that want to use money from others.

Although there is a need to increase the overseeing of governance structures, this is not an easy task. As mentioned by James Wolfensohn,[4] former president of World Bank:

> a number of high profile failures in 2001–2002 have brought a renewed focus on corporate governance, bringing the topic to a broader audience ... the basic principles are the same everywhere: fairness, transparency, accountability, and responsibility. These are minimum standards that provide legitimacy in the corporation, reduce vulnerability to financial crisis, and broaden and deepen access to capital. However, applying these standards across a wide variety of legal, economic, and social systems is not easy. Capacity is often weak, vested interests prevail, and incentives are uncertain.

The high visibility heaped on corporate governance, sparked by the scandals at the beginning of the twenty-first century, brought attention to lacking governance policies in more specific disciplines. In the early 1990s, information technology executives perceived a crying need to put order into the then chaotic industry. Various programs and standards were developed, such that IT governance has become a solid cornerstone of the profession. (Details about IT governance are given in Chapter 11.) After the turn of the century, a similar need became evident in the burgeoning field of project management.

The evolution has been from the management of single projects to multiple projects and then to the development of project management offices, corporate project management offices, and chief project officers. To gather all this under one governing roof, Enterprise Project Governance is making the scene.

From Corporate Governance to Enterprise Project Governance

Enterprise Project Governance helps fill the voids left in loosely woven corporate governance policies, primarily with respect to transparency, accountability, and responsibility. Effective EPG ensures that corporate initiatives and endeavors are appropriately defined with respect to policies and accountability.

More importantly, EPG is a natural evolution in organizations that wrestle with countless demands for new projects to be completed within tightened time frames, at lower cost, and with fewer resources. Indeed the pressures from faulty corporate governance have influenced companies' trends to include EPG policies, but in fact the need for EPG is simultaneously becoming apparent as the world becomes increasingly projectized, with more and more projects clamoring for attention. The demand to undertake, manage, and complete multiple projects creates a need to provide greater governance and structure. Whereas corporate governance also includes the concerns of the ongoing organization with its status quo activities and operational issues, EPG focuses on new and changing factors, thus on the projectized parts of organizations.

The book provides definitions and insights regarding the essence, variations, and myriad subtleties of EPG. Capsule summaries of each chapter follow:

Chapter 2: The Essence of Enterprise Project Governance. The need for the integration of projects with the business environment led the Association for Project Management in the United Kingdom to spotlight the need for improved project governance. This concept evolved to a broader view that encompasses portfolios and programs and that is called Enterprise Project Governance. It is a framework extending from corporate governance with a set of principles and key components: strategic alignment, risk management, portfolio management, organization and stakeholder management, performance evaluation, and business transformation.

Chapter 3: Linking Strategy to Portfolio. Related yet unique worlds hold in balance the essence of an organization's success. The first world, one of strategy and direction, is populated by business strategists whose calling is to divine the future and develop a winning business strategy. The second, related to translating intentions into results, is dominated by project managers obsessed with getting things done. Each looks at the world through different lenses. Since gaps exist between the responsibilities and the mind-sets of the key players, challenges in communications are commonplace. An effective strategy is designed to surround, permeate, and guide daily business. Therefore, major alignment is called for, aimed at dealing with the fuzzy area that lies between strategic planning and project implementation and in which roles and responsibilities may be unclear and communications and relationships equally opaque.

Chapter 4: Risk Management: Dealing with Uncertainty. Using the ISO 31000 risk standard definition that risk is "the effect of uncertainty on objectives," it becomes possible to relate risks to the different levels of objectives: strategic, tactical, and operational. The outputs from successful risk management include compliance with applicable governance requirements, assurance to stakeholders regarding the management of risk, and enhanced decision making. External reports may be produced in response to mandatory requirements, such as Sarbanes-Oxley, or to provide external assurance that risks have been adequately managed. These outputs improve the efficiency of operations, the effectiveness of tactics through the articulation of a portfolio of programs and projects, and the efficacy of the organization's strategy.

Chapter 5: Project Portfolio Management: The Right Combination of Right Projects. Modern organizations are dynamic, turbulent, living organisms. They call for new ways to bring order to the demands imposed by the topsy-turvy times. Projects organized and managed under a portfolio with defined criteria and priorities represent a solution to this challenge. Although organizations still possess numerous operational activities to be managed, the future of companies depends on the content and successful management of their portfolio of projects. New projects are the key to staying ahead of the survival curve and to ensuring an organization's growth and prosperity. This is why project portfolio management is an essential component of Enterprise Project Governance.

Chapter 6: Turning Strategy into Reality. Once the portfolio is aligned with company strategies, focus turns to making projects transform strategies into the desired results. This means that each project must meet its goals as chartered and that the project portfolio is balanced and implemented in the proper order and sequence. Here, basic project management comes into play in order to make sure that projects produce the benefits prescribed and that the relationships among projects continue to be complementary. Attention to the overall balance of project portfolios is required to ensure that strategies do indeed become reality.

Chapter 7: Organizing for Enterprise Project Governance. The interface between business strategists (upper management and business planners) and the implementers (program and project managers) requires organization and structure in order to put into practice project governance policies and sort out the challenges of managing a multitude of projects competing for scarce resources across the enterprise. Three groups of stakeholders influence the way EPG is structured and manifests itself in organizations. A board committee may lay out generic EPG policies as guidelines for the organization. Or it may prefer simply to comply with corporate regulatory requirements and leave the essence of EPG to the executive level under the CEO. In this setting, the CEO may elect to delegate responsibility to executives in specific business units or heads of major departments.

Chapter 8: Stakeholder Management and the Pivotal Role of the Sponsor. Stakeholder management deals with interfacing issues such as power, politics, and influence; therefore it is highly relevant to EPG. Special interests, hidden agendas, and interpersonal conflicts also come into play in stakeholder management, so a structured approach for dealing with these people issues becomes relevant. The sponsor provides a connection between the formal organization and the projects designed to carry out company strategies. This crucial role is normally taken on by senior executives because experienced top managers are likely to have credibility to interact effectively with other executives on the impact of projects with competing strategic issues.

Chapter 9: EPG Performance: Beyond Time, Cost, and Quality. Billions of dollars go to waste annually when projects fail to deliver what is expected or when projects are aborted due to faulty strategizing or unexpected swings in the economy. Such waste includes the time and effort expended to make a project produce, as well as the cost of lost opportunity. Businesses continue to expand the number of projects in spite of constrained resources. As projects become more complex, enterprises are tasked to deal with conflicting objectives and shorter delivery cycle times. In this environment, executing projects successfully is a key business requirement. Avoiding the project pitfalls discussed in this chapter will help corporations navigate the challenges and better position their projects for success.

Chapter 10: EPG in Mega Projects, Joint Ventures, and Alliances. Compared to their counterparts in the past, twenty-first century projects are bigger, more complex, and more ambiguous, and they require a closer focus on integration to deal with the growing number of interfaces. Great flexibility and a tenacity to deliver in the face of unknown obstacles and difficulties are also required, along with skills to manage the surge in interconnections and interdependencies. Traditional project management tools and techniques, while still necessary, are insufficient to guide the most complex of projects through to delivery on time and within cost and performance targets. Different approaches for Enterprise Project Governance are applicable for different types of projects and stages in project life cycles. This is particularly true for mega projects and joint ventures. Specific governance policies are required for each project, since multiple partners are involved. One way of dealing with these projects is called *alliancing,* which is a form of collaborative contracting based on the concepts of collaboration, transparency, and mutual trust between the owner and contracting parties.

Chapter 11: EPG for Different Types of Projects. Certain industries have peculiarities and require special governance approaches. Examples are given for information technology (IT), for research and development (R&D), and for organizational change programs. Governance in IT projects came into focus in the early 1990s, when executives identified the need to align these projects with corporate direction. After early failures, major advances have been made in the organization and governance of IT projects. R&D projects have points in common with IT endeavors. The final product for both types of projects is rarely perfectly clear, and the pathway for arriving at a final result invariably contains twists and turns. R&D efforts range from process improvement to new product development to breakthrough discoveries. These projects are challenging because by definition, researchers don't know in advance exactly how to achieve the desired results. Organizational change programs face the political scenario and behavioral issues of such ventures, as well as the resulting challenges for leadership. Project management skills are essential, yet these must be coupled with business experience and knowledgeable sponsorship.

Chapter 12: The EPG Plan: A Roadmap to Transformation and Success. An EPG plan maps out a journey between a point of departure, with tollgates along the way, to a destination—a vision of success in the future where a transformed state is expected. The plan outlines steps for implementing an overall governance of portfolios, programs, and projects through direction, control, assurance, and support by people across the organization's strategic, tactical, and operational layers. The resulting deliverables of this plan become a guide to consolidating the policies, standards, and lessons learned resulting from the implementation of the actions involving the EPG framework. Three cases are presented in the chapter, each referring to specific situations. EPG deals with people and changing the culture of an organization. The examples outlined are suitable for application in an array of companies and organizations, and they may be used as a basis for new EPG plans.

Chapter 13: Challenges and Roadblocks. Challenges are bound to appear along the pathway to EPG. Challenges to overcome include the justification factor, the motivation for change, and how to organize and prepare people. To get around roadblocks, displaying the facts is not enough because organizational change is strongly affected by other factors, such as tradition, opinions, and politics. Ways to prevent potential challenges involve situational analysis and planning and implementing a customized change program. Corrective approaches to unexpected roadblocks include backtracking, reanalysis, and replanning. The individual components of EPG, such as project portfolio management, program management, PMOs, and management of individual projects, are often implemented independently from EPG, and they also present challenges and roadblocks that ultimately have impacts on the effort to institute project management seamlessly across the enterprise.

Conclusions

Project management began with the intuitive logic of ancient architects and evolved through successive stages of development: single projects, methodologies, software, multiple projects, programs, project portfolios, project management offices, and issues of governance. So the view of project management has broadened over the years. This view has evolved to the level of project governance, which is the umbrella of policies and criteria that comprise the laws for the components of the world of projects.

EPG has evolved in part due to the dynamic changes that have affected overall corporate governance beginning in the 1990s. Pressures from the marketplace, governments, and regulatory agencies have placed a disconcerting spotlight on company boards to ensure that decisions and corresponding actions are fully traceable from the top down. Since a major part of organizational survival depends on new projects, EPG adds that measure of traceability and corresponding accountability to the basics of corporate governance.

2

The Essence of Enterprise Project Governance

The challenge for organizations that rely on projects, programs, and portfolios to instigate change and to grow value is monumental. It calls for moving from ad hoc execution to an integrated, robust, repeatable, and auditable system aimed at increasing the predictability of an organization's future state. When these requirements are combined with the enhanced expectations of stakeholders, a significant requirement for such robust, predictable, and auditable processes emerges.

Enterprise Project Governance resides under the umbrella of top management and corporate governance. It is about ensuring that projects are aligned with overall strategy, are balanced with respect to corporate priorities, and succeed by establishing a well-defined approach that all parties understand and agree to. The approach must be followed throughout the life cycle of portfolios, programs, and projects, and progress must be measured and actions proactively taken to confirm that everything stays on track and that the agreed benefits, products, or services are delivered.

Part of this development can be found within corporate governance circles and may be seen as a different way of connecting projects to their parent organization, the owner, or the financing party. In addition, some countries, such as the United Kingdom and Norway, place an increasing focus on the role of government in public investment. International organizations, such as the World Bank, and professional project management associations have developed governance frameworks aimed at defining how to improve the initiation and execution of projects through control and support. Four pertinent views from some international organizations on the governance of project management are discussed next.

Association for Project Management

The need for greater integration of projects with the business environment in which they exist led the Association for Project Management (APM) in the United Kingdom to produce the document "Directing Change—A Guide to the Governance of Project Management."[1] The publication describes the principles of effective project governance and the information a board needs to be confident that the organization's projects are managed in accordance with the governing principles. Organizations striving for project success are encouraged to lift their perspectives beyond the delivery of the project itself and onto the broader issues of the project's benefits and effects on the business.

According to the document, four governance areas enable the achievement of the principles outlined:

1. *Portfolio direction* is concerned with ensuring that the project portfolio is aligned with the organization's objectives, including profitability, customer service, reputation, and sustainability.

2. *Project sponsorship* is the effective linkage between senior management and the management of the project. At its heart is leadership and decision making for the benefit of achieving the project objectives. It is the communication route through which project managers report

progress and issues upward to the board and obtain authority and decisions on issues affecting their project. It owns the business case and is responsible for ensuring that the intended benefits become the project objectives and are delivered accordingly.

The APM publication lays out the principles of effective project governance:

- The board has overall responsibility for the governance of project management.
- The roles, responsibilities, and performance criteria for the governance of project management are clearly defined.
- Disciplined governance arrangements, supported by appropriate methods and controls, are applied throughout the project life cycle.
- A coherent and supportive relationship is demonstrated between the overall business strategy and the project portfolio.
- All projects have an approved plan containing authorization points at which the business case is reviewed and approved. Decisions made at authorization points are recorded and communicated.
- Members of delegated authorization bodies have sufficient representation, competence, authority, and resources to enable them to make appropriate decisions.
- The project business case is supported by relevant and realistic information that provides a reliable basis for making authorization decisions.
- The board or its delegated agents decide when independent scrutiny of projects and project management systems is required, and implement such scrutiny accordingly.
- There are clearly defined criteria for reporting project status and for the escalation of risks and issues to the levels required by the organization.
- The organization fosters a culture of improvement and of frank internal disclosure of project information.
- Project stakeholders are engaged at a level that is commensurate with their importance to the organization and in a manner that fosters trust.

3. *Project management* addresses the capability and competence of the teams assigned to the management of projects, the appropriateness of the levels of decision-making authority delegated to project teams, and their ability to deliver the project objectives. Team capability is about the competence of the people involved at all levels, the resources they have available to perform their roles, and the processes or management systems they are able to deploy in fulfilling their function.

4. *Disclosure and reporting* in an open and honest environment is paramount for effective reporting. What is reported is to be open, honest, efficient, timely, relevant, and reliable. When disclosure and reporting are poor and ineffective, there is inevitably weak project sponsorship and project management because this component is the most reliant on the culture of the organization.

Project Management Institute

Working from another angle of effective project governance, the Project Management Institute (PMI) developed an integrated set of foundational standards addressing the processes required to manage projects, programs, and portfolios and one focusing on the project maturity of organizations. The component standards are *A Guide to the Project Management Body of Knowledge*, *The Standard for Program Management*, and *The Standard for Portfolio Management*, while the *Organizational Project Management Maturity Model (OPM3)* covers the management of projects on a broader scale.

According to PMI, the OPM3[2] standard is designed to provide benefits to organizations and senior management, such as:

- Strengthening the link between strategy and execution, so that project outcomes are predictable.
- Providing best practices to support the implementation of organizational strategy through projects.
- Offering a basis from which organizations can make improvement in their project management processes.

The standard acknowledges that corporate governance is the force that drives the realization of strategies through portfolios, programs, and projects. If an organization correctly understands the complementarities between corporate governance, strategy execution, and project portfolio management, then it can successfully pursue its strategic goals.

Office of Government and Commerce

Another organization with a strong focus on project governance is the Office of Government and Commerce (OGC), a department within the U.K. government with a remit to help public sector organizations gain better value from procurements and deliver improved success from programs and projects. OGC is the owner of PRINCE2, a well-known methodology for project development, and the IT best-practice framework ITIL.

OGC also has a *Portfolio, Programme and Project Management Maturity Model*[3] (*P3M3*). The standard describes the portfolio-, program-, and project-related activities within seven perspectives (management control, benefits management, financial management, stakeholder management, risk management, corporate governance, and resource management) addressing governance issues that correlate to improved performance at five levels (recognition, repeatable, defined, managed, optimized). Knowing the positioning level of each perspective helps determine what actions to target.

International Organization for Standardization

The ISO 21500, Guidance on Project Management,[4] is intended to provide orientation for the needs and effects of projects in organizations. The standard, launched by the International Organization for Standardization (ISO), is not for accreditation but for guidance purposes only, providing organizations with a solid baseline from which to evaluate the development of projects; it incorporates the work of several national standards. However, the most significant value is the establishment of a global, common understandable guideline from which the principles of project management can be further developed and refined across each national standard organization, toward the overall improvement of project performance.

The ISO norm recognizes that projects usually exist within a larger context, that they are often the means to accomplish strategic goals, and that the creation of required project deliverables contribute to the achievement of benefits associated with those goals. It also considers that project governance is concerned with those areas of corporate governance specifically related to project activities, including such aspects as defining the management structure; the policies, processes, and methodologies to be used; limits of authority for decision making; stakeholder responsibilities and accountabilities; and interactions such as reporting and the escalation of issues or risks. The responsibility for maintaining the appropriate governance of a project is commonly assigned either to the project sponsor or to a project steering committee.

...

These four views are congruent with the definitions of EPG and its components as presented in this book. Indeed, they reinforce the need for a framework such as EPG with the objective of successfully creating a governance structure for overseeing the pathway from strategy to value creation.

Two Schools on Enterprise Project Governance

The first school (*board-sponsored EPG*) is based on logic proposed by organizations having knowledge and connections with the field of project management. Here, Enterprise Project Governance extends the principles of corporate governance and the ones considered by APM, PMI, OGC, and ISO 21500 into the management of projects through governance structures and oversight at a business level. It aims at guaranteeing that programs and projects are delivered effectively and efficiently or are cancelled when appropriate. Under the school of board-sponsored EPG, the board establishes a related committee such as strategic planning, special projects, or EPG itself to provide input and oversight for enterprise-wide ventures.

Many boards, however, concentrate only on broad issues related to business ethics, risks, auditing, CEO succession, and internal board administration. All other subjects are handled by the permanent executive staff under the leadership of the CEO. So, although the second school (*CEO-sponsored EPG*) is similar in concept to the first, in this case, the board delegates full responsibility to the CEO and executive committee. Therefore, the board provides no input or oversight to projects in the enterprise. Enterprise Project Governance takes place fully within the scope of the company's full-time professional leadership. Policies, structures, and procedures for EPG are therefore developed under the umbrella of the CEO and C-level colleagues, and delegated to appropriate levels within the organization.

Air Navigation and EPG

Air navigation provides an easy analogy for understanding Enterprise Project Governance. Airways Corporation of New Zealand Limited is a public company, controlling over a million aircraft movements a year, whose shareholders are the Minister for State-Owned Enterprises and the Minister of Finance. The vision of Airways is to be a key player in global air navigation services by demonstrating world's best practices. For Airways, each airplane, as shown in Exhibit 2-1, is controlled by its flight crew, yet has to follow the orders of overseeing governing structures, including:

- *Air Traffic Control.* Primarily the separation of aircrafts in flight, to standards determined by the Civil Aviation Authority in New Zealand, using radar or other means.
- *Air Traffic Management.* The management of aircraft in flight to maximize access to the most efficient flight paths as determined by the customer, limited only by the constraints of safe delivery of an Air Traffic Control service.
- *Navigation Services.* The navigation infrastructure and supporting services used by aircraft to navigate.

Airways' *Vision 2015*[5] outlines the expectations, deliverables, and benefits of adopting an enterprise portfolio management approach to meet the future air traffic management requirements in New Zealand. This *Vision* is built on

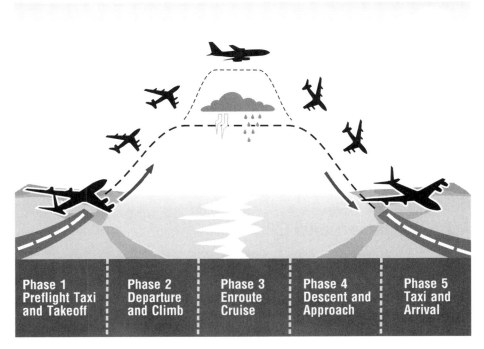

| Phase 1
Preflight Taxi
and Takeoff | Phase 2
Departure
and Climb | Phase 3
Enroute
Cruise | Phase 4
Descent and
Approach | Phase 5
Taxi and
Arrival |

Exhibit 2-1. Flight Phases from Preflight to Arrival

the work of industry-driven project teams involving Airways New Zealand, the New Zealand Civil Aviation Authority, and aviation group representatives including the airlines, the military, and aviation interest groups. The *Vision* is influenced by and linked to a number of other planning initiatives within New Zealand and overseas. In addition, the approach taken considers the complex interprogram relationships not only in air traffic management, but also in the ground infrastructure and aircraft equipage.

Airways New Zealand provides a good analogy for the application of EPG. Time and effort are needed at the highest levels in an organization for the project governance arrangements to function correctly and provide stakeholders with confidence in the arrangements. The project governance structure also serves as a reference document for independent project reviews. The *Vision*, for example, highlights key authorization points and ties these in with the schedule of governance meetings and other stakeholders' engagement points.

Enterprise Project Governance Principles

The air navigation analogy provides a background reference for principles essential for good EPG. Here are six key principles:

1. *Identify a single point of accountability.* Identify the persons accountable for the success of the portfolio, programs, and projects. Equally, all personnel involved in the project governance structure need to know what they are accountable and responsible for. Accountability cannot be shared—more than one person, or a committee, cannot be held accountable for the success of a project—or delegated. Without a single point of accountability, projects lack clear authority because the validity of any decision is questionable since the authority behind the decision has not been established. In the case of overall EPG, responsible parties might be the CEO, CPO, and head of CPMO.

2. *Ensure that Enterprise Project Governance is value focused.* The focus on value creation is guaranteed by the EPG structure that considers three decision layers:

   - *Strategic Decisions—What?* Strategic decision making creates the forward thrust in the business. Corporations often capture their overall business strategy in a statement of intent, and it's an excellent term for describing strategic decision making. Failure to examine the big picture can lead to stagnation in the business and an inability to move forward.

   - *Tactical Decisions—How?* Tactical decisions involve the establishment of key initiatives to achieve the overall strategy. This layer of decision making can sometimes be overlooked, yet it is the glue that creates a strong connection between long-term vision and day-to-day activities.

   - *Operational Decisions—How will we deploy resources?* Operational decisions determine how activities actually get done. They are the grassroots decisions about who is going to do what and when. Operational decisions are often made in real time and are the result of needing to make quick adjustments or changes to achieve the desired outcome.

3. *Separate EPG and Corporate Governance.* EPG and corporate governance are complementary, yet require separation in order to reduce the number of project decision nodes because decision paths will not normally follow the organizational line of command.

4. *Separate Stakeholder Management and Decisions.* Stakeholder management and project decision making are separate functions and call for separate forums to be addressed. When the two are confused, decision-making forums become clogged with stakeholders, resulting in labored decision making. While many people may need to be aware of a project and have input into shaping it, not everyone needs to participate in each project decision. Achieving separation reduces the number of people required in project decision forums while maintaining the essential input provided by key stakeholders. Effective stakeholder management is essential for the success of any project. Supporting the needs of stakeholders requires establishing communication channels and developing reporting frameworks. Stakeholders need the opportunity to have their issues and concerns raised and addressed. These tasks can, however, be done separately to the function of decision making.

5. *Timely Decision Making.* Timely decisions, accurately communicated, are essential for project momentum, and such decisions must be capable of being implemented. Particularly at some stages, the ability of the project governance arrangements to resolve complex issues, some of which will have conflicting requirements that will need trade-offs and compromises, is fundamental for the progress of the project.

6. *Control and Communication of Information.* This requirement ensures that the project is where it should be, that the key work streams are visible, and that any formal disclosure requirements are made.

Exhibit 2-2 shows that EPG is separate from governance of operations and linked to the strategy that guarantees projects and program alignment and the capture of the desired benefits leading to value creation.

Actively managing such a framework is complex and is strongly impacted by external events and changing conditions. Therefore, an effective set of governance functions is essential to provide the means to identify, assess, and respond to internal and external events and changes by adjusting portfolio, program, and project components. A poor governance structure will be in a continuously reactive state, constantly struggling to catch up with an ever changing panorama.

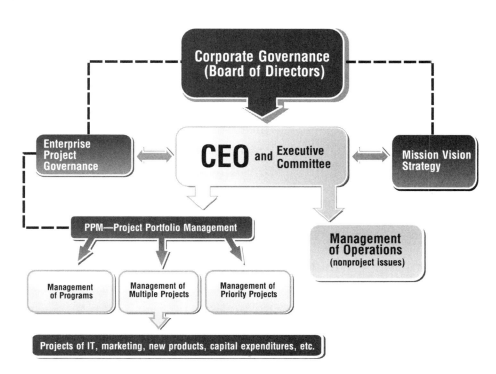

Exhibit 2-2. Relationship of EPG to Corporate Governance, Projects, and Operations

Key Components of Enterprise Project Governance

In fulfilling the EPG role, key activities for project sponsors and steering committee members to address are:

- Strategic Alignment
- Risk Management
- Portfolio Management
- Organization
- Stakeholder Management
- Performance Evaluation
- Business Transformation

Implementing project governance requires a framework based on these major components, as presented in Exhibit 2-3.

Strategic Alignment

A responsibility of EPG is to ensure that projects are consistent with company strategies and goals and that the projects are implemented productively and effectively. All investment activities are subject to the governance process in that they need to be resourced and financed adequately. For mandatory projects, the decision is not whether to undertake the project but how to manage it in order to meet the required standard with minimum risk. For discretionary projects, there needs to be more focus on the go/no-go decision and whether the project supports the strategic objectives and whether the investment gives the best value compared to other alternatives.

Risk Management

Risk management is a systematic process of identifying and assessing company risks and taking actions to protect a company against them. Companies need risk management to analyze possible risks in order to balance potential gains against potential losses and avoid expensive mistakes. Risk management is best used as a preventive measure rather than as a reactive measure. Managing risk in an integrated way can mean everything from using financial instruments

Exhibit 2-3. Components of EPG

to managing specific financial exposures, from effectively responding to rapid changes in the organizational environment to reacting to natural disasters and political instability.

Portfolio Management

The project portfolio provides a big-picture view. It enables managers to become aware of all of the individual projects in the portfolio and provides a deeper understanding of the collection as a whole. It facilitates sensible sorting, adding, and removing projects from the collection. A single project inventory can be constructed containing all the organization's ongoing and proposed projects. Alternatively, multiple project inventories can be created representing project portfolios for different departments, programs, or businesses. Since project portfolio management can be conducted at any level, the choice of one portfolio versus many depends on the size of the organization, its structure, and the nature and interrelationships among the projects being conducted.

Organization

Effective governance starts with leadership, commitment, and support from the top. However, such leadership, while crucial, is not enough. Appropriate organizational structure and the roles and responsibilities for all participants are required. There are three main organizational components to EPG: executive leadership, the portfolio management team, and the program and project managers. To be effective, the individuals who direct and those who oversee governance activities must be organized, and their contributions must be modeled to ensure that authority and decision making has a clear source, that the work of management and oversight is efficient, and that the needs for direction and decisions are all addressed. The bulk of Enterprise Project Governance work is carried out by committees and, for many organizations, multiple committees work at different levels. The committees used depend on organizational structures, culture, and other issues; not all organizations will employ all of these committees at the same time. EPG is a collaborative process, and there must be a healthy mix of corporate, business units, and support services.

Stakeholder Management

In every undertaking, there are parties with a vested interest in the activities and results of the project. These parties are called *stakeholders*: individuals with some kind of stake, claim, share, or interest in the activities and results of the project. Identifying stakeholders early on leads to better stakeholder management throughout the project.

All people have expectations that drive the way they interact. Expectations reflect their vision of a future state or action; many of their expectations are unstated but critical to the project's success. Understanding these expectations and responding to them is an art, and expectation management is useful in any area in which human beings must collaborate effectively to achieve a shared result. Failure to recognize that people are bound to have positive and negative reactions will only result in disaster.

Most stakeholders have interests outside the project. They will not be effective in supporting the project's delivery unless they are accurately and currently informed about the progress of a project and consulted on the challenges it is facing. One of the aims of project governance is to build a common sense of ownership of the project, such as by informing and listening and by creating an environment of trust between the dedicated project delivery team and the wider stakeholder community.

Performance Evaluation

For EPG to be effective, it has to be measured and its performance monitored on a periodic and ongoing basis to ensure that it contributes to business objectives while being effective and responsive to the changing environment. Typically, performance is evaluated during execution and, quite often, it is forgotten after the product or service is delivered.

Business Transformation

Business transformation should be a continuous process, essential to any organization in implementing its business strategy and achieving its vision. It is an ongoing requirement because vision and strategy always need adapting and refining as changing economic influences make their impact. Business agility, or the ability to achieve business transformation, is therefore a true measure of both management and corporate success and, as such, must be considered on the EPG structure. Developing the internal capability for change management is an essential step in assuring the successful implementation of any change project. Establishing change capability enables clients to continue optimizing performance in response to changing service demands and new strategic drivers.

The components of EPG, however, do not operate in a vacuum. They are part of a larger context as illustrated in Exhibit 2-4.

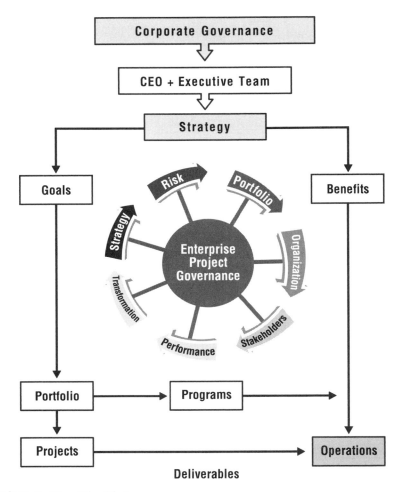

Exhibit 2-4. The Big Picture

The Case of Metronet

The U.K. government announced in March 1998 that it would create a publicly owned operating company, London Underground Limited (LUL), with responsibility for running trains and stations and for setting fares. Three new companies, owned and operated by the private sector, would be responsible for maintaining and improving infrastructure such as stations, trains, track, and signaling under public private partnership (PPP) contracts with London Underground.[6]

Since London Underground transported around a billion passengers per year, the government planned to enhance oversight by separating operations from infrastructure improvements and maintenance, under three separate 30-year PPP contracts funded by the government.

In 2003, the consortium Metronet won two of the three contracts for upgrading and maintaining two-thirds of the lines. As shown in Exhibit 2-5, Metronet had five shareholders who formed the board and who were also the suppliers responsible for delivering the contracts. A subsidiary, Trans4m, composed of four of the five shareholders, was created to carry out station renovations. The organization created had the power to charge bills to Metronet and to reject penalties for failure because the members were also on the board. The result was a cumbersome decision process with conflicting interests, poorly aligned with the objectives of the consortium. The suppliers-shareholders in charge of

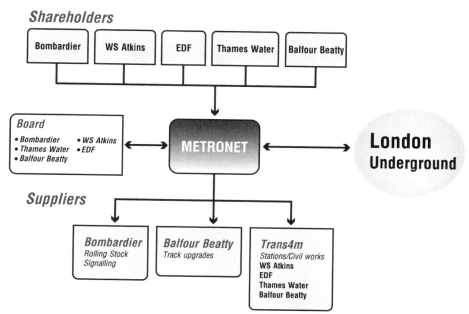

Exhibit 2-5. Metronet's Governance Structure

the work provided inadequate cost information to the executive management, making it difficult to monitor costs and maintain sound communication with London Underground. The poorly documented performance and cost information also hindered the development of substantiated requests for claims.

By March 2006, Metronet was well behind schedule with 11 stations renovated and 44 kilometers of track remodeled of the originally planned 35 stations and 69 kilometers of track. The PPP arbiter in the annual review indicated that the organization and contractual relationships were unsatisfactory and that contracts outside the internal Metronet supply chain should be awarded through competitive tender. But it was already too late to fix something that started wrong since its inception. Metronet ran out of cash and entered third-party administration in July 2007. In May 2008, Metronet was taken over by Transport of London, a governmental agency.

Given that Metronet was an organization assembled specifically for the purpose of developing and delivering a number of projects, failure in adequately structuring and implementing an effective EPG was a major cause for its downfall.

Conclusions

Enterprise Project Governance offers a transformational route for organizations striving to deliver strategy through improved oversight of portfolios, projects, and programs. The discipline of EPG ensures that portfolios and programs are composed of the right projects and that the best resources are available to manage them. When EPG's multiple components are successfully coordinated and integrated, the optimal combination of the right projects are completed as planned, thus ensuring growth and prosperity. Corporate governance is the umbrella held by the board under which the CEO and executive teams implement a portfolio of projects and programs that produces the desired benefits. EPG is the bridge that spans the gap between an organization's best of intentions and actual goals achieved.

CHAPTER

3

Linking Strategy to Portfolio

Connections between strategies and putting the strategies into play are critical for organizations. When strategists neglect the transition of ideas to implementation, strategy goes awry and the seeds of failure are sowed. Although executives might understand this instinctively, they may lack a systematic approach for moving strategies from good intentions onto the transformation highway toward results.

This gap between strategic concepts and implementation arises from assumptions about how strategy is to be converted into understandable work and to what extent the organization is capable of managing the transformation needed to implement upper management's ambitions. People at all levels affect the transition process.

Two Worlds, Shared Objectives

Related yet unique worlds hold in balance the essence of business and organization success. The first world, one of strategy and direction, is populated by business strategists whose calling is to divine the future and develop a winning business strategy. The second, related to translating intentions into results, is populated by project managers obsessed with getting things done. Each looks at the world through very different lenses. But in spite of these differences, both worlds must conspire to move companies toward their goals. The functions differ, yet they are highly complementary.

Since gaps exist between the responsibilities and the mind-sets of the key players in these differing worlds, challenges in communications are commonplace. Just as all of an astronaut's in-flight behaviors (e.g., navigating, daily routines, conducting experiments) are carried out in the context of the mission's environment, an organization's behaviors (e.g., research, innovation, marketing, investments, operations) are carried out in the context of its strategy. An effective strategy is not separate from an organization's endeavors. To the contrary, it surrounds, permeates, and guides them. Therefore, major alignment is called for, aimed at dealing with the fuzzy area between strategic planning and project implementation where roles and responsibilities may be unclear and communications and relationships equally opaque.

Projects at Unilever

In February 2000, Antony Burgmans and Niall Fitzgerald, chairmen of the giant Unilever, one of the largest consumer goods companies, announced a €5 billion, five-year growth strategy to align the entire organization behind ambitious plans.[1] The aims were to accelerate growth and expand margins, commit to double-digit earnings growth, and bring about a significant improvement in its performance. The initiative, named Path to Growth Strategy,[2] involved a comprehensive restructuring of operations and businesses and cutting down on its unwieldy portfolio of 1,600 brands and focusing on the top 400.

Unilever decided to concentrate on four major areas:

- *Brand Portfolio.* Emphasizing leading brands and supporting them with strong innovation and focused marketing strategies.
- *Capabilities.* Recognizing the need to ensure world-class status in each

of their core processes—everything from innovation to shopper marketing, from customer management to supply chain.

- *Organization and Ways of Working.* Increasing the speed of decision making and simplifying business processes.
- *Culture and Behaviors.* Essential to fit the aspects of the transformation together—new strategic priorities, new capabilities, and a new organization.

In 2004, Path to Growth was showing some success. Unilever had had just four billion-dollar-a-year brands in 2000, it now had increased to 12 such brands. Moreover, its profit margins doubled over the previous four years. However, revenue growth was stalled. Unilever took a hard look in the mirror and saw that the previous change was not enough. The mirror reflected a complex and fragmented picture. As an example, Unilever's employees in 24 countries used 18 ERP systems and hundreds of different finance processes. Because Unilever's business groups operated as a loose federation, they created duplication, high cost, and varying quality.

Path to Growth initiated a transformation process targeting brand focus and improved profitability. But there was still much to do. According to Patrick Cescau, Unilever's first group chief executive, with respect to the strategy in place before his mandate:

> It did not address important aspects of Unilever's business model. It was clear that we needed a new business model for Unilever. One that combined a more active, aggressive, top-down approach to managing and building our brand portfolio, together with an organization to support this growth strategy. Ultimately, execution is what counts, but strategic clarity, total alignment, the right governance and mindset... are all preconditions for good execution. The starting point for the growth strategy was a rigorous, unsentimental assessment of the strengths and weaknesses of our portfolio.[3]

Unilever's administration felt the need for more integration and launched One Unilever, a broad program aimed at rethinking the business. A new mission was crafted, declaring that "Unilever's new mission is to add vitality to life. We meet everyday needs for nutrition, hygiene, and personal care with products that help people feel good, look good, and get more out of life." This broad statement intended to help managers and employees connect their work activities to consumers' increased attention to health, nutrition, and well-being.

One Unilever had as its goals to streamline the business, achieve substantial savings, become more consumer focused, act more effectively against its competitors, and increase growth. In Europe, the ambition included establishing a European supply chain. In February 2005, a series of significant changes was made to its management and leadership structure, including the abandonment of its dual-chair CEO structure with separate bosses in London and Rotterdam. Patrick Cescau, having been announced as their first group chief executive, stated, "The de-layering of the top management brings simplicity, clarity of leadership and greater accountability. And now we have the right people in the right roles focusing on the right issues. We are all determined to return Unilever to the kind of performance the shareholders expect."[4]

In January 2009, amid the global financial storm, Patrick Cescau retired, and Paul Polman, a former Nestlé and Procter & Gamble veteran, was named chief executive ahead of four internal candidates.[5] As the result of Unilever's strategy at that point, the top 25 brands were responsible for three-quarters of Unilever sales, and management headcount had been reduced by 40 percent.

A new initiative, known as the Compass,[6] was launched that contained, according to Polman, an energizing vision and strategy to bring the company back to sustainable growth based on a passion for getting the consumer (end user) and customer (wholesaler) squarely back on the agenda. The new vision was to double the business and outperform market growth, at the same time reducing overall environmental impact. The Compass (Exhibit 3-1) was used as the basis for providing alignment in a company with more than 160,000 employees and operating in more than 150 countries around the globe.

As seen from the Unilever example, transformation is a journey that begins with leadership. It took nine years to transition from a dual leadership toward hiring an external CEO who would act in an environment where shaping

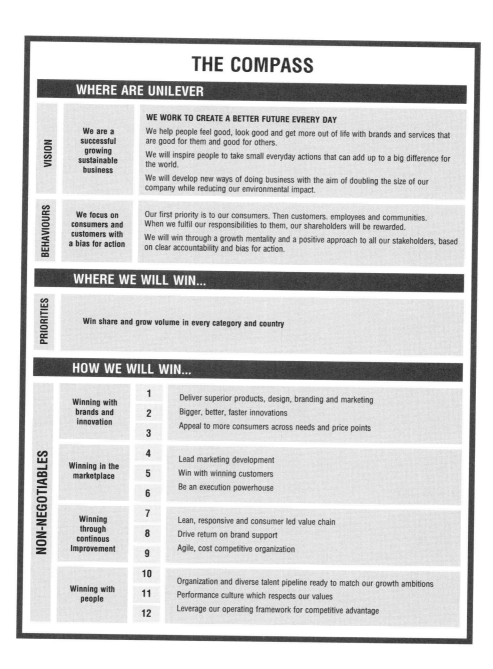

Exhibit 3-1. Unilever's Compass

strategy and building value are facilitated by the previous work of de-layering their various management levels around the globe.

Once leadership is in place, the next step is to establish direction and create an agenda. Then come people alignment and the development of a human network for achieving the agenda. To get the agenda executed, people need to be inspired and motivated to produce change that results in the outcomes associated with strategy. This is achieved by:

- *Communicating the Strategy Throughout the Organization.* The alignment of players in support of a common business strategy is a key factor to achieve success in all company settings. Alignment implies being lined up and heading in the same direction, so that the organization converges toward the business strategy. Thus management style and corporate culture come into play, expressly to align the hearts and minds of people behind the organization's strategic intent.

- *Adopting Portfolio Selection and the Management of Individual Projects as well as Program Management Practices.* Whereas a business strategy lays out broad directions and determines what is to be accomplished, the portfolio of projects defines how the strategy is to be put into effect.

Projects are the true traction points for strategic execution. They develop new businesses, markets, products, services, systems, skills, and alliances. A company's project portfolio drives its future value. Successful strategic execution requires tightly aligning the project portfolio to the corporate strategy. These projects then become part of the portfolio of projects, and the players involved marshal forces behind each project, in turn contributing to the overall company goal.

The aggregate of an organization's wide range of projects is encompassed in its portfolio of projects. Some of those projects may be freshly approved, others are in the planning or implementation phases, and yet others are zeroing in on completion. Aside from the timing variances, they are likely to vary in nature, including strategic initiatives, capital expenditure, product launch, and operational improvement. The challenge for top management includes keeping a company's project portfolio aligned with the business strategy and available resources, at the same time ensuring that projects are aligned with one another and with the organizational structure. Only by continuously reviewing the project portfolio, carefully allocating available resources, and consciously realigning the organization can a company bring its proposed strategy to life.

An organization's portfolio of projects is the offspring of the business strategy. Based on those strategies, projects are developed aimed at generating the benefits envisioned by the strategists. The project portfolio lies at the crossroads where vision, leadership, and strategy meet culture, people, processes, systems, performance, and results. There is simply no effective way to execute strategy other than making it fully formalized or delegated within the organization. The portfolio is the true materialization of an organization's intent, direction, and progress.

For all that to happen, collaboration is required between business strategists and project strategists, and the collaboration must be aimed at answering the following questions:

- How many projects should make up the core of the portfolio?
- What kinds of projects are needed?
- How should they be organized?
- Who will be responsible?
- When will they be launched?
- Are sufficient resources available?

The answers to these questions depend on company culture, previous practices, present needs, market demand, and stakeholders' opinions. Once these factors have been taken into account and the corresponding project portfolio criteria determined, much of the alignment challenge is taken care of.

Execution, however, guarantees that the aligned hierarchy of strategy, goals, objectives, projects, and programs results in business change produced by outputs, outcomes, and benefits. Once the hierarchy is aligned, benefits realization can start as simple as evaluating a small number of projects and comparing their results with initial expectations.

In practice, things may work out differently. Scenarios change while projects are underway; priorities fluctuate as different players move in and out of the scene; projects—sometimes based on personal agendas—spring up out of the woodwork and try to nestle themselves into the portfolio of projects.

Although top-down, strategy-to-project alignment is indeed a major priority for an organization's portfolio of projects, a process is required to ensure that the bottom-up project proposals are appropriately screened so that they are aligned with company strategy.

Apple's Revival

It's easy to forget just how desperate Apple was during the 1990s. It was widely believed to be on the path to extinction. For example, Michael Dell, the founder of Dell, stated before a crowd of several thousand IT executives, "What would I do? I'd shut it down and give the money back to the shareholders."[7] Around the same time, Microsoft's chief technology officer called Apple "already dead."[8]

Steve Jobs's return to Apple in 1996 marked the beginning of Apple's revival, and his subsequent work makes for a good example of how strategy is deployed and executed to create value. In 2002, Jobs commented to *The New York Times* about his competitive strategy: "I would rather compete with Sony than compete in another product category with Microsoft.... . We're the only company that owns the whole widget, the hardware, the software, and the operating system. We can take full responsibility for the user experience. We can do things the other guys can't do." Clearly, he was carefully evaluating opportunities in the marketplace.[9]

While most high-tech firms focus on one or two sectors, Apple does all of them at once. Apple makes its own hardware, it makes the operating system that runs on that hardware, and it makes programs that run on that operating system. It also makes the consumer-electronics devices that connect to all those things, and it runs the online service that furnishes content for those devices. Bringing together Microsoft, Dell, and Sony into one company, you would have something like the diversity of the Apple technological biosphere.

Steve Jobs's instructive parable about the concept explains how Apple does it:

> You know how you see a show car, and it's really cool, and then four years later you see the production car, and it sucks? What happened? What happened was the designers came up with this really great idea. Then they take it to the engineers, and the engineers go, "Nah, we can't do that. That's impossible." And so it gets a lot worse. Then they take it to the manufacturing people, and they go, "We can't build that!" And it gets a lot worse.[10]

That was the situation he found when he returned to Apple.

The two lessons to be drawn from that story are about collaboration and control. Apple employees talk incessantly about what they call *cross-pollination*. This means that products get worked on in parallel by all departments in endless rounds of interdisciplinary design reviews in a very collaborative, integrated way. In this sort of environment, it is fundamental to keep everybody on track and aligned with the vision and strategy, which in the case of Apple was in Jobs's head.

Steve Jobs's strategy was 100 percent focused on customer-centered innovation. Apple's innovation difference is less about an inward focus on how to squeeze every dollar out of some process or on reducing costs and more about addressing customer frustrations, needs, and expectations. However, if the prime target is innovation, you can't just go out and ask people what the next big thing should be. Innovation requires the capacity to interpret needs and expectations.[11] As Henry Ford once said, if he had asked customers what they wanted, they would have said, "A faster horse!"

Rather than taking a weak company that was struggling to stay afloat and challenge the dominant market maker, Steve Jobs directed Apple innovation strategy to focus on the integration of technology and entertainment. The iMac created a new market for one-piece, no-wires, no-hassle Internet PCs. The iPod created a new market for an integrated hardware–software–service trilogy for digital music appreciation. The iPhone created a new market by unifying hitherto disjointed phone, Internet, and media consumption in a single device. In January 2010, the company introduced iPad, a multipurpose mobile device for browsing the Web, reading and sending email, viewing photos, watching videos, listening to music, and playing games. iPad is based on the company's multitouch technology and allows customers to connect with their applications and content more interactively.

The strategy of focusing on technology and entertainment created outputs such as the iPod, iMac, iPhone, and iPad. These produced client satisfaction and led to the development of a brand image that resulted in benefits like increased sales with high margins, therefore delivering value for Apple customers as well as stockholders.

The company entered the mobile phone industry with an altogether different business strategy known as *value innovation*—making the competition irrelevant by opening up new and untapped markets and by creating a leap in value for consumers. With the iPhone, Apple upstaged Nokia, until 2007 the dominant brand in mobile phones. An interesting fact is that, five years before Apple introduced the iPhone and three years before it launched an online applications store, Nokia was ready to introduce its own Internet-ready touch screen handset with a large display and had an early design of an online applications store. So what happened?

Apparently, Nokia was not able to coordinate decisions and activities across departments or levels of management. With lack of cross-organizational coordination and cooperation, Nokia wasn't able to improve their proprietary operating system, Symbian, which would have allowed it to support a more sophisticated smartphone. The lesson learned is that conflicting organizational activities, silos, redundant processes, and confusing governance policies all contribute to blocking effective and consistent execution.

Nokia's market value took a downward slide in 2007, the year Apple launched the iPhone. In 2006, Nokia had almost 50 percent of the mobile phone market. Four years later, in 2010, its participation went down to 33 percent, demonstrating the company's incapacity to react to a new wave of smartphones. Nokia had to do something.

In September 2010, Stephen Elop joined Nokia as the president and CEO. He announced:

My role, as the leader of Nokia, is to lead this team through this period of change, take the organization through a period of disruption. My job is to create an environment where opportunities are properly captured, to ultimately ensure we are meeting the needs of our customers, while delivering superior financial result.[12]

In February 2011, in an open letter to all employees, Elop posed a question: While competitors poured flames on our market share, what happened at Nokia? We fell behind, we missed big trends, and we lost time. At that time, we thought we were making the right decisions; but, with the benefit of hindsight, we now find ourselves years behind. The first iPhone was shipped in 2007, and we still don't have a product that is close to their experience. Android came on the scene just over 2 years ago, and they have taken our leadership position in smartphone volumes. Unbelievable.[13]

After the letter, Elop announced Nokia's new strategy, including a management shakeup, a significant number of layoffs, and a realignment of their business units. But the boldest change is their embrace of a third-party smartphone platform in Windows Phone 7.

Only time will tell whether Nokia will be capable of aligning their strategy to a desired destination. But one thing is certain: Strategy and alignment require effective implementation with special emphasis on timing, speed, and momentum.

Lessons Learned from Apple and Nokia

For companies like Apple and Nokia to recover from past slumps, once the right strategies are worked out, success rests with effectively implementing those strategies. Success implies having in place all the major components of EPG, including project governance, macroprocesses, culture, and competency. For that to happen, a solid plan toward creating an enterprise-wide project management culture is fundamental. Here are guidelines for making the essential link between strategies and the portfolio of projects.

Key characteristics for organizations to align strategies with project portfolios are:

- *Communication and Coordination.* Failure to communicate, coordinate, and educate is a critical factor in alignment. Project players respond best when they feel informed and are part of the planning and execution process.

- *Strong Link Between Strategy and Project Selection.* Projects tied directly to organizations' strategic objectives make substantial contributions toward companies' results and overall performance.
- *Aborting Questionable Projects.* If changes have occurred such that a project in progress is not contributing to the realization of benefits as intended, project termination should be evaluated.
- *Prioritized Resource Allocation.* Focus by management on prioritizing and balancing resources avoids the pressure to multitask, as well as unexpected errors by overloaded professionals.
- *The Quality of Information.* Regardless of the quality and sophistication of the portfolio selection and decision tools, information quality is essential for making accurate decisions.
- *Project Governance.* A solid governance framework keeps project investment tied to the organization's strategy and precludes having to prioritize work based on nonobjective criteria like personal agendas or internal politics.

Enterprise Project Governance enables organizations to manage the interrelationships of all underlying initiatives comprising a strategic goal. It also provides the boundaries and checkpoints needed to keep programs and projects in alignment with plan goals. Organizations that have established an effective governance model can ensure that all the programs and their underlying projects are managed and harvested for the necessary metrics and progress reporting.

Aligning business strategy remains one of the top issues that business executives wrestle with. One of the major obstacles for achieving strategy alignment is that many organizations do a poor job of communicating strategy. When people who are key to executing strategy don't know what the strategy is or fail to understand how their day-to-day activities contribute to strategy execution, it's likely that the overall enterprise performance will suffer. Strategy maps are one way to shore up communication and ensure alignment with strategy.

Strategy Maps and JetBlue

A strategy map is a generic architecture for describing strategy that helps organizations develop an integrated and systemic way of viewing their strategy. At their simplest, strategy maps describe how the organization creates value, showing cause and effect linkages among the four balanced scorecard perspectives: financial, customer, internal business processes, and learning and growth. The map forces an organization to think about its strategy, to develop the outcomes and drivers of the strategy, and to draw the linkages among them.

Strategy map development is a top-down process that drives an organization to first reach a consensus on its strategy and related objectives and then to develop expected outcomes and their dependent drivers. Financial and customer perspectives represent the expected outcomes of strategy, whereas the internal process and learning and growth perspectives represent the drivers of those outcomes.

Strategy maps create a single language to communicate strategy and objectives proactively by driving consensus on strategy and by creating a common language; it also serves as the entry point to implementing a project portfolio.

Founder David Neeleman started JetBlue Airways in 2000 with the vision of bringing humanity back to air travel. The goal was to be a discount airline carrier that offered comfort and service to its customers. This included providing new planes with leather seats and personal televisions for passengers. It also included never overselling flights, focusing on being on time, updating check-in and boarding procedures, and more. JetBlue was the first airline to implement paperless cockpit flight technology and to have 100 percent e-tickets.

The company grew rapidly based on an expanding fleet of Airbus and Embraer jets. By 2007, JetBlue had been awarded the Best Domestic Airline from Condé Nast Traveller for the fifth consecutive year. In February 2007, a severe snowstorm affected JetBlue's main hub at John F. Kennedy International Airport in New York. This resulted in thousands of passengers grounded in the terminal and in planes on the tarmac. The company was not prepared to face a crisis of such proportion, with more than a thousand flights cancelled and accumulated losses of around US$30 million with ticket refunding, lodging, and overtime crews.[14] Worst of all, the company's shining reputation was tarnished. On top of that, 2007 was a year with high fuel prices affecting operational costs.

JetBlue was aware that, after seven years of phenomenal growth, the time had come for deep reflection. In 2008, the company adopted a new strategy focused on reevaluation of assets, cost reduction, and selective growth. Aircrafts were sold, and delivery for new ones postponed.

The 2009 annual report focused on strategic objectives such as the delivery of the desired benefits, disciplined growth, managing the fleet size, optimization of the route network, cost control, and unit revenue optimization. One of the instruments used to ensure JetBlue's alignment toward the desired goals were strategy maps,[15] as shown in Exhibit 3-2, designed to link management intentions with metrics in order to measure accomplishments. The company's performance management system and bonus program were reformatted to be consistent with the strategy maps.

Strategy alignment is key for the success of EPG and the use of strategy maps is one of the enablers.

Reaping Benefits Through Projects

Interest in managing projects in the context of benefits and outcomes is emerging as the understanding of project management matures. For some, it is a response to concerns around project failure. The aim is the coordination of a portfolio of projects that transforms organizations through the achievement of expected benefits. In this development model, value delivery is linked to business strategy through the integration of the outputs (deliverables) and workflows of multiple interdependent projects. Delivering projects on time and on budget may be appropriate in the development of outputs; however, this approach fails to recognize that projects can still fail if they do not deliver the required benefits to the organization.

Benefits realization focuses on the benefits that a program, project, or portfolio will deliver for the business and begins with the following fundamental questions:

- Why is the initiative being undertaken?

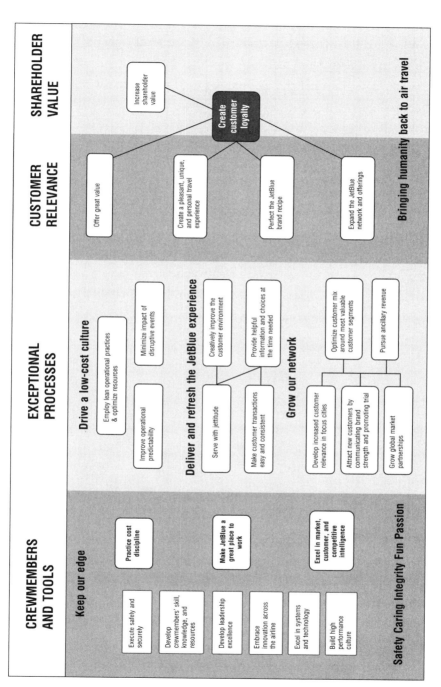

Exhibit 3-2. JetBlue Strategy Map

- What are the planned outcomes and long-term benefits the project aims to achieve?
- What organizational changes are required to realize the planned outcomes?
- Who is responsible and accountable?

Project outputs are integrated into outcomes, benefits, and the ultimate value creation as shown in Exhibit 3-3.

On the one hand, the main concern for project and program definition is to understand how impacts are connected to the needs on both a strategic and a tactical level. What impacts will give shareholders maximum value? Reality shows that, when asked for impacts, executives seem to have a very difficult time articulating clear end results. If the problem is the inability to articulate impacts, then there is little point in developing an elegant strategy.

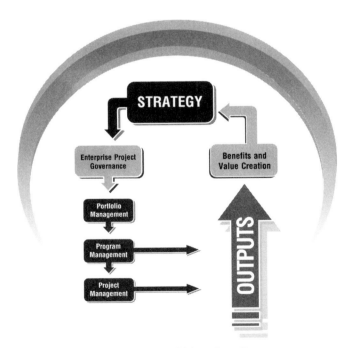

Exhibit 3-3. From Strategic Thinking to Value Creation

John Thorp, author of the best seller *The Information Paradox*, in an interview for APM,[16] observed that "benefits don't just happen and they rarely happen according to plan. They need to be managed. Much of the activity today is still focused on the front end and getting the money rather than full life-cycle management." He further observed that benefits management is portrayed as entering the mainstream of project and program management and is increasingly perceived as a broader governance issue, not just an IT governance issue.

The following are the topics that the executive team must reach a common understanding on in order to establish the connections between strategy and their expected impacts:

- The future value creation resulting from an adopted strategy
- The links to overall organizational strategy deployment and the resulting business change
- Assumptions made on cascading strategy
- How impacts are to be measured
- The tangible work product in terms of project outputs that must be created to reach the outcome

The Logframe Approach

The logical framework (Logframe) has come to play a central role in the planning and management of development interventions. Originally developed by the U.S. Department of Defense, it was then adapted for the U.S. space agency NASA before being adopted by USAID (United States Agency for International Development) for development projects in the late 1960s. It was picked up by European development organizations in the 1980s and, by the end of the 1990s, Logframe had become the standard approach required by many donors for grant applications.

Logframe has been in use at the World Bank[17] since 1997, when it became a standard attachment to project appraisal for investment operations. It is used by private companies, municipalities, and international development organizations when assessing and making follow-ups and evaluations of projects and programs. Logframe is a tool that has the power to communicate the essential elements of a complex project clearly and succinctly throughout the project cycle.

Managing program performance in the public sector has always been a challenge because of the difficulty to measure the effectiveness of government programs to achieve expected benefits. Governments commonly express the range of programs delivered in the context of a logical framework, such as the Australian Government Outcomes and Outputs Framework.

The Australian framework[18] has placed a strong emphasis on outcomes as the foundation for performance information for more than two decades with the objectives of improving agencies' corporate governance and enhancing public accountability. The framework is defined in the context of governments delivering benefits to the Australian community, primarily through programs, goods, and services (outputs), which are delivered against specific performance indicators, as shown in Exhibit 3-4. The benefits, outcomes, and outputs are the drivers of strategic decision making.

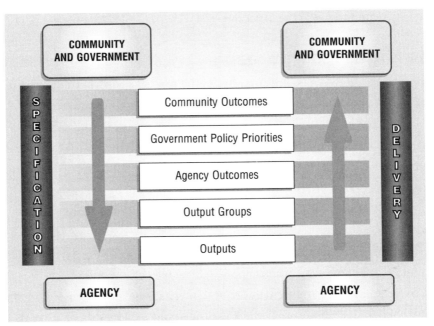

Exhibit 3-4. Relationship Between Outcomes and Outputs

Strategy alignment requires formal interfacing to make sure that completed projects contribute substantially toward corporate value creation and requires major improvement over the well-known grenade-over-the-wall approach. In this view, the business planning staff identifies and characterizes strategies and then tosses the goals over to an uninformed and uninvolved project management team that is shackled with successfully completing a project, which may or may not be fully aligned with company objectives. Exhibit 3-5 shows a simple logical framework approach that can be applied to projects. The purpose of creating these sorts of matrixes is on the one hand to guarantee that nothing is lost along the deployment between strategy and each of the associated projects, especially all the assumptions. People have a tendency to assume that everyone knows the assumptions embedded in a project. Nothing is more wrong! On the other hand, there is a necessity to make sure that the expected benefits are being realized. Linking the two poles are the established metrics for progress evaluation.

Strategy Alignment Through a CPMO

An approach to facilitate the governance of aligning strategy is to organize

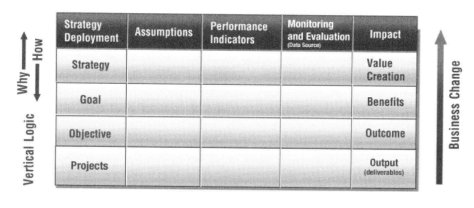

Exhibit 3-5. Connecting Strategy Deployment to Business Change

a corporate project management office (CPMO), sometimes called a strategic project office. CPMO is a value-adding structure to provide the coordination and the broad perspective needed to select, prioritize, and monitor projects and programs that contribute to the attainment of corporate strategy. The CPMO provides the organizational home for communicating the strategy throughout the organization and converting it into a portfolio of programs and projects.

The structure is guided by the CPMO steering committee. This committee is normally made up of the director of the CPMO, the heads of the business units, and the heads of supporting organizations, such as IT. This committee is formed and is active on a continuing basis to select, prioritize, and evaluate the entire corporate portfolio of projects. When major issues or problems must be escalated, the CPMO steering committee provides a forum for issue or problem resolution.

Finally, cascading and aligning strategy downward and upward in an organization requires governance, part of which is operationalized through programs and projects that will produce benefits capable of translating intention into execution. Some necessary projects are as follows:

- Strategy mapping
- Facilitated sessions for structuring goal setting
- Incentive system redesign
- Executive compensation realignment
- Organizing a corporate project management office
- Facilitated sessions for structuring the why-how framework
- Establishing a monitoring and follow-up calendar

Conclusions

Business strategists and project managers may appear to come from different worlds, yet they have strongly shared roles. The key to linking strategies to the right project portfolio is overall alignment. The governance framework associated with strategy alignment ensures that decisions are made coherently up and down the organization and that a set of responsibilities and practices is defined and exercised by executive management with the following goals:

- The strategic direction is clearly understood throughout the organization, and business units and levels of management are focused on aligning themselves to this strategic direction.

- The execution of strategic objectives is permanently monitored to measure performance.

The link between strategy and value creation is a waterfall in which corporate strategy is translated into a portfolio of programs and projects cascading across business and supporting units. It is designed to carry out the strategic rationale in a decision environment that is the result of a wave of impacts (outputs, outcomes, and benefits) that ultimately will result in value creation. Along this journey, measurement is critical in order to monitor progress and to evaluate whether intentions are being translated into execution toward the right direction.

4

Risk Management: Dealing with Uncertainty

In February 2002, during a news briefing, U.S. Secretary of Defense Donald Rumsfeld addressed the absence of evidence linking the government of Iraq with the supply of weapons of mass destruction to terrorist groups by making a dodging statement:

> As we know, there are known knowns; there are things we know we know. We also know there are known unknowns; that is to say we know there are some things we do not know. But there are also unknown unknowns; the ones we don't know we don't know. And if one looks throughout the history of our country and other free countries, it is the latter category that tends to be the difficult ones.[1]

The quote, long in use within the United States military establishment, was based on the classic *On War* from the famous Prussian, General Clausewitz. In the book he commented that "three quarters of the factors on which action in war is based are wrapped in a log of greater or lesser uncertainty. ... Many intelligence reports in war are contradictory; even more are false, and most are uncertain."[2]

NASA exploration involves numerous unknowns in missions involving difficult, dangerous, and dynamic operations, ranging from earth orbits to planetary and universe exploration. These missions push the limits of human, technological, and theoretical knowledge boundaries. With all its success, NASA has had failures that cost billions of dollars, experienced lost opportunities for scientific advancement, and resulted in the loss of human lives.

Uncertainties in NASA missions are countless, and they involve known-knowns, known-unknowns, and unknown-unknowns. Universe exploration is about developing complex systems and diving into the unknown-unknown. As the commission that investigated the loss of the Columbia space shuttle noted, "Complex systems almost always fail in complex ways."[3] And, most of the time, the failures happen in unpredictable ways. Worth noting is that these mishaps are frequently rooted in the organization's culture, management, and structure.

In 2000, NASA released a series of reports in response to failures in the Mars Program, shuttle wiring problems, and a generic assessment of NASA's approach to executing "faster, better, cheaper" projects. The need for improving risk management was flagged as the highest priority. For example, *the Enhancing Mission Success, a Framework for the Future from NASA Integrated Action Team* report recommended: "Improve and enhance NASA and contractor knowledge and ability to identify, assess, mitigate, and track risk through the definition of success criteria, acceptable risk, utilization of existing and new tools, and proper policy and guidance."[4]

The principles of risk highlighted in the NASA report are equally applicable in other corporate or governmental agency settings and are essential parts of an organization's EPG policies. The report pinpointed causes for failures and proposed preventive measures aimed at mitigating the risks in future space missions.

From Outer Space to Subsea

Aside from NASA's space probes, other forms of exploration also constitute risky business. In April 2010, in the Gulf of Mexico, the largest marine oil spill in history occurred, caused by an explosion on the *Deepwater Horizon* offshore oil platform. The platform was owned by Transocean, under contract with British Petroleum to drill an exploratory well in the Macondo oil field, a joint venture of British Petroleum (65 percent), the operator, Anadarko Petroleum (25 percent), and Mitsui Oil Exploration (10 percent).

At the time of the explosion, Halliburton, another contractor, had recently completed the cementing of casings in the well, and BP and Transocean were closing the well in anticipation of later production. Eleven crew members died and others were seriously injured as fire engulfed and ultimately destroyed the rig.

Over a 90-day period, BP's failed attempts to stop or mitigate the oil flow spotlighted the sharp contrast between the industry's ability to successfully extract oil from deeper offshore sites and the necessary capability to predict and deal with accidents when they occur. As exploration moved into deeper and riskier waters, regulatory agencies were late in recommending independent monitoring or mandating preparation for disaster recovery.

The BP internal investigation report[5] assigned partial blame to itself and repeatedly focused on the failure of cement barriers in the well, placing blame on work done by Halliburton. It also pointed out the responsibility of the rig's owner, stating that "Transocean was solely responsible for operation of the drilling rig and for operations safety. It was required to maintain well control equipment and use all reasonable means to control and prevent fire and blowouts."

In response, Transocean dismissed the BP report as a "self-serving report … that attempted to conceal the critical factor that set the stage for the Macondo incident, BP's fatally flawed well design. In both its design and construction, BP made a series of cost-saving decisions that increased risk, in some cases, severely." Halliburton also pointed to a number of substantial omissions and inaccuracies by BP. [6]

On May 2010, President Barack Obama announced the creation of the National Commission on the BP Deepwater Horizon Oil Spill and Offshore Drilling, an independent, nonpartisan entity, directed to provide a thorough analysis and impartial judgment. The Commission report issued in January 2011 concluded that:

> the explosive loss of the Macondo well could have been prevented. ... The immediate causes of the Macondo well blowout can be traced to a series of identifiable mistakes made by BP, Halliburton, and Transocean that reveal such systematic failures in risk management that they place in doubt the safety culture of the entire industry. ... The Deepwater Horizon disaster exhibits the costs of a culture of complacency. There are recurring themes of missed warning signals, failure to share information, and a general lack of appreciation for the risks involved. In the view of the Commission, these findings highlight the importance of organizational culture and a consistent commitment to safety by industry, from the highest management levels on down.[7]

Unquestionably BP, Halliburton, and Transocean have detailed standards and procedures to address operational functionality or to tackle health and safety issues. However, the beliefs and attitudes toward these standards, associated with a lack of team integration, were the root causes of an accident that spiraled into corporate and ecological disaster.

Deepwater Horizon remains as a beacon indicating that the development of a risk-mature culture within organizations requires recognizing the interdependence of risks at the strategic, tactical, and operational level of the enterprise and that they must be managed proactively. An integrated approach to risk management can create competitive advantage by bridging level gaps to enable the realization of business benefits and to avoid disasters and crisis.

Lessons learned from most business disasters can be traced back to bad risk taking. When managers overreach and expose their businesses to the wrong type of risks or accept too much risk, investors in these firms bear the brunt of the unfortunate decisions. Decision makers are responsible for taking the right amount of risk.

The Development of Risk Management

Until the early 1980s, risk was relatively new to those outside the insurance industry. Up to that time, companies were able to transfer certain risks to insurance companies. These transferred risks related to natural catastrophes, accidents, human error, or fraud. Later, companies began to look more closely at financial risks, like exchange rates, commodity prices, interest rates, and stock prices. This was the beginning of financial risk management as a formal system.

A major drive toward more formalized approaches to risk management, corporate governance, and internal controls resulted from the high-profile collapses of major corporations since the late 1990s. These scandals found executives testifying that they were unaware of unethical activities carried on by their companies. This prompted new regulatory environments such as Sarbanes-Oxley (SOX) in the United States, the Combined Code on Corporate Governance in the United Kingdom, and the Basel II Accord for the banking sector, all with a strong focus on internal controls and on making company executives responsible for establishing, evaluating, and monitoring the effectiveness of their company's internal control structure. The most widely accepted definition of internal control was developed by the Committee of Sponsoring Organizations (COSO) of the Treadway Commission:

> a process, effected by an entity's board of directors, management, and other personnel, designed to provide reasonable assurance regarding the achievement of objectives in the following categories: effectiveness and efficiency of operations; reliability of financial reporting; compliance with applicable laws and regulations.[8]

The most contentious aspect of SOX is Section 404, which requires management to produce an annual internal control report that must affirm the responsibility of management for establishing and maintaining an adequate internal control structure and procedures for financial reporting. The report must also contain an assessment of the effectiveness of the internal control structure and procedures of the issuer for financial reporting.

Internal controls are fundamental to the successful operation and day-to-day running of a business and to assisting the company in achieving their business objectives. The scope of internal controls is very broad. It encompasses all controls incorporated into the strategic, governance, and management processes, covering the company's entire range of activities and operations, not just those directly related to financial operations and reporting. The scope is not confined to the aspects of a business that could broadly be defined as compliance but extends also to the performance aspects.

In the same way that internal control is a key aspect of corporate governance, risk management is a vital element of internal control because bad risk management may affect the internal controls in all organizational areas. Identifying risks and creating systems and safeguards to ameliorate them is one way to create a sound internal control framework. As a result, internal controls depend on effective risk management to guarantee quality performance and compliance for organizations to achieve their business objectives, as shown in Exhibit 4-1.

Because CEOs and CFOs are obliged to make public statements attesting to the effectiveness of internal control, a framework is required that is based on objective criteria and that is subject to measurement.

As the field of risk management expanded, proposals were formed toward creating a corporate culture able to hurdle the risks associated with rapidly

Exhibit 4-1. Internal Control Framework

changing business environments. The concept was tagged *enterprise risk management (ERM)*. The overarching principle of ERM is that it must produce value for the organization, producing a net effect that is more than the cost of risk management and risk controls.

For risk to be seen as adding value to an organization, a view broader than the conventional meaning of "danger" is required.

The word *risk* is depicted in Chinese by two characters that give insight to a more holistic meaning. The first character signifies "threat" and the other "opportunity."

$$危機$$

In this sense, risk can be seen as having a downside and an upside, where indeed the threatening component exists, yet opportunities also present themselves. Enterprise risk management effectively boils down to avoiding unnecessary exposure that might endanger meeting projected goals, at the same time staying alert for opportunities to add value.

Risk Management at BHP Billiton

BHP Billiton focuses on long-term value creation through the development of natural resources operating in steelmaking, raw materials, copper, coal, nickel, uranium, and oil and gas in more than 25 countries. Risk management is embedded throughout the organization from the top down.

The company began implementing enterprise risk management (ERM) in 2002, after the merger of BHP and Billiton. It was board driven. Their board governance statement set the mandate for risk management, stating that "… the identification and management of risk is central to achieving the corporate objective of delivering long-term value to shareholders."[9] Documents were approved and implemented requiring a systematic approach to identifying and managing risk. That was supported by a risk management policy that outlines principles, performance standards, guidelines, and methodologies. The document was signed by the CEO and countersigned by the asset presidents and displayed at site level.

Over 80,000 risks are identified online and documented at BHP Billiton. Asset managers responsible for those risks are expected to demonstrate that risk management is indeed an integral part of their management duties by showing that risks are monitored and controlled and that necessary corrective action is taken.[10]

At each BHP Billiton asset, risk management is conducted regularly. Each asset reports key material risks through to senior management and ultimately the board level. Twice a year, BHP's risk profile is reviewed to ensure that appropriate controls have been put in place. Ultimately, the vice president of risk management must provide a reasonable assurance to the CEO that the processes and controls are in place and working.

Having reached a high stage of maturity with ERM and its risk financing program, they targeted simplification. For example, the number of risk management guidelines has been reduced from 14 to two and the standards from seven to four. Simplifying the process ensures that key risks are identified.

The risk methodology is established in an enterprise-wide policy, approved by the BHP Billiton CEO and by senior management of each asset. Olympic Dam, the world's largest uranium resource and fourth largest copper deposit, is an example of such an asset.

A global BHP Billiton policy, overseen by a risk management steering committee, ensures that the importance of risk management is understood by personnel in all assets. The steering committee's role includes overall risk governance aimed at limiting uncertainty by managing exposures, and it includes evaluating each asset's risk profile, as well as tracking over time changes to potential risks. Strategies for risk mitigation are also part of the committee's responsibilities.

The risk management plan indicates specific goals and strategies for Olympic Dam, and it is prepared in conjunction with the asset management team based on a two-stage business continuity management model. When an issue is detected that could affect business continuity, the short-term, initial response is control and containment, meaning that the crisis is to be managed and the stakeholders informed. Once the crisis is contained, the resumption and consolidation phase begins, if required. An on-site incident management team trains regularly to handle crisis situations. The final phase includes business impact analysis, as well as the identification of vulnerabilities, critical assets, and events that could cause any extended downtime.

Proactive risk management, however, doesn't preclude potential disasters, so contingency plans for potential occurrences are still required at Olympic Dam, as well as other BHP Billiton assets, has a program for identifying major risk liabilities, along with appropriate plans to deal with the consequences of the unfavorable occurrences. While a robust risk management program continues to be the best preventive measure to avoid disasters, well thought-out remedial plans are also part of dealing with risks.

The Maturity Continuum

Risk management takes on different forms in different organizations. The responsibility may rest solely with a part-time professional or, at another extreme, require a full-fledged department to deal with an array of multibillion-dollar issues. At Mars Corporation, a worldwide multibillion-dollar corporation noted for chocolate bars, an ERM program was approved by the board and implemented over a four-year period. A series of implementation workshops was conducted throughout the organization to help create a solid base for reaping benefits from risk management. Having established the basic risk culture, Mars began to integrate ERM into other managerial pillars, such as strategic planning and performance management. The risk management framework was also used to interact with the business units for identifying and mitigating strategic and operational risks at that level.

The Mars ERM team takes a proactive stance in working with leaders throughout the organization by conducting annual workshops that provide opportunity for the open exchange of views about potential risks and how to deal with them. Risks of all natures are examined, including strategic and operational, as well as those related to portfolios, programs, and projects.

Another organization that embraced ERM is Hydro One,[11] the largest electricity company in Ontario, Canada. In 1999, when the company began to adopt ERM, the board and management had established ambitious goals for high achievement with excellent corporate governance and superior performance through the use of best practices. The company perceived risk management as an integrated way to identify both threats and opportunities in the allocation of resources in a scenario that involves ever increasing oversight by government regulatory agencies.

Hydro One's senior management established a team, called the Corporate Risk Management Group, to show the value of ERM and fixed a six-month time frame to provide proof for a go-ahead with the program. Two full-time professionals, a part-time chief risk officer, and as-needed consulting support comprised the team.

The team initially produced an ERM policy document that laid out broad principles for governance, responsibilities, and accountabilities. An ERM framework was also prepared, which set forth pragmatic how-to procedures for managing risk. Still requiring solid evidence to justify a full-scale program, the board recommended doing a pilot study with one of the subsidiaries, which would then be subject to the approval of board committees.

A workshop approach was used in the pilot study to help clarify the business objectives and to address the related risks. Risk was defined as "having potential to threaten the achievement of business objectives," so the clarification of those objectives was particularly important. The workshop discussions revealed that many risk-related issues had been thought about but not openly discussed and evaluated. Through the pilot program, a common understanding of risks was attained and a corporate plan for prioritizing and managing risks developed. The pilot was a success, and the program was approved by the board for overall implementation.

The ERM program implementation took about five years. It delivered benefits such as a positive reaction of the credit rating agencies, the resulting reduction in the company's cost of debt, and the improvement of capital expenditure taking into account the benefit of risk reduction in all major risk categories.

Risk Management Maturity Continuum

Overall risk management in organizations evolves over time and is impacted by a learning process, as shown in Exhibit 4-2. First, organizations begin reacting to risks and are managed in silos with no common language to communicate throughout the company. Once organizations recognize the need for an integrated approach, a common vocabulary begins, and key organizational risks are identified. More and more, the organization understands the need for structuring.

Finally, risk management becomes part of the enterprise strategic thinking. The adoption of an overall risk management policy helps create awareness and commitment, keeping senior management focused on high-level risks that will affect results and the organizations' capacity to meet its objectives. Nevertheless, there is a wide perception that the current state of maturity is low. A 2010 COSO survey highlighted that the state of ERM appears immature, with 60 percent of respondents saying that their risk tracking is mostly informal and applied in silos and that there is a notable level of dissatisfaction with how organizations are currently overseeing enterprise-wide risks.[12]

ISO 31000 and ERM

The International Organization for Standardization (ISO) noncertifiable Standard 31000, Risk Management: Principles and Guidelines, published in 2009 with the participation of 30 countries, seeks to answer differing views on risk

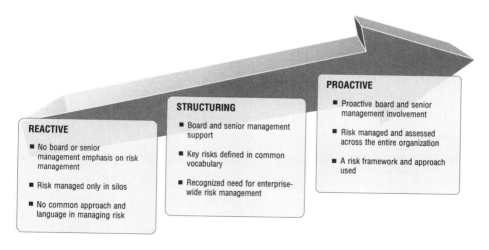

Exhibit 4-2. Risk Maturity Management Continuum

and risk management.[13] The standard supports a simple way of thinking about risk and risk management and is designed to resolve the many inconsistencies and ambiguities among differing approaches and definitions.

Every organization has its own unique risk footprint and its own risk management challenges. The aim is to establish a consistent framework that can be integrated across various industries and regions and adopted by any organization—including public, private, not-for-profit, and government entities—to benefit all organizations confronting the always problematic challenges of managing risk.

ISO 31000 defines risk as the effect of uncertainty on objectives. Risk is the consequence of an organization's setting and pursuing objectives against an uncertain environment. The uncertainty is driven by internal and external factors that may prevent the organization from achieving its objectives. Striving toward business goals always carries an element of risk and uncertainty, and the effective management of that risk makes possible meeting the established goals. This definition is totally aligned with the top management aims of driving the organization to a desired point in the future.

The ISO standard is built around three fundamental pillars: principles, framework, and processes (Exhibit 4-3). *Principles* position risk management as fundamental in the success of the organization rather than a wearisome burden. As such, risk management must be considered to create and protect value, and it must be an integral part of the organization's processes and decision making. Each decision maker is accountable for risk management as a critical discipline, including the identification, analysis, and evaluation of any risks.

The standard also states that, to be successful, risk management should function within a risk management *framework* that provides the foundations and organizational arrangements that embed it throughout the organization at all levels. The risk management framework is the management system that defines and describes how risk management will permeate the organization. Once commitment is established, using a systematic, structured, and timely approach makes risk management a continual and active process, not a once-a-year exercise that can be left on the shelf to gather dust.

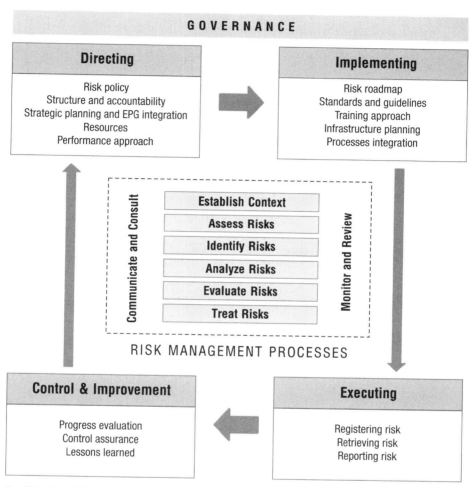

Exhibit 4-3. ISO 31000 Structure

This is in full alignment with regulators, such as in Basel II, which considers board and senior management oversight a main feature of rigorous, forward-looking stress testing that identifies possible events or changes in market conditions that could adversely impact the organization. The board of directors should ensure that "the formality and sophistication of the risk management processes are appropriate in light of the risk profile and business plan."[14]

Finally, the standard addresses the *processes* for managing risk with five primary activities:

1. Communication and consultation
2. Establishing the context
3. Risk assessment, where risk is identified, analyzed, and evaluated
4. Risk treatment
5. Monitoring and review

The standard is intended to be used throughout an organization. Deployment timing and sequence may vary by organization, but it serves to reinforce the concept of formality and structure.

By simplifying complex concepts and coupling the framework with the process and principles, ISO 31000 is likely to subsume all the existing risk management standards by providing a platform for developing effective management of risk, no matter where a company's operations are located. Some of the benefits resulting from managing risk are:

- Full integration in the organization's governance structure (in which EPG is included)
- Improved governance
- Increased likelihood of achieving objectives
- Improved identification of opportunities and threats
- Compliance with relevant legal and regulatory environment and improve controls

Exhibit 4-3 presents the integration of the organization's governance, the risk framework, and the risk management processes to be deployed throughout the organization as indicated in ISO 31000.

ERM and EPG

Managing risk in an integrated way can mean everything from using financial instruments to managing specific financial exposures, from effectively responding to rapid reactions in the organizational environment to natural disasters and political instability. Within this wider understanding of integrated risk management, the ability to tackle the risks involved across the strategy/execution gap is mandatory, as discussed in previous chapters.

The EPG realm addresses the strategy-execution gap by considering risk management as part of portfolio, program, and project management processes already covered by well-known standards. But one could appropriately question that risks are within the focus of ERM. In reality, EPG benefits from the overall structure for ERM while supporting ERM with well-established processes to identify, analyze, and mitigate risks. It is critical to start alignment and integration between ERM and EPG at the top, as shown in the directing block of the framework in Exhibit 4-3. The effective implementation of integrated risk management can produce a number of benefits to the organization that are not available from the typical limited scope of analyzing only risk processes without considering the broader context of the permanent organization.

This is the only way of providing useful information to decision makers when the environment is uncertain in order to support the best possible decisions at all levels, of creating space to manage uncertainty in advance with planned responses to known risks, and of minimizing threats and maximizing opportunities and so increasing the likelihood of achieving strategic objectives.

Conclusions

Risk management can be applied to an entire organization and has earned increasing attention at executive levels. It is also part of portfolio, program, and project management and, as such, an integral part of Enterprise Project Governance. High-tech mega projects, such as space shots and deep-sea oil explorations, require particularly effective risk prevention measures due to the possibility of potential catastrophes. Yet, although perhaps less dramatic, major organizations also face possible disasters when risk management is lacking in their portfolio of projects. For this reason, risk management is a component of EPG, and a link with ERM must be established. In reality, care should be taken to guarantee an integration and articulation between ERM, EPG, strategic planning, and auditing.

The ISO 31000 is designed to be applicable across various industries and regions and adoptable by any organization. When the standard is implemented and maintained accordingly, the ground is prepared for the development of a risk-mature culture within the organization, recognizing that risk exists in all levels of the enterprise but that risk can and should be managed proactively in order to deliver benefits. After all, the greatest risk of all is to take no risk at all.

5

Project Portfolio Management: The Right Combination of the Right Projects

An organization can be seen as a portfolio of projects. Although most organizations have a major component of operational business-as-usual activities, the growing number of project initiatives demands major time from top executives and managers. So the view of a company as a portfolio of projects makes perfect sense for achieving the goals set by an organization. That's how organizations keep up with the demands heaped upon them by racing evolution and pile-driving external pressures—by dreaming up and putting into practice projects that meet the needs of company strategy and the cravings of the marketplace. New projects are the key to staying ahead of the survival curve and ensuring growth and prosperity.[1]

The aggregate results of an organization's project are what constitute a substantial part of a company's bottom line. Missions, objectives, strategies, and goals are transformed into company-wide programs that translate corporate intentions into actions. Those programs are, in turn, broken down into projects. Corporate results are then viewed from an aggregate project perspective as opposed to the conventional department template.

Two Views: Strategy Alignment versus Execution

Effective project portfolios naturally mirror the company's strategic direction, as outlined in Chapter 3. Good strategy is the bedrock of successful project portfolio management, and part of portfolio management consists of ensuring that projects remain aligned with the organization's strategy. Portfolio management, therefore, includes the responsibility for questioning the timelines of project strategies and for articulating necessary adjustments.

The other side of managing project portfolios encompasses seeing that projects are implemented in accordance with the priorities, quality, cost, and time lines. For projects to yield the proposed benefit, they have to be executed effectively and efficiently. In all scenarios, the job of portfolio management is to correct situations when things aren't going right, with the solutions ranging from aborting a project that strays drastically off course to implementing a recovery approach for a lagging initiative. Project portfolio management includes looking at competing investment opportunities and prioritizing those that promise the greatest impact on strategic objectives.[2]

The project portfolio provides a big-picture view. It enables managers to size up all projects in the portfolio and provides an understanding of the collection as a whole. It facilitates the sensible sorting, adding, and removal of projects from the collection based on real-time information.

A consolidated project inventory is constructed by listing all the organization's ongoing and proposed projects. Alternatively, multiple project inventories can be created representing portfolios for different departments, programs, or businesses. Since project portfolio management can be conducted at any level, the choice of one portfolio versus many depends on the size of the organization, its structure, and the nature and interrelationships among the projects being conducted.

Grouping projects using common resources is key to leveraging the knowledge and expertise needed to manage the portfolio. When multiple-project portfolios are defined, related projects are organized into common portfolios. Portfolios of highly interrelated projects are referred to as *programs*—groups of projects selected and managed in a coordinated way in order to maximize success. Exhibit 5-1 illustrates a relationship among portfolios in a large organization.[3]

Value is the key element in portfolio decision making; however, quantifying value is not always straightforward. Creating high-value projects is a snap when the factors that create or destroy individual project value are clearly identified and quantified. Assessing overall portfolio value, however, is more complex. Although individual projects are managed for value, the overall portfolio

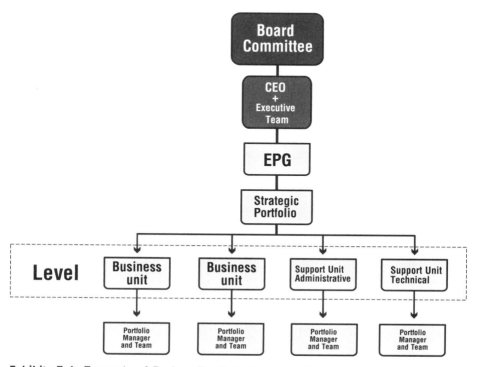

Exhibits 5-1. Example of Project Portfolio Organization

requires a balanced set of projects to ensure alignment with resource availability and company strategies. For instance, a great project for a new product will produce little gain for the organization if marketing doesn't have a corresponding product launch project in the works.

Exhibit 5-1 shows programs and projects composed of a project portfolio designed to support high-level strategies on a corporate level or individual business units. Since the nature of projects varies substantially, it makes sense to look at groups of projects from distinct viewpoints. For instance, the following groups may call for a customized approach both for portfolio selection and subsequent performance tracking:

1. *Strategic.* Projects that create substantial value.
2. *Operational.* Upgrade or improvement projects that make the organization more efficient.
3. *Compliance.* Must-do projects that are required to comply with government regulations.

Why Manage Project Portfolios

Motives abound for using a structured approach for managing an organization's project portfolio. Although company portfolios have always been managed, either intuitively or under existing organizational criteria, structured approaches stand to deal more effectively with growing challenges, such as:

- Burgeoning bottom-up demand from within the organization for improvement projects.
- The need to innovate and develop new products to guarantee organizational sustainability.
- Limited resources, limiting the number of projects.
- The requirement for balance among projects.

A structured approach to project portfolio management ensures the alignment of projects with corporate strategies and optimizes resource allocation. It's the bridge that connects strategic decision making to project execution. Although project portfolio management may be practiced at multiple levels in organizations, the focus in this chapter is on overall project portfolio management. That focus zeroes in on critical strategic projects and programs, as well as those that require integration across the organization, thus not including other project portfolios focused on specific or departmental units such as IT. This corporate approach provides an agile platform for selecting the right projects and for filtering out the wrong ones. It also puts forth a mechanism for the effective use of resources, along with a means for tweaking the portfolio to meet market fluctuations.

Project Portfolio Management: Two Major Components

What does it take to manage a portfolio of projects across an enterprise? How does the management of the portfolio fit into the corporate picture? The foundation for dealing with projects is established by the principles of Enterprise Project Governance, as outlined in Chapter 2. This provides the umbrella under which *project portfolio management (PPM)* is carried out. The global strategy's link with project prioritization and execution is thus guaranteed, and the components of portfolio management are dealt with coherently.

The project portfolio scope typically includes a combination of processes, including opportunity assessment, business case analysis, approvals, and execution tracking. The processes are assessed and adjusted continually with a strong spotlight on management decision making. Items such as cost, benefit, time, and risk require follow-up throughout the process, and projects require wrap-up in terms of postproject evaluation and lessons learned. What follows are the major components of portfolio management.

The Right Projects: Sizing Up Opportunities and Prioritizing

Candidates for comprising the project portfolio come from different areas. Some proposed projects come from market-driven needs that are required to keep pace with the evolving times. Others fall into the category of innovation, where new ideas are tested in hopes of creating a niche of opportunity. Regulatory projects also demand their space because they are must-do government-required undertakings. Improvement projects also filter up from within the organization and compete for space in the portfolio. Initially, all these new initiatives and project ideas are collected, so that they can be preselected as worthy candidates for further analysis.

Invariably, more projects reach out for a slot on the portfolio of projects than resources and time allow. The first part of portfolio management involves sizing up the most promising opportunities so that they can subsequently be filtered and prioritized.

The best use of limited organization resources requires a decision process to evaluate which projects to start, which to keep ongoing, and which projects to abort.[4] As illustrated in Exhibit 5-2, the so-called project filter moves ideas through the stages of planning and development before reaching the execution and development stages of the ideas that are not rejected during the process. Finally, the surviving projects move on to operation.

Here's what has to happen to make sure the organization focuses on the right projects:

- Ensure balance of candidate projects.
- Require a business case for each project.
- Carry out filtering process based on established business criteria.

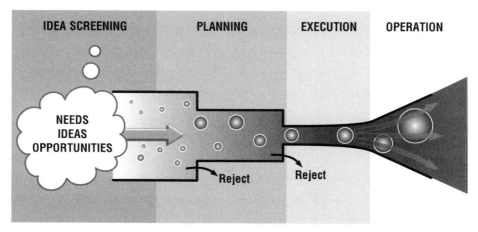

Exhibits 5-2. Managing the Project Portfolio Filter

Support for sizing up the opportunities may be provided by business analysts, who may be connected directly with portfolio management when a formal PPM structure is in place. In other settings, business analysis may be assigned to a strategic support group or financial area or simply left in the hands of an executive committee to sort out.

Once the opportunities and needs have been assessed, the candidate projects move on to the selection and prioritization phase. Aside from the business case already available, more information, such as a detailed project charter, containing basic budget and schedule milestones, facilitates the selection process.

Classically, for a project to get through the project portfolio filter, it has to measure up to three criteria: fit, utility, and balance (FUB):

- *Fit* means alignment with corporate strategic direction. Is there a basic logic for carrying out the project in terms of the organization's overall focus? Will the project indeed spawn benefit to the organization and contribute to achieving its goals?

- *Utility* refers to the relative usefulness of the project. In what way does it contribute to the cause? Does it provide a solid bottom-line result? Or is the benefit more indirect in nature, by bettering motivation, synergy, and productivity? The utility of a project is measured by its usefulness and value, and it is typically defined by costs, benefits, and risks.

- *Balance* refers to the mix of projects in the portfolio. Is there an appropriate ratio of projects from the key areas of the organization, such as marketing, production, finance, operations, and logistics? Or is the ratio lopsided, with project overload—say on operational expansion—without enough punch programmed for marketing and sales?

Since projects compete for resources and funding, somehow a decision has to be made to ferret out the chosen few. The FUB criteria are generic in nature and provide philosophical guidance regarding project selection. Structured paths are also tools for screening and classifying potential projects.

Two applicable approaches are the simplified weighted matrix approach and the analytic hierarchy process.

Simplified Weighted Matrix Approach

This technique uses common decision criteria, against which each project is compared. It is useful for an initial analysis of the relationships among competing projects. The criteria are weighted to establish their relative importance because some factors are more crucial than others. This allows the organization to calculate a score for each project using values for each criteria and applying the relative weights. Exhibit 5-3 shows an example for scoring projects where the criteria chosen to determine the potential contribution of each project are:

- Increases revenue (4).
- Decreases costs (2).
- Optimizes operations (1.5).
- Satisfies clients (1.5).
- Innovates (1).

The relative importance established by the organization for each of these factors for the example given is indicated in parentheses.

Projects	Type	Increases Revenue	Decreases Costs	Optimizes Operations	Satisfies Clients	Innovates	Weighted Sum	Priority
Weighted Factors		4X	2X	1,5X	1,5X	1X		
Project A	IT	2 = 8	2 = 4	4 = 6	2 = 3	1 = 1	22	4
Project B	Market	2 = 8	0 = 0	0 = 0	3 = 4.5	3 = 3	15.5	6
Project C	R&D	1 = 4	1 = 2	1 = 1.5	2 = 3	4 = 4	14.5	7
Project D	Market	3 = 12	1 = 2	1 = 1.5	3 = 4.5	3 = 3	23	3
Project E	Capital expenditure	4 = 16	3 = 6	2 = 3	3 = 4.5	1 = 1	30.5	2
Project F	New product	3 = 12	1 = 2	0 = 0	2 = 3	4 = 4	21	5
Project G	Capital expenditure	4 = 16	3 = 6	2 = 3	2 = 3	3 =3	31	1

Legend for scoring: 0= Not applicable;   1= Low impact;   2 = Medium impact;   3 = High impact;   4 = Very high impact

Exhibit 5-3. Sample of Simplified Weighted Matrix

These criteria vary depending on the nature of the business in question. For each project, the criteria are scored on a scale from 0 to 4; those numbers, summed, give a final weighted sum. These sums are then compared and priorities established based on the relative position of the scores, from highest to lowest.

The simplified weighted matrix is useful as an overall size-up for prioritizing strategic projects. Additional study and analysis are required to come up with the final prioritization because other factors not covered by the matrix come into play. Intuition and organizational politics are also relevant influencing factors.

Analytic Hierarchy Process (AHP)

Sophisticated decision support systems for choosing the right projects are appropriate in complex contexts. The analytic hierarchy process, developed in the early 1970s, is such an approach and has been increasingly applied to the selection process of portfolio management. The principle involves dividing a complex decision into smaller, manageable pieces, which are then recombined into a final metric.

In essence, AHP provides a rational framework for attacking a decision-making scenario, quantifying its elements, relating those elements to overall goals, and sizing up alternative solutions.[5] Here are the steps:

1. Model the project selection process as a hierarchy containing the goal, the alternatives for reaching it, and the criteria for evaluating the alternatives.
2. Establish criteria for establishing priorities among the elements of the hierarchy by making judgments based on comparisons of the elements. For example, for a major investment project, ROI might be the highest of priorities, whereas for certain IT projects, quality and functionality might prevail over cost.
3. Summarize these premises to serve as a priority backdrop for the selection process.
4. Check the consistency of the judgments and premises established.
5. Make decisions based on the results of this process.

Whereas the procedure outlined implies a simple one-through-five pathway to balanced and consistent portfolio selection, in fact, it requires a substantial degree of iteration to yield the right criteria and premises.

Although the simplified weighted matrix approach and the AHP conceptually share a common logic, the difference lies in the degree of complexity and detail involved. Both require a set of assumptions. In the simplified model, the assumptions regarding the weighting of pertinent criteria, for instance, are broad in nature. In AHP, the process precludes the need to break down assumptions in great detail. The technical literature is ample with case studies, and specific software programs have been developed to facilitate the process.

Projects Done Right

The text so far has referred to the up-front part of PPM, which boils down to choosing the right projects, which is obviously essential for effective portfolio management. Once that's done, the second half of the managing project portfolios comes into play. This means making sure that the chosen projects are done right, that is, performed so that they produce the benefits as projected in the selection phase.

This requires tracking projects and the project portfolios to ensure that they do not stray off course. It also means analyzing different portfolio scenarios and replanning for changes in strategy or financial scenarios. So each project's business value requires monitoring, and that information is then used for repositioning the organization's project portfolio as required.[6] Chapter 6 outlines in detail the steps for ensuring that the projects are done right and that the overall performance of the portfolio is consistent with company directives.

Portfolio Management—An Iterative Process

Although PPM consists of two major components as described—choosing the right projects and making sure the projects are done right—the process is highly iterative and involves subphases. PPM is dynamic, interrelated, and ongoing, and it requires artful management to keep pace with changing markets, organizational shifts, budgetary hiccups, and project statuses.

The first iteration involves the project inventory, where candidate projects are submitted for entrance into the project portfolio. That inventory already includes active and proposed projects as well as those on hold or delayed. The existing projects in the portfolio contain the business case information, including data on schedule and cost, dependencies, strategic relevance, expected benefits, risk evaluation, and priority. As new candidate projects appear, this sets off a need to filter the incoming projects and to reassess the existing projects.

So the portfolio requires periodic analysis, which entails another iterative process. The new projects are sized up in terms of fit, utility, and balance, and the overall portfolio is reviewed with regard to priority. The new projects face screening on the entrance criteria with regard to the organizational strategy and contribution to the organization. How do new and ongoing projects relate to each other? How can the project mix be optimized? Periodic portfolio analysis is essential for prioritizing the portfolio and maximizing the benefit to the organization within its available resources. Support techniques, such as the weighted matrix or the AHP, are helpful in evaluating the relative importance of factors such as budget, strategic alignment, marketing, and risk. Relationships among the projects influence ultimate portfolio prioritization, and they include factors such as resource allocation, financial restraints, and timing. So the analysis phase calls for multiple iterations resulting in trade-off decisions and adjustments to the portfolio.

Once projects are selected and initiated, additional iteration is required in the project planning phase. Here the resources are allocated and projects scheduled. Thus project planning becomes integrated with portfolio planning, where resource and schedule decisions are made holistically in view of the portfolio requirements.

PPM includes tracking the portfolio of projects against a standard of metrics established to assess the performance of each project. Large, multistage projects may need to be evaluated at specified gates to ensure that they are on track and meeting their milestones, as shown in Exhibit 5-4. Gate reviews give early signs that could trigger reevaluation or even immediate project termination.

Exhibit 5-4. Project Gate Reviews

Stage gate evaluations are part of the tracking process and involve go/no-go decisions, where projects are given the green light, put on hold, or aborted.

Project portfolio reviews also involve double-checking to ensure the continued validity of the business cases, as well as a comparative analysis of projects in terms of relative priorities, which may have been affected by changing business, technological, and market scenarios. The iterations involved in shifting conditions result in the realignment of the portfolio and, as a result, replanning is required, including changes in resource allocation and scheduling.

In successfully managed project portfolios, iteration permeates the process from the time candidate projects are considered and analyzed through the planning and execution phases. This means that major synergy is required between project management and project portfolio management.[7]

Aligning Projects with Each Other

Project teams tend to be sharply focused and sometimes develop a tunnel view of priorities with respect to their projects, so the alignment of projects presents a challenge. Veritable tugs-of-war may develop over scarce resources. Since all project managers and respective teams are ultimately judged based on how well they complete their projects, collaboration between projects is not an easy task. The project team that tugs the most tends to gain the resources, even if a company does not derive the most benefit from that result. Perhaps another project could produce greater impact if it were accelerated with increased resources.

In resource-scarce settings, a superior power is needed to referee between the conflicting priorities. Project teams unable to peacefully resolve the quest for gaining limited resources need to be able to appeal to a higher authority.

Exceptions to the rule are independent projects having budgets that allow them to reach outside the organization when resources are inadequate.

Aligning the Portfolio with Available Resources

The clamor for resources is constant in the arena of projects. With the ever present pressure to do more with less, resources of all natures are invariably scarce. Although all resources can be translated into money, the shortfalls usually take on the form of sparse information, space, people, material, or equipment. Poor performance on projects is often linked to a shortage of one or more of these factors.

Because resources in all organizations are limited, the challenge that both business planners and project planners face revolves around getting the most mileage out of available resources. The demands sometimes require an almost magical ability to conciliate the conflicting priorities—resource juggling. Although magic may happen in spurts, solid resource management is the best way to handle the perennial resource problem.

What if the portfolio's requirements cannot be aligned with available resources? Let's say an organization's ambitions far outdistance the traditional levels of investment. And assume that company goals can be met only by reaching out beyond available resources. Does this make alignment impossible? No, the situation is just different. In this case, the answer resides in obtaining outside resources. Although the resources are not readily available (whether they be material, equipment, labor, intellectual, or purely monetary), the projected return on investment for the portfolio of projects justifies rounding up external support to bring the full portfolio in on time.

Monitoring Portfolio Performance

Even originally well-conceived projects rapidly become misaligned because of shifting and evolving business goals, with projects straying over time and over budget. However, misalignment is a natural and expected outcome. The real key is to identify the misalignments and to take corrective actions and objective go/kill/hold/fix decisions.

Failure to systematically monitor the corporate or business unit portfolio can lead to resource bottlenecks, the duplication of efforts, and budgets that are constantly revised upward with unnecessary incurred costs. Under such circumstances, achieving corporate objectives becomes a hit-or-miss affair. Monitoring a portfolio's performance allows detecting the materialization of risks and opportunities for reducing or enhancing its influence on strategy execution. For instance, the shortage of resources may be a manifested risk that delays benefits realization.

Braskem is a Brazilian petrochemical group present in more than 60 countries and the leading thermoplastic resin producer of the Americas; the company operates 28 industrial units in Brazil and three in the United States. Braskem's agenda is based on the development of products and services with added value for customers and growth projects in attractive market segments. The growth is based on value creation across the petrochemical and plastics production chain, on the expansion and protection of core Latin America businesses, on the assurance of low-cost materials and energy supplies, and on access to attractive markets (Exhibit 5-5).

The company has two portfolio approaches: one for capital investments and another for R&D. Both are based on four steps: (1) identifying projects, (2) characterizing and centralizing, (3) prioritizing, and (4) executing projects and programs, as shown on Exhibit 5-6.

The investment program is aimed at modernizing assets, capacity expansion, and acquisitions, and it is realized in accordance with financial discipline and return on investment criteria. In 2010, this included a US$2.5 billion petrochemical complex in Mexico; a US$3 billion petrochemical complex in Venezuela, and studies for the implementation of a petrochemical complex in Peru. The approach for managing capital expenditures is shown in Exhibit 5-7.

Braskem's state-of-the-art US$150 million Technology and Innovation Center is one of best equipped in Latin America, with over 250 patents in Brazil, the United States, and Europe. The R&D approach is managed as a portfolio, aimed at innovation that creates value beginning with ideas that are filtered to create projects, which are then managed under a portfolio. Some

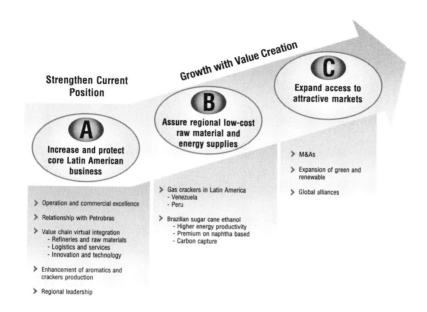

Exhibit 5-5. Braskem Value Creation Intentions

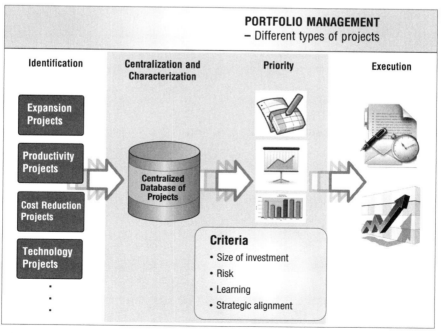

Exhibit 5-6. Braskem Portfolio Phases

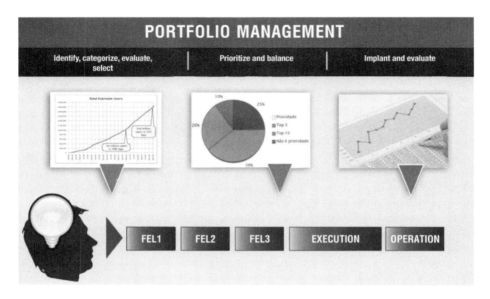

Exhibit 5-7. Capital Investment Portfolio

research projects are developed through the alliance concept as presented in Chapter 10.

The following questions provide insight into the health of an organization's portfolio management effort:

- Are projects aligned with the organization's strategies?
- Is there a formal process to ensure such alignment?
- Is there a process for realignment in the case of changing strategies?
- Do approved projects have a business case?
- Is priority given to projects that provide the highest return?
- Is there a formal process to ensure that the most important projects are given priority treatment?
- Is the number of projects limited to the resources available?
- Is there a gate process (go/no-go) that allows for aborting projects?
- Is there a formal structure (committee, department, project office) for managing the portfolio issues?

- Are there clear channels of communications between portfolio management and upper management?
- Is there an appropriate balance between the company disciplines in the overall portfolio?
- Are short-term, mid-term, and long-term issues appropriately addressed?
- Has the impact of regulatory projects been taken into account?
- Are there enough resources to carry out the projects?

Software for Managing Project Portfolios

Commercial software programs are available as support for managing the portfolio. The selection process for such software starts with understanding the needs and objectives of the organization. Some of the tools available are quite comprehensive; care must be taken in the implementation process so as not to overwhelm potential users. A gradual process is recommended, introducing one feature at a time. Here are some features that comprise a good project portfolio management system:

- Project progress reporting
- Executive dashboard capability
- Communications criteria
- Project evaluation methodology
- Cost and benefits tracking
- Issues log and tracking
- Capacity planning (resources)

Project portfolio management software provides information for management to periodically review the portfolio, providing a solid basis for making key financial and business decisions for the organization.

Conclusions

Although organizations possess numerous operational activities that require managerial attention, the future of companies depends on the content and successful management of their portfolio of projects. New projects are the key to staying ahead of the survival curve and to ensuring an organization's growth and prosperity. Therefore, project portfolio management is an essential component of Enterprise Project Governance.

Effective project portfolios mirror the company's strategic direction and are managed in such a way as to maintain that direction. Conducting the selection and prioritization of projects falls within the scope of PPM. Support techniques, such as the weighted decision matrix and the analytical tool AHP, are helpful in choosing and prioritizing the right projects. The other part of managing project portfolios encompasses the oversight of projects to ensure implementations in accordance with the priorities, quality, cost, and time lines. That's the overall challenge of project portfolio management—to ensure that the right combination of the right projects is done right.

CHAPTER

6

Turning Strategy into Reality

Putting strategic initiatives into effect in organizations is like turning an ocean liner at full steam. Although the captain's command may echo loud and clear, and even if the turning procedure is underway, no direction change is apparent for the first few moments. The inertia of these giant vessels, measuring hundreds of yards in length, is so great that a quick response is out of the question. It takes planning ahead and allowance for reaction time to make the right change in an ocean liner's course.

This same challenge permeates the corporate world. While top decision makers may mandate a given strategy, overcoming the business-as-usual inertia takes time. Allowing for the inertia-related time lag is crucial for the success of strategic projects. So the time lapse for the course-changing process has to be built into the components of Enterprise Project Governance. This chapter pinpoints the policies and practices to be defined in EPG to ensure that strategies are duly implemented and translated into results.

The starting point is the strategy itself. This assumes that a solid portrait of the desired results exists, formalized in terms of strategic initiatives. That overall strategy then acts as the bedrock that sustains the implementation of the projects designed to paint the picture visualized by the organization's strategists. When the strategies are swiftly and effectively put into place, the odds are good that they will bear benefits. A great strategy, nimbly implemented, guarantees success and generates benefits, fulfillment, and rewards. The actual success rates for implementing strategies, however, leave room for improvement. Consider a few dismal numbers:

- A 2004 survey by *The Economist* of 276 senior operating executives found that 57 percent of the companies had been unsuccessful in executing strategic initiatives over the previous three years.[1]
- In a 2006 survey of more than 1,500 executives by the American Management Association and the Human Resource Institute, only 3 percent of respondents rated their companies as very successful at executing corporate strategies, whereas 62 percent described their organizations as mediocre or worse.[2]
- In 2007, the Conference Board asked 700 executives to list their top 10 challenges. Excellence in execution and consistent execution of strategy by top management ranked first and third, respectively, as the greatest concerns. Clearly, the ability to transform strategic plans into action is a universal concern.[3]

Therefore, even an inspired strategy poorly implemented may spell failure. For instance, a beautifully balanced portfolio is of little use if its projects run helter-skelter, overtop their budgets, and without the intended outcomes. On the other hand, a superbly managed project that finishes out of synch may inadvertently sabotage a well-designed strategic campaign. For instance, if the strategy is to be first-to-market, and if the execution phase lacks agility, then the strategy might not work at all. Aside from schedule overruns, other barriers can roadblock a good strategy. Rampaging costs make return-on-investment figures look discouraging. Quality glitches are another source of sabotage for even the most enlightened strategies.[4]

Four Views for Getting Things Done

The enduring success of organizations depends on two dimensions: strategy (decisions on the paths to follow) and execution (getting things done along the pathways). Expanding on the classic combinations of strategy versus execution presented in Chapter 5, Exhibit 6-1 shows how these dimensions unfold into the four performance quadrants.

Each quadrant has specific performance characteristics:

- *Quadrant I—Movie Watching.* In this quadrant, a business has a strong strategy poorly executed, which means that the organization will stay where it is. The strategy is like a powerful creative movie but with an audience passively watching it without being motivated. Although a clear vision is established, the organization is incapable of moving in that direction. The dreams are not translated into the desired outcomes and benefits.

- *Quadrant II—Bridge Building.* Quadrant II requires a disciplined organization, one that addresses the needs of today yet builds for tomorrow. In this quadrant, good strategy is matched with good execution. This means consistently maintaining the right strategies along with

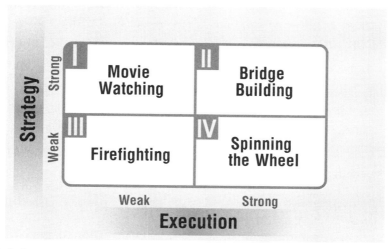

Exhibit 6-1. Performance Quadrants

agile execution of the strategic projects. Richard Lepsinger, author of *Closing the Execution Gap*, says that five bridges help people traverse the execution gap: (1) the ability to manage change, (2) a structure that supports execution, (3) employee involvement in decision making, (4) alignment between leader actions and company values and priorities, and (5) company-wide coordination and cooperation. Organizations in this quadrant are capable of correctly building the bridges between strategy and execution.

- *Quadrant III—Firefighting.* Companies operating in this quadrant are focused on operations, using poor processes and involving management and employees who are overworked, confused, and feeling hopeless due to the critical issues without resolution. Robert Kaplan, author of several books on the Balanced Scorecard, says, "Though executives may formulate an excellent strategy, it easily fades from memory as the organization tackles day-to-day operations issues." He adds that this creates a situation of "fighting fires making employees react to issues within the business rather than managing the business itself." Since strategy is weak and the execution is chaotic, the priority is for resolving the always urgent and present issues, leaving the future for a tomorrow that never comes.

- *Quadrant IV—Spinning the Wheel.* A business without a strategy, or with a bad one, but good at execution may do well for a while, but sooner or later it will fall victim to a competitor or the ever mutant environment. However, no amount of operational excellence can prevent failure stemming from poor decisions and a bad strategy. For firms that want to remain competitive in the marketplace, operational excellence is necessary but not sufficient. Such firms may go under or become targets for takeovers.

Moving Around the Quadrants

Ice cream accompaniments manufacturer Askey's was founded in 1910. The business was sold to Kellogg's, the American food manufacturing giant, in

1965. Under the new ownership, Askey's was used solely as a manufacturing site, with support services being run from Kellogg's U.K. head office. During this period, the factory concentrated on the mass production of a limited range of standard cones and wafers sold to ice cream parlors and kiosks, ice cream vans, and other outside caterers. However, through the 1980s, the market took a turn, and sales through supermarkets became the headliner. By the 1990s, the vast majority of Askey's products were channeled through the major supermarkets. Sales to the catering trade and ice cream vendors were diminishing. Under the relentless downward price pressure exerted by the supermarkets, profitability plummeted. Nonetheless, Askey's retained its position as the largest British manufacturer of ice cream accompaniments, but little effort was put into articulating a strategy that could create new products or geographic expansion. Askey's was merely spinning the wheel.

In 1995, Askey's was acquired by two experienced food industry executives, financed by venture capitalists. The new owners set about extending the product range. Though this takeover seemingly heralded a fresh start for the firm after a period of underinvestment, it wasn't long before cracks appeared. A new strategy was tried based on the creation of new products, but it resulted only in short-term profit, which was not sustainable over the long run due to the lack of investments. The company entered into the firefighting quadrant because of the expansion without a clear articulated strategy. After more than a decade of steady firefighting, the business was bought out again.

In 2004, Askey's was sold to Silver Spoon, Britain's largest sugar and sweetener producer. The company's strategy was to continue expanding the business through exploring new markets, expanding existing ones, and new product development. This resulted in a jump up to an 80 percent share of the U.K. retail market for ice cream peripherals and a significant share of the market for restaurants, cafés, and ice cream vans. The company thus moved on to the bridge-building quadrant.

In the years since 1910, Askey's moved through three of the four quadrants, lacking only movie watching, which depicts a good strategy poorly implemented. Over time, companies naturally pass through periods of change regarding the relationship of strategy to execution, as they strive for the ideal. A vigorous strategy-execution balance is the obvious pathway for achieving healthy organizations. Strong strategies, coupled with great execution, represent the magic formula for reaching the organizational nirvana suggested in quadrant II.

While this balance is sometimes attained by companies for periods of time, market trends, technological breakthroughs, and shifts in the worldwide economy invariably bump even the most effective organizations off course from time to time. An example follows of how a highly successful industry over the years comes to terms with strategies and execution during dramatically changing times.

Big Pharma: An Industry Faced with Challenges

Competitive and technological changes in the pharmaceutical industry are reshaping the business.[5] No fewer than nine of the pharmaceutical industry's 10 biggest blockbusters go off patent and face low-cost generic competition by 2016. This has a gigantic impact on big pharma, as the large pharmaceutical companies are called. By some estimates, expiring prescription drug patents will cost the pharmaceutical industry over US$50 billion in revenues by 2020. These pressures strain the traditional, vertically integrated business model of big pharma. Best sellers like Pfizer's cholesterol-lowering Lipitor, the world's most prescribed medicine, lost patent protection in 2011. The drug is responsible for 20 percent of the largest big pharma's annual revenue. As cholesterol drugs go off patent, a new stream of high cholesterol–controlling drugs enters the market. Yet the question arises: Will they evolve fast enough to offset the losses from generics?

A survey of global pharmaceutical executives by Germany's Roland Berger Strategy Consultants,[6] with participating companies covering 40 percent of global pharmaceutical revenues and including seven out of the global top 10 players, found that 65 percent of those polled said the sector faced a "strategic crisis." Nearly half of those questioned agreed that current investments in research and development would yield a negative return. Changing health care environments, budget pressures, challenging market access, and massive patent expirations caused a major upset in the traditional business model, which has focused exclusively on high-margin and patent-protected innovative medicine.

As a result, the industry began reshaping and altering the way business was conducted—from R&D to sales and marketing. Big pharma faces the challenge of improving individual patient outcomes and health outcome predictability through the tailoring of treatments. For that to happen, a move is required from the present model of one size fits all with lower predictability of outcomes to a more tailored approach stratifying populations and optimizing outcomes based on biomarkers as a step to targeted therapy.

To meet the challenge, drug giant GSK (GlaxoSmithKline) established the following strategies aimed at increasing growth, reducing risk, and improving long-term financial performance:[7]

- Grow a diversified global business.
- Deliver more products of value.
- Simplify GSK's operating model.
- GSK's corporate structure includes a position of chief strategy officer, whose task is to formulate appropriate strategies based on market information and input from stakeholders and to interface with other areas to ensure that the strategies become reality.

To make the complementary strategies become reality, GSK counts on a solid set of Enterprise Project Governance principles and structures. For starters, a corporate-level PMO is part of the CEO's office and is charged with tracking strategic projects and seeing that they are appropriately supported. Business units also have their own PMOs and basic project management methodology and support are part of the GSK organization.

Under the emerging scenario, corporate strategies are aimed less at milking blockbuster discoveries and more at a market mix that involves both organic growth and acquisitions in areas such as biotechnology, dermatology, oncology, and generics. This creates a fragmented portfolio of projects and a need for an enterprise-wide project culture capable of managing projects at strategic, tactical, and operational levels. Change management, marketing, and organizational restructuring projects are particularly relevant in the increasingly dynamic scenario.

At GSK, manufacturing and R&D projects continue to be managed under a traditional portfolio of projects. Increased attention, however, is given to the broad array of the emerging organizational, administrative, and commercial projects demanded by the changing marketplace. Initiatives called "critical business drivers" (those that strongly affect business outcomes), are labeled as strategic projects and given high priority. Whereas in a given region such as Latin America, comprised of 37 countries, hundreds of individual projects may vie for budget resources, as few as seven projects may be chosen for high-profile attention and tracking at an executive level. Other approved tactical and operational projects are dealt with at the country level.

Big pharma is a striking example of industries impacted by sweeping changes in the marketplace. Invariably, major marketplace turmoil calls for an overhaul not only in strategic direction, but also in transforming those strategies into reality as quickly as possible. When the right strategies are done right and put into place on a timely basis, good things happen for the organization. Yet if the organization lacks both project management expertise and the drive to turn the strategies swiftly into reality, great strategies are of little avail.

How to Transform Strategies into Reality

A principal function of Enterprise Project Governance is to make sure that policies are defined and put into place for the right composition of projects to be managed effectively. Turning strategies into results requires a three-pronged approach once the strategic projects have been selected and prioritized, as outlined in Chapter 5. There's no off-the-shelf package for managing these strategic projects; a customized approach is called for.

Here are key management actions for making sure the portfolio of projects spawns the benefits aspired to by corporate decision makers:[8]

- Balance the overall portfolio.
- Use program management to group and coordinate related projects.
- Apply stage gate tracking for individual strategic projects.

- Apply classic project management principles.
- Analyze benefits management.

Keeping the Portfolio Balanced

Chapter 5 sums up the challenges of forming and balancing project portfolios. This balance is vital for successfully implementing the organization's strategy. The right design of project mix sets the stage for turning strategy into results. Yet portfolio design and planning are only part of the equation. Other factors are crucial to optimize desired results. For instance, keeping the portfolio balanced over time is as important as starting off right. For that equilibrium to remain, periodic reviews are required. These may happen semiannually, quarterly, or as often as monthly depending on organizational dynamics.

Portfolio reviews are worth the effort because they force upper management to size up benefits over time. They are fruitful when proactive decisions are made, such as accelerating projects, putting some on hold, and aborting others. Here are issues that merit reflection during a project portfolio review session:

- Balance between short-term and long-term projects
- Budget adjustments as time progresses
- Balance between risks and rewards
- Cash flow implications
- Operational impacts of completed projects

Portfolio reviews take place in various organizational settings. For instance:

- *Strategic PMO.* Typically, the scope of strategic PMOs includes running periodic portfolio alignment reviews. This involves the participation of appropriate stakeholders, who may vary depending on the projects under review.
- *Portfolio Management Committee.* Another option is for the portfolio reviews to be carried out by a committee convened for this purpose.
- *Executive Committee.* Ultimately, the review may land on the agenda of an executive committee, tasked with overall management responsibilities.

Where the review takes place is not important as long as it is effective, touches on the right topics, and results in proactive decision making. It is ultimately the responsibility of EPG to make sure that firm policies are fixed so that effective project portfolio reviews are carried out periodically.

Keeping Related Projects Aligned: Program Management

The continuous alignment of related projects can be guaranteed by gathering them under the umbrella of an overarching program. Program management is designed to direct interrelated projects toward achieving strategic results. The links between projects in a given program vary from being tightly to loosely connected. Such is the case of the overall space exploration program managed by NASA, which includes specific programs of interconnected projects aimed at earth-related studies, manned space flight, planets and asteroids, science and technology, stars and the cosmos, and the sun. Each of these groups congregates interrelated projects, and the programs themselves are also loosely linked because they are all space related.

Keeping Individual Projects on Course: Stage Gates

Stage gates are check points along a project's pathway to completion, aimed at ensuring that the previous stage has been completed and that all is clear to move on to the next stage. These gates help in shining a light on status, in sizing up the business situation, and in evaluating assigned resources. Stage gates provide decision makers with the information to review status in the light of new developments.

Various names are used for this checkpoint concept, including stage gates, review points, gates, design reviews, and project gates. The terminology used for capital expenditure projects like offshore oil rigs, for instance, identifies three major gates: FEL 1, FEL 2, and FEL 3. FEL means "front end loading," referring to early rites of passage prior to the outlay of major investments, thus optimizing design and avoiding rework and unnecessary costs, as shown in Exhibit 6-2.

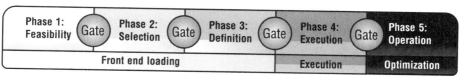

Exhibit 6-2. FEL in the Stage Gate Process

In this model, FEL 1 refers to kickoff activities such as project charter development and initial feasibility. FEL 2 embodies the preliminary scope for equipment design, layout, schedule, and estimates. Finally, FEL 3 includes detailed information about major equipment specifications, final estimate, project execution plan, preliminary 3-D model, and equipment lists.

The FEL approach is also known as preproject planning. No matter what the moniker, the stage gate technique provides powerful input toward reducing uncertainty, so that cost–time–quality parameters are met to the satisfaction of the sponsoring organization. In these early stages of major projects, optimizing tools such as VIPs (value-improving practices, which use techniques like value engineering) are also instrumental in ensuring effective stage gating.

In some cases, only three gates are appropriate, yet as many as six might make sense in other settings, with the number left to the discretion of the sponsor or to best practices in the specific industry. Here are factors that influence the decision regarding the number of gates:

- The stability of the business case as related to changes in the strategic environment
- The empowerment appropriate for the project manager to make decisions that are aligned with the strategy
- The nature of the project and the extent to which periodic external review is appropriate
- The quality of metrics available to both the project team and the sponsor

Effective Enterprise Project Governance policies do not specify the number of stages or their content, yet they do determine the use of a stage gate approach for making sure that projects are strategically monitored.

Doing Individual Projects Right: Methodologies, Best Practices, and Standards

Making strategies happen depends on the implementation of the projects that unfold from the strategies. That implementation requires focus on completing enterprises and projects within cost parameters, time constraints, and quality specifications. For that to occur, the best practices of project management come into play.

Since a project approach is needed to make the leap from strategy to results, it makes sense to draw from the accumulated know-how of the project management profession. It is the responsibility of Enterprise Project Governance to make sure the fundamentals of project management are defined and in place in the organization.

Projects are carried out over a time frame, known as the *project life cycle*. This is true for projects of all natures, whether strategic, operational, or innovative. Since projects, like people, are finite by definition, they are designed to be born and to be terminated. Projects also live a life and go through distinct phases. Exhibit 6-3 shows an example of a life cycle.

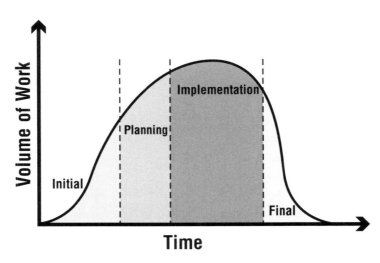

Exhibit 6-3. Example of a Project Life Cycle

Here are pertinent questions for sponsors and reviewers to raise through-out the project life cycle:

Preproject Phase

- Does the project meet company standards in terms of profitability or return on investment? Are resources available to carry out the project?
- Are the premises and numbers used in the feasibility study valid?

Concept Phase

- Does a project charter define the project mission and primary objectives?
- Is the overall scope of the project clearly defined?
- Is all the information needed for the project to proceed available and organized?
- Have the design assumptions been validated?
- Have the client requirements been formally confirmed?
- Has a macro risk assessment been carried out?
- Are key stakeholders involved?
- How about the project manager? Does he need more support or on-the-job training? Or could she use additional guidance during a given phase?
- Has formal project kickoff been planned? What format is planned? Meeting? Workshop?

Planning Phase

- Has a quality assurance plan been developed?
- Are project management and implementation strategies and methodologies in place?
- Have project risks been identified, quantified, and risk responses identified?
- Are systems for document management, activity scheduling and

tracking, procurement management, estimating, budgeting, and cost control in place?

- Have the systems been debugged, and is the staff competent at operating them?
- Has an overall, technically oriented detailed project plan been developed? (What is to be done on the project and how will the work be performed?)
- Has a project management plan been developed (how will the project be managed)?
- Is there a stakeholder management plan?
- Have statements of work (SOWs) been written for the work packages?
- Has the project communications plan been developed?
- Have the meeting and reporting criteria been developed?

Implementation Phase

- Are regular tracking meetings taking place?
- Is change management being formally managed?
- Is decision making proactive and solution oriented?

Final Phase

- Have project closeout procedures been developed, and are they in place?
- Has a transition plan (from project completion to operation phase) been prepared, and is it being followed?

Postproject Phase

- What was done right on the project, and what needs improvement on the next one?
- How did the project size up with other comparable projects within or outside the company?
- What lessons learned need to be shared with others in the company?
- How can project results be used for marketing and promotional purposes?

Views of Project Management from Professional Associations

The essence of project management was traditionally represented by a triangle, depicting the need to manage time, cost, and quality. These core areas have long since morphed into a square, depicting quadruple constraints, with the addition of scope management because scope is so tightly intertwined with the elements of the classic triangle. So time, cost, quality, and scope are the pillars for turning strategic projects into results.

PMI

These four basic areas have since evolved into nine knowledge areas as outlined by PMI: management of time, scope, quality, cost, risk, communication, procurement, human resources, and integration.[9] All of these areas have to be managed to make things work. A slipup in any area is enough to start a domino effect that can go crashing into all other areas. For instance, a communication glitch in the procurement cycle might set off an unscheduled time delay that affects quality and amasses a cost overrun. This may put the project in danger and have a strong impact on human resources. So intimate connections exist among all the areas. The PMI model is dynamic and evolves as new perceptions are recognized. For instance, the topic of project stakeholder management is gaining increased attention in the literature as researchers and practitioners perceive the substantial impact it has on the success or failure of projects. Exhibit 6-4 shows the knowledge areas as defined by PMI.

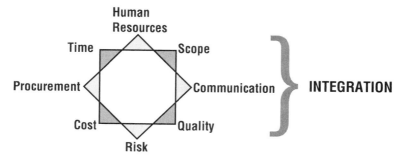

Exhibit 6-4. Integrating the Basic Project Management Areas

International Project Management Association

The International Project Management Association (IPMA) represents more than 50 project management associations from all continents and offers another basic model. The IPMA Competence Baseline (ICB)[10] is the basis for a certification system and serves as a standard for practitioners and stakeholders. This model assumes that professionals must have competency in three basic areas: behavioral, technical, and contextual.

Standards Related to Executing Projects

Over the years, PMI has developed a library of global standards. Five themes reflect the expansive nature of the project management profession: projects, programs, people, organizations, and profession. IPMA also periodically updates its competence baseline standard. The U.K. Office of Government Commerce (OGC) also provides policy standards and guidance on best practice in procurement, projects, and estate management, and it monitors and challenges departments' performance against these standards, grounded in an evidence base of information and assurance. Their publications include the themes of portfolio, programs, and projects as well as the widely accepted Prince 2 methodology.

As project management continues to grow and gain recognition globally, since 2006 the International Organization for Standardization (ISO) has been developing Standard 21500, Guidance on Project Management, with final delivery expected by 2013. Over 30 countries participate in its development.

Keeping Benefits Realization on Track: Using the Why-How Framework

Execution is the crucial step in realizing benefits. Execution can free up resources or transform the organizational portfolio into a never-ending story of great goals. Execution is the interface between strategy carriers, programs and projects, and operations. Failure to achieve successful execution leaves strategies incomplete and resources unavailable for other projects. Successful execution requires strong sponsorship, coordination of commissioning and testing, attention to managing change produced by projects' outputs, and feedback from operations to the portfolio team and from them to the strategic planners.

An Implementation Strategy in Practice

The Virginia Department of Transportation (VDOT), based in Alexandria, faced major challenges in implementing its strategy to construct a US$1.4 billion high-occupancy toll lane infrastructure project, which started in 2007.[11] Here was the scenario:

- The project was structured as a design-build public-private partnership (PPP) between VDOT, Fluor-Lane, partnering contractors, and Transurban, a toll road developer and investor.
- It was situated in a congested travel corridor around Washington, D.C.
- The work involved new construction, replacing aging infrastructure, relocating houses, and adding toll lanes.
- The economy was in a downturn.
- The project involved 300 contractors, working at off hours and weekends.

The governance of the project was mandated by the State of Virginia's Public-Private Transportation Act of 1995, a legislative framework enabling the Virginia Department of Transportation to enter into agreements authorizing private sector entities to develop and/or operate transportation facilities. The governing criteria established by the act include policies related to quality control, an independent review panel, state transportation board recommendations, the selection of detailed proposals, negotiations, and final legal review of agreement.

Under these governing guidelines, the project was managed using classic project management techniques such as planning, organization, and control. The knowledge areas of project management also came into play, including the effective management of scope, time, cost, quality, procurement, human resources, communications, risk, and integration. Since things do not always come out as planned, implementing strategies called for adjustment when things swung off course. This was the case for VDOT.

VDOT's strategy was to carry out the billion-dollar-plus project with minimum disruption of traffic under the governance umbrella of a design-build public-private partnership. That said, the question became how to make it happen. The design-build format was new for the state, as was the public-private partnership model. Although turning strategy into reality is, in principle, a matter of applying the basics of project management, twists and turns are normal along the pathway, as revealed on the VDOT project.

As construction started at the end of 2007, it became apparent that a basic piece in the project governance was missing. While VDOT became focused on evaluating every contract package, the Fluor-Lane team became increasingly anxious to get the bids out, and this created tension early on between the partners. To meet the ambitious time lines fixed for the project, VDOT didn't have the manpower or expertise to evaluate and approve the bid packages as required. As a result, due to the lack of approved designs, some contractors found themselves on site without the drawings to proceed. This meant scrambling for alternative ways to utilize the labor force until the bidding procedure could be completed.

To resolve this, VDOT brought in an additional player to help meet the demands. ATCS CH2M Hill, a joint venture between two U.S.-based engineering companies, was contracted to take on the responsibility for managing the mega project, acting as the technical manager and administrative arm. ATCS CH2M Hill consequently became an additional stakeholder in the project's governance structure. The joint venture's major challenge was to strike a balance between the competing needs for appropriate oversight and urgent action.

Turning strategies into reality calls for applying the basics of project management and then going beyond. Constant evaluation and fine-tuning are also parts of the formula for making strategies actually happen. In the case of the VDOT mega project, a major issue of governance was overlooked in the beginning and ended up causing turmoil. Although the act established a solid base for governance, a basic structural link was missing with respect to the hands-on management of the project. Once the governance issue was fixed by bringing in an engineering consortium to act as project managers in support of the client, the project was pulled back on course.

Bridge Building

Over the years, people have been struggling with how to create a model for successful strategy implementation. Getting from strategy to execution requires a coherent and reinforcing set of supporting practices and structures. One model that has persisted is the McKinsey 7S model, which involves seven interdependent factors, which are categorized as either hard elements (strategy, structure, and systems) or soft elements (shared values, skills, style, and staff). The model is based on the theory that, for an organization to perform well, these seven elements need to be aligned and mutually reinforcing.

The 7S model is adequate for analyzing a current situation and a proposed future situation and for identifying gaps and inconsistencies that must be addressed in order to make the journey successful. It's then a question of adjusting the elements to ensure that the organization works effectively to reach the desired endpoint. Let's look at each of the elements:

- *Strategy.* The integrated vision and direction of the company, as well as the manner in which it derives, articulates, communicates, and implements that vision to maintain and build competitive advantage.
- *Structure.* How the company is organized to execute strategy, including the policies and procedures that govern how the organization acts within itself and within its environment, as well as the way who reports to whom.
- *Systems.* The decision-making systems within the organization that can range from management intuition, to manual policies and procedures, to structured computer systems.
- *Shared Values.* The principles adopted by the company to guide its style and behavior. (The values and desired behavior must be communicated to and embraced by the entire organization.)
- *Style.* The shared and common way of thinking and behaving, involving the organization culture and leadership style and reflecting the

manner in which the company interacts with stakeholders, customers, and regulators.

- *Staff.* The employees and their general capabilities. (Effective people management is about creating the right workforce to achieve the desired objectives. It means that the company has hired able people, trained them well, and assigned them to the right jobs.)
- *Skills.* The actual skills and competencies of the employees working for the company. (It refers to the fact that employees have the skills needed to carry out the company's strategy.)

All this may appear simple, but it is not. The main message is that a multiplicity of factors influence an organization's ability to change. And a crucial point is that organizations don't always get the people side of implementation right (shared values, style, staff, and skills) and their reaction to the change involved.

In reality, bridging the strategy execution gap requires a program to manage all the projects and initiatives to accomplish the expected results, all under the EPG oversight framework.

Conclusions

The chapter encompasses approaches for implementing projects coherently with corporate strategy. Since it takes projects to implement strategies, the basics of project management are outlined. Three approaches are shown to ensure the alignment of projects and portfolio with the organization's strategies: (1) project portfolio balancing, (2) program management, and (3) stage gate reviews. Also, establishing strong strategy associated with strong execution (bridge building) requires a set of integrated and reinforcing practices. Effective EPG prescribes policies to ensure that the practices outlined in this chapter are ingrained in the project management culture of the organization. The implementation of strategies calls for applying the basics of project management, beginning with project governance, and then customizing portfolio, program, and project management to fit the organization.

CHAPTER

7

Organizing for Enterprise
Project Governance

For EPG to become a reality, the fundamentals for managing projects across an enterprise must be in place. Those elements for effectively implementing and making operational EPG are many, as outlined in previous chapters, but they fall into four categories:

- *Governance.* This group includes alignment with corporate governance and top management, as well as establishing overall policies for the management of portfolios, programs, and projects. Project management governance also entails establishing criteria for organization, management, and support for project activities, as well as adhering to best practices for industry-related projects.

- *Competency.* The competency group oversees the alignment of project management competency with existing corporate-wide competency models. Professional profiling and career path design also belong to

109

this group. In terms of upgrading project management competency, developmental activities, such as education programs, on-the-job training, coaching, and mentoring, are the essential elements for improving overall performance on projects.

- *Processes.* The process group embodies the methodologies and techniques for making sure that projects across the enterprise are managed effectively. It also includes the systems and automated tools that add speed and synergy to managing multiple projects. Other parts of the process group are the measurement of maturity in project management and ensuring continuous improvement in the approaches used.

- *Culture.* To make EPG a part of an organization's way of life requires developing a project management culture. This requires *change* to ensure that project concepts and practices permeate professionals throughout the organization. Toward that end, change management is the recommended practice to ease the transition from operational culture toward the dynamics of project management. Also essential to achieve a PM culture is knowledge management encompassing project management practices, experiences, and lessons learned, as related to the company and its industry.

Exhibit 7-1 shows the four groupings of the elements that comprise Enterprise Project Governance. Emphasis in this chapter is given to the governance group that deals with organizational issues. The remaining groups—competence, processes, and culture—are complementary and round out the elements required to implement Enterprise Project Governance.

Putting EPG in place requires sizing up the situation, planning, implementation, and maintenance. The plans necessarily encompass the elements summarized in the four groups listed in the chapter introduction. The intensity of a given EPG implementation program varies and depends on the degree of project management maturity in an organization. How it will be done also depends on the surrounding contextual factors.

Exhibit 7-1. Organizing for EPG

Three Scenarios

The structure of Enterprise Project Governance in organizations depends in part on how corporate governance is formulated. The board may opt for a prescriptive approach in which it lays out some project-related policies for the organization. Or it may prefer to dictate the bare minimum to comply with corporate regulatory requirements and leave the rest to the executive level under the responsibility of the CEO. In this second setting, once again the approach may be prescriptive where structures and policies are predetermined, or these may be left to executives in specific business units or heads of major departments. So EPG may be developed in three scenarios:

- Corporate board committee
- CEO and executive team
- Grassroots movement

Scenario One

In this first scenario, corporate governance creates specific committees related to EPG with names like "strategic planning and implementation," "operations oversight," "product development," or "events and programs." These committees can influence EPG policies as well as maintain oversight rights. Organizations with corporate governance committees having scopes that relate to the governance of projects include:

- *The Global Fund.* A major organization aimed at fighting AIDS, tuberculosis, and malaria under a Portfolio and Implementation Committee.[1]
- *L'Oreal.* The French cosmetics conglomerate that maintains a Strategy and Implementation Committee.[2]

How might these committees help shape EPG policies? Although overall executive responsibility for implementing projects resides with the CEO and management team, a board-level committee can exert an influence on the selection and implementation of strategic projects—those that ultimately affect the company's future. Here are actions appropriate for board-level committees that propose to focus on issues such as planning, strategy, and implementation:

- Require policies for selecting and prioritizing strategic projects.
- Require the organization to address issues of Enterprise Project Governance, including project portfolio management.
- Set up a policy for the oversight review of a few key initiatives (but avoiding micromanagement).
- Establish appropriate communication channels.
- Require periodic project management maturity assessments.

Scenario Two

In the second setting, board governance makes no mention of strategic issues and their implementation. Traditionally, board committees are limited to issues such as auditing, executive remuneration, nominating, and executive governance. They may also include such topics as risk, finance, product development, marketing and sales, ethics, and research. In this scenario, corporate governance restricts itself to basic compliance regarding auditing, financial, and ethical practices, as well as to the running of the board itself, which requires a nominating committee for new board members and for CEO selection, as well as an executive committee for ad hoc issues that pop up between formal board meetings.

So, in this context, corporate governance does not mandate policies for EPG but rather delegates all project-related issues, as well as operational and general management matters, to the CEO, who has overall responsibility for the organization. EPG then is just one of several responsibilities of the CEO, who is charged with making projects and everything else work effectively. The board's role regarding EPG is limited to hiring and firing the CEO, who hopefully will be enlightened with respect to project governance policies. This limited EPG scope for board committees is prevalent in the corporate world and is adopted in organizations such as General Electric, Accenture, Roche, and Volkswagen. EPG then is a matter to be organized and structured by the CEO and the executive team.

When corporate governance has delegated full responsibility to the CEO to deal with all management and organizational matters, including strategies and projects, then the CEO needs to provide for the interface between the strategists (upper management and business planners) and the implementers (program and project managers). Here are some of the ways the CEO can effectively deal with the project-related issues across the organization.

The *chief project officer* (CPO) is one option. Other titles, such as VP for special projects or head of program management, are also used to describe the same function. In large organizations, the challenge of effectively coordinating hundreds of complex projects can be too much for a conventional hierarchical organization to handle. A solution to this is to designate a project-wise C-level executive to help coordinate the governance and oversight of multiple projects and major programs.

This executive, called the chief project officer, shoulders the overall responsibility for EPG in the organization. How a CPO operates depends on the maturity level of the organization with respect to project management (methodologies, experience, and support), on the size and complexity of the projects, and on the conviction of top management with regard to using an enterprise project approach to managing. It also depends on the nature of the organization—whether it's project driven, as in an engineering company, or functionally based, as in a manufacturer of toothpaste that uses project management as a means to an end. The CPO function makes particular sense in organizations that are global and multidisciplined and that require the timely delivery of multiple, complex projects.

A CPO's responsibility is to care for the organizations' portfolio of projects—from the business case to final implementation, including:

- Involvement in the business decisions that result in new projects
- Strategic project planning
- Setting priorities and negotiating resources for projects
- Oversight of strategic project implementation
- Oversight of an enterprise-wide project management system
- Development of project management awareness and capability throughout the organization
- Periodic project review, including the decision to discontinue projects
- Top-level stakeholder management, facilitation, and mentoring

The *corporate project management office* (*CPMO*), sometimes called the strategic project office, is another option. This is a small, strategic group that acts as the link between the executive vision and the project-related work of the organization. Its functions include overseeing strategic items such as project management maturity, project culture, enterprise-wide systems integration, managing quality and resources across projects and portfolios, and project portfolio management.[3]

The CPMO is responsible for the project portfolio management process and ensures that the organization's projects are linked to corporate strategies. The CPMO ensures that the organization's project portfolio continues to meet the needs of the business, even as these needs change over time. It serves as the critical link between business strategy and the execution of tactical plans.

A third option is the *program management office* (abbreviated *PgMO* to distinguish it from the project management office, or PMO). This office operates at a less strategic level than the CPMO and is designed to provide coordination and alignment for projects that are interrelated under the umbrella of a given program.

Committees offer still another approach for dealing with EPG issues. This option involves the use of committees to provide strategic guidance and oversight coverage for project management endeavors. Examples are the committee for strategic projects, strategic steering committee, and portfolio review committee. These committees have authority for prioritizing projects that cut across functional departments and that are composed of executives from all over the organization to ensure consensus and balance.

The CEO thus has multiple options for providing strategic guidance for managing projects across the enterprise. Which approach is the best fit and how the organization will be structured depend on existing company culture, the developing needs within the organization, and the opinions of the principal decision makers.

Scenario Three

The third approach operates under the following assumptions: Corporate governance provides no committee coverage for EPG, and the organization under the CEO establishes no formal structure such as a CPO or CPMO to deal with issues related to portfolios, programs, and projects. Here, the challenge of dealing with multiple projects of sundry natures persists, yet the responsibility is scattered throughout the organization. How to deal with this?

When guidance is lacking from above, the leadership for minimizing potential project chaos is taken on by business unit heads or leaders of major departments. Areas like IT and engineering have often implemented PMOs due to the heavy concentration of projects in those disciplines. Many large business units are sufficiently independent to set up their own approaches for dealing with EPG issues. They may have a beefed-up PMO to support the projects in the business unit or department in question. For EPG to happen in this type of setting, a bottom-up movement is required. Here the awareness for the benefits of project management, when applied across the organization, begins at a grassroots level. This means that upper leadership in the organization is concentrating on other priorities and that EPG issues are not high on the strategic radar. Thus awareness needs to be raised at the upper levels.

The grassroots movement involves a bottom-up approach. In this setting, a growing awareness exists at the middle management and professional levels regarding the need for a coherent enterprise-wide set of policies, competencies, and methodologies for managing projects of all natures and types. At this hands-on level, benefits for an EPG-type approach is evident to participating stakeholders because this holistic view implies that the organization will be supported with appropriate systems, trained personnel, and an overall project culture.

The awareness, however, is not so evident to upper management. Proposals to top decision makers for an overarching program like EPG fall on deaf ears, leaving the interested parties with two options. The first is to go with the flow—keep plugging away as best as possible and hope that something will sway opinions in the future. The other option is to take a proactive stance and embark on a policy of advocacy for the EPG cause. This implies using techniques of influence management to create interest and awareness. Here are some effective approaches:

- Target potential champions that might help carry the flag for the EPG cause.
- Distribute published literature, including magazines and Internet publications, that documents how competitors or other organizations take project management to higher levels.
- Use indirect influencing by involving people who have access to the ears of the decision makers.
- Prepare a business case showing feasibility and proposing a step-by-step approach.

Such a bottom-up approach may be articulated by existing PMOs because they surely have awareness and interest in articulating such a movement.

PMOs come in all shapes and sizes. They can be staffed on a part-time basis or managed virtually. The focus may be limited to planning and reporting. In other cases, PMOs may have departmental status with responsibility for overseeing, managing, and reporting on multiple projects.

The names for PMOs vary and mirror the diverse range of activities carried out in different types of organizations. The wide array of titles include program office, project management initiative, product management office, project support office, program support office, project support group, project control group, group program office, virtual PMO, division program office, project management center of excellence, organization support project office, project management competency center, and business support initiative.

No matter what their scope, PMOs are an indispensable link in the chain of effective Enterprise Project Governance. Regardless of its structure, an effective PMO includes minimally in its scope of activities:

- Control and reporting
- Support, methodology, and resources
- Competency and training in project management

In many cases, PMOs evolve over time to meet needs as they arise. This is common in areas of IT and construction, and this evolutionary approach often fits the intended purpose.

For broader, organizational applications, however, an overview diagnosis is recommended before structuring a PMO. This establishes a basis for developing a customized design that fits both the immediate and future needs of the organization. Here are issues that require reflection and evaluation prior to initiating PMO design:

- Reporting level within the organization: corporate, departmental, or program?
- Desired outputs: information for management, support and internal consulting for projects, standardization of methodologies, implementation of cutting-edge technologies, stakeholder articulation?
- Size of the organization: global or otherwise geographically widespread,

local and concentrated? Is the target audience only a part of the entire organization?

- Probable roadblocks: lack of upper management support, strong resistance from the grassroots, underestimating the change management necessary to implement the concept?
- Characteristics of the organization: project-driven (construction, software development) or product-driven (consumer products)?

These questions set the scene for the PMO design process. Based on the issues raised in the initial evaluation, a detailed analysis is required focusing on the myriad variables that affect the design and the subsequent performance of the PMO. Here are the principal questions that require definition in order to develop an effective design.

Context
- Is the need for a PMO market driven or internally driven?
- Who are the principal articulators: top management, middle management, a specific area?
- What is the implementation intent: revolutionary or evolutionary?
- Is the intended scope of PO aimed only at the implementation of projects, or is it also tied to business strategy?

Organization and People
- Will the PMO have a line or staff function?
- To whom does the PMO report: CEO, department head, committee?
- What is the scope of the projects: all projects, strategic projects, area projects?
- Who has responsibility for project people: recruiting, training, allocating, support?
- What is the size of the PMO: large group, two or three people, part-time, mostly virtual?

Scope of Support Function

- What is the methodology for responsibility: develop, implement, monitor?
- What PM tools will be used: selection, adaptation, training?
- How are records kept: for all projects or just for priority projects?
- What type of support is needed: proactive or upon request?

Project Execution Responsibilities

- Tracking and reporting: all-inclusive for management or project by project?
- Auditing: support function for PMs or for upper management control?
- Planning and scheduling: support for projects or hands-on assignments?
- Communications: enterprise-wide or single-project support?
- Change management: proactive management or procedural support?

After the PMO design parameters are fixed, the next step is to define and formalize them in written documents:

- A charter for the PMO project
- Internal organization and external interfaces
- Policies and procedures
- Roles, responsibilities, and position descriptions
- Competency and training requirements

As for any other project, starting up a project management office requires a logical sequence of actions. A PMO project involves both technical and behavioral issues.[4] Here is the sequential order:

- *Situation Size-Up and Conceptual Design.* Assess current practices and develop a concept that will be coherent with company needs.
- *Detailed Design and Solution Development.* Develop the solution, including methodology and system requirements, as well as organizational requirements.

- *Testing.* Test the proposed solutions on a specific project.
- *Implementation.* Use the solutions on a broader scale with special attention to the behavioral side of change management.
- *Maintenance.* Manage the processes and train.

The proper fit of the PMO in the organization is essential. When EPG is already in place, an organizational framework exists for ensuring that the new PMO initiatives add value to the overall cause of managing projects. In this ideal environment, a logical relationship exists among company strategies, portfolio policies, and communications regarding project-related topics. A new PMO would then reside under the protective umbrella of EPG and blend seamlessly into the organization's project management scenery.

In a less than ideal setting, however, EPG may not be in place, such as when PMOs of sundry sorts have sprouted to meet specific departmental or business unit needs. This means that alignment is likely lacking among the PMOs and that probably the wheel has been reinvented and efforts duplicated. Here, special care is called for when designing a new PMO. The timing might be right to gather lessons learned from existing PMOs and to plant seeds for establishing an EPG movement—or at least to beef up communications channels in the organization's project management community.

The success of PMO design is measured by the degree to which it focuses on the project issues at hand and interfaces effectively with the organization to ensure that projects perform within procedures and in line with organizational strategies. Meeting that goal requires custom tailoring based on the design questions and parameters outlined because, in the case of the project management office, one size does not fit all!

Communication and Building Commitment for EPG Implementation

The pieces that comprise the EPG concept are sundry. Mapping out the vision and strategy for EPG, using the variables given, is a giant step in the right direction toward implementing the concept. Yet developing the vision is not enough to make EPG actually happen. Although the right EPG concept is a critical success factor, how the view is sold to the rest of the organization is equally important.

While the design of EPG is primarily an intellectual process, communicating and gaining buy-in of the idea is a behavioral issue. Selling the idea involves the human ego, reaction to change, turf battles, and allowing time for the new concepts to sink in. So once the EPG concept has been launched, behavioral-based planning is called for to garner support to make the idea actually happen.

Getting principal stakeholders like project managers, vice presidents, functional managers, and support staff to heartily embrace EPG requires a process for understanding, acceptance, and buy-in. To develop understanding, exposure of the idea is essential, along with allowance for the idea to mature. This may involve hearing a speech on the topic, participating in a workshop, surfing the Web for more details, reading about it in the literature, and discussing it with colleagues. Some people make need weeks and others may need months just to understand what EPG is all about.

Getting people to buy in involves other issues as well. For instance, stakeholders may struggle with questions like these:

- What's in it for me?
- How will EPG affect my present status?
- Will someone be invading my turf?
- What risks will I run?
- Who else supports the idea?
- How does the EPG affect internal politics?

It takes time for stakeholders to find answers to such questions and move on to full acceptance.

Buy-in for EPG means understanding and embracing the concept and being ready to put it into practice. For this to happen, prerequisites are required, such as enthusiasm, planning, implementation, and persistent follow-up. In practice, the implementation of Enterprise Project Governance must follow a pathway that ensures commitment to the cause by the principal stakeholders. Actions that facilitate buy-in include:

- Campaigns to promote understanding including such actions as lectures, intranet postings, and literature distribution
- Forums for stimulating discussion via seminars, workshops, and intranet
- Start-up workshops or integration seminars to ensure that stakeholders work toward the same goals

So the implementation of EPG depends not only on the right vision for the organization, but also on how the concept is communicated to primary stakeholders and the rest of the organization. That communication is sensitive to the need for people to understand the EPG concept, to accept it as valid, and to buy into the idea and fully support it.

A Major Multinational Corporation

Managing multiple types of projects effectively across an enterprise requires structure and organization. A major global player in consumer products with annual sales exceeding £12 billion includes the corporate PMO in the area of strategy and planning. PMOs are also established in each of five worldwide regions, each of which maintains a matrix relationship with the regional director and the corporate-level PMO. Regional PMO managers coordinate subordinate geographical-area PMO managers and at least one staff support person.[5]

Areas of PMO responsibility include:

- Portfolio management, involving maintaining the governance model, strategic alignment, prioritization and resource allocation, and support for decision making
- Center of excellence, including internal business consultancy, best practices and lessons learned, developing competencies, and heartbeat quality checkups
- Support, which includes interfacing, risk management, benefits realization, processes, and tools

The portfolio of projects of the organization focuses on business change initiatives. These initiatives are managed through projects because change is usually ad hoc in nature and carried out through a project approach. The projects are managed through existing project management structures and often involve temporary professional staffing. Success is measured against business objectives at the end of the project after delivery.

PMOs across the organization have the responsibility for reporting to management on progress, risks, and issues that require attention and decision making. The PMOs monitor these communications' best practices as part of an overall EGP philosophy. Here are samples of reports used.

- *Highlight Reports.* The objective is to provide the project board and key stakeholders with a periodic executive summary of project status. The project board uses the report to monitor project progress. The project manager uses it as a communications tool to advise the project board of potential problems or areas where the board needs to provide support or make a decision. Report topics include budget status, schedule status, products completed during the reporting period, actual or potential problems and risk update, actions to be completed during next period, status of project issues, impact of any changes on budget and schedule, and status of quality.

- *Postproject Review.* Also part of the PMO tool kit are actions taken once projects come to an end. The objectives here are to:

- Define how to measure benefits.

- Learn whether the final product has caused any problems in use.

- Understand whether products are delivering the benefits defined in the business case.

- Check the costs generated by the products against the business case.

- Verify KPIs/metrics to show project effectiveness.

- Check recommended corrective actions.

- *Monthly Meeting Updates.* This one-hour report is given during the executive team meeting. The focus is on decision making and priority action with respect to the portfolio.

Conclusions

For EPG to become a reality, the fundamentals for managing projects across an enterprise must be in place. The fundamental elements for effectively implementing and making operational EPG are many, but they can be grouped into four categories: (1) governance in project management, (2) culture, (3) macroprocesses, and (4) competency. EPG can be developed under distinct leadership in three scenarios: (1) corporate board committee, (2) CEO and executive team, and (3) grassroots movement. Some of the organizational options are CPO (chief project officer), CPMO (corporate project management office), PgMO (program management office), and project committees, as well as variations of the classic PMO. The fit of each of these essential pieces of the EPG puzzle is essential. Implementation of EPG and its respective components requires design to meet the organization's requirements, as well as communication and commitment building. An example of a global consumer products company shows the importance of structuring project management on an enterprise-wide basis so that the concepts permeate the organization.

8

Stakeholder Management and the Pivotal Role of the Sponsor

Stakeholder management is a basic cornerstone in Enterprise Project Governance. It deals with organizational relationship issues and includes interfacing approaches such as power, politics, and influence. Special interests, hidden agendas, negotiations, and interpersonal conflicts also come into play in stakeholder management. Although sometimes perceived as a collection of *soft* behavioral methods, in fact, stakeholder management often calls for hard-knuckled action to effectively deal with the issues.

To implement Enterprise Project Governance, which demands a change in organizational mind-set, a start-up stakeholder approach is required—one that focuses on the unique issues of managing an organizational change project. Even when an enterprise philosophy already reigns, stakeholders have to be managed to keep the organization lively and productive.

EPG also serves as a bastion for solid stakeholder policies for projects that are vital to the strategic success of the organization. EPG is all about making sure the right combination of projects are done right , in particular, mega projects or other highly strategic ventures. So EPG has a role for ensuring that key project-related executives, sponsors, and professionals across the organization are up to speed on managing all the players affecting their projects.

A Stakeholder Threesome

A case in point involves the complex stakeholder issues associated with the construction of a gigantic military aircraft for the Indian Air Force (IAF). The IAF partnered with the U.S. Air Force (USAF) and subsequently signed with aeronautics contractor Lockheed Martin in March 2008 to design and build six high-tech C-130J Super Hercules planes.

The complex aircraft fabrication project included more than just building planes, thus involving stakeholders outside the manufacturing process. Support systems, spare parts supply and warehousing, maintenance equipment, and training programs were also part of the picture. Personnel were required in the primary settings of the stakeholders: New Delhi (IAF), Washington, D.C. (USAF), and Marietta, Georgia (Lockheed Martin).[1]

For Lockheed Martin, the three-way relationship among major stakeholders was not normal practice. "The IAF didn't understand the process of working through the U.S. government or Lockheed Martin's foreign military sales process," said Lockheed's Director and Project Manager Abhay Paranjape. "And Lockheed Martin had to realize that this was the first aircraft India has bought from the United States in decades. So we didn't have a good understanding of IAF requirements, procedures, and processes."

The stakeholder issues were successfully managed through a combination of long-distance virtual communications, periodic face-to-face group meetings, and effective governance practices among the three major players. This combination contributed heavily to the two-months-ahead-of-schedule delivery of the first aircraft in December 2010.

The triangular relationship created challenges in stakeholder management and raised issues on project governance. Early on, it was recognized that the collaborative relationship between the two air forces would require extensive dialogue and adjustment. Thus the parties established governance practices that ensured smooth communications throughout the project. When Lockheed Martin entered the scene, additional negotiations involving the full stakeholder threesome took place to ensure overall stakeholder alignment. For the IAF C-130 project and other major undertakings that are vital to the goals of contracting parties, the issues of stakeholder management and project governance are key success factors. Part of the mission of EPG is to make sure that those issues are systematically dealt with on all projects across the enterprise.

Power, Politics, and Influence

EPG is all about power, politics, and influence. Although structure and procedures are also relevant factors, these more amorphous issues are what ultimately determines the effectiveness of Enterprise Project Governance. The concepts are described in this chapter. If these views are not part of the culture of the organization, it is recommended that a workshop program be carried out to ensure that the primary stakeholders know how to navigate in the waters of EPG.

EPG and Power

"Power is the ultimate aphrodisiac," Henry Kissinger said when he was U.S. Secretary of State. The statement suggests that power has an almost sensual attraction; people are drawn to power by a magnetic, quasi erotic force. Whether this is true or not, it's a fact that power is necessary for executives and other important project players to get their jobs done. Power provides the energy to take initiative, to lay out plans, and to follow up on results. From a company standpoint, the attraction people feel to power is a healthy influence because, when power is properly used, it moves an enterprise in the right direction. For Enterprise Project Governance, here are the prevalent forms of power:

- *Formal.* Stemming from position power, formal power indicates that the player has received some charter to do a job. A scope of work is associated with that job, which is to be carried out according to the culture and values of the company. Formal power is the easiest kind to see and understand. It is usually expressed in an up-front manner.

- *Relationship.* "It's not what you know, but who you know" goes the old expression. Access is a form of power, whether that access is through blood relationships, an good-old-boy network, or church or community acquaintances. Relationship power opens doors.

- *Knowledge-Based.* While authority can be formal, it can also be couched in knowledge. Nobel Prize winners, for instance, are not always steeped in formal power, but their recognized knowledge makes them leading authorities, which in turn becomes power. Thus power and authority go hand in hand.

- *Competence.* Competence power transcends that of knowledge, in that the person is recognized as someone who gets things done. Power derived from competence stems both from technical knowledge and from behavioral and political skills.

Cultivating one or a combination of these power factors considerably boosts the potential power of executives and other significant players in an enterprise. From a stakeholder management viewpoint, it makes good sense to establish a firm power base and even to brandish power when necessary, provided that ethics and people's feelings are respected. It takes power to get things done, particularly in a wide-reaching web of power brokers exercising their influence across the enterprise. Here are tips on how executives and other players can use power effectively in the organization:

- *Understand the organization.* All organizations have a fundamental culture. They have traditions and a history. Even though major surgery may be needed, understanding the essence of an organization is fundamental to putting together the governance of a project-oriented enterprise.

- *Polish up on interpersonal skills.* For Enterprise Project Governance to work, both senior executives and project team members must have high levels of the emotional quotient of behavioral and political skills needed to deal intelligently with the power factors present.

- *Build up image.* Just as products need to be marketed to convey an image, all key players in a project setting need to keep personal images polished. Call it self-marketing, blowing your own horn, or whatever, the personal image as a competent and articulate project-based player deserves constant nurturing.

- *Develop and cultivate allies.* Enterprise Project Governance is like a team sport. Individual actions become significant only within the context of a series of actions. As in volleyball, where one player receives the ball, and a second sets it up for the third player to spike, players in projectized organizations require support from teammates.

EPG and Politics

Politics has been described in government circles as the "art of the possible." The possible in companies depends on the art of conciliating differing interests and opinions among the people who make up the network of power in the organization. Executives, therefore, need to act politically to influence the company's decision-making process in order to bring about decisions consistent with their interests and opinions—and that at the same time are possible. The key to politics lies in understanding that facts are not the important factor in making political decisions. Much more important are the interests at stake, such as departmental or sectorial interests, power-based interests, economic and financial interests, and personal agendas. And most important, the opinions of individuals, formed for whatever historical, cultural, or psychological reasons, are the essence of everything political. When managing stakeholders in an enterprise setting, here are some recommended techniques for successful politicking in favor of a given cause:

- Plant seeds of action by casually remarking on issues, circulating articles, or citing third parties.

- Don't press the issue; give people time to absorb and process new ideas and issues.

- Involve others because politics by its nature includes and affects groups of people.

- Give details in support of your cause as discussions evolve.
- Include the suggestions of others, and negotiate any details involving the interests of all.

EPG and Influence

In an enterprise setting, influence is closely related to competence. The greater the level is of technical and behavioral competence, the greater the level of influence will be. Because of the large number of network and matrix relationships in an enterprise setting, power and politics have to be wielded in a subtle fashion, using different forms of influence. Here are the assumptions for effective influence management:

- Most executives possess the basic experience and knowledge necessary to exercise influence management, yet they do not fully utilize that potential.
- An easy way to influence others is to give positive feedback, provided the feedback is timely, relevant, and sincere.
- The art of listening, although an apparently passive stance, is a powerful technique for influencing others. It creates a bond that inevitably pays dividends in terms of relationships and goodwill.
- The classic approach of different strokes for different folks continues to be valid when it comes to influencing other people. This means customizing behavior for individuals with differing characteristics so that each person gets made-to-order treatment.
- Interface management, or the building of bridges for communication and conciliating interests between company stakeholders, is a key activity in projectized organizations.
- Multidirectional relationships between executives and key project players, involving vertical, horizontal, and diagonal communications, are the norm in organizations that are managed via projects.
- Conflict management is part of the executive's job in any organization; in organizations managed by projects, the propensity for conflict is even greater because of the multiple relationships.

Structured Stakeholder Management

The power, politics, and influence issues involved in managing projects across an enterprise can be looked at using a structured format. A stakeholder management plan maps out a structured way to influence each player. The key word is "structured," as opposed to using a purely intuitive approach. Although stakeholders have always been managed in some form, structured stakeholder management allows for the comprehensive planning and staging of what needs to be done to influence the doers and opinion makers.

Dealing with stakeholders in a customized, needs-based manner boosts the chances for smooth sailing in a project environment. Conversely, the lack of a systematic slant on handling both the obvious decision makers and the behind-the-scenes opinion makers is an open invitation to disaster: Sooner or later a disgruntled stakeholder will toss a curveball. At minimum, the fix for an unexpected situation entails backtracking, rework, and the management of grief.

Walmart, Battling for the Hearts and Minds of Stakeholders

Walmart's worldwide status as the number one company in retailing has been frequently documented on *Fortune* magazine's annual lists. The company is famous for its values of hard work, customer satisfaction, and employee appreciation, expressed since the beginning by founder Sam Walton in 1962.

In spite of these admirable qualities, since 2000, Walmart has been the target of severe criticism with respect to its business practices. Accusations leading to lawsuits included low wages, gender discrimination, and the use of illegal immigrant labor.[2] The University of Michigan's American Customer Satisfaction Index has rated Walmart at the low end of its list since the index's inception in 2004.

Consumer interest groups, as well as politicians and nongovernmental organizations (NGOs), launched campaigns against the company using techniques like lobbying, media movements, and grassroots initiatives. The consumer groups aim to influence the entire consumer market by targeting the worldwide leader. Walmart Watch's mission is to hold Walmart accountable for its impact on communities, the workforce, the retail sector, the environment, and the nation's economy. Walmart Watch challenges the company to fully embrace its corporate responsibilities and to live up to its position as the largest corporation in the United States.[3, 4]

Walmart's public relations and reputation management (PR) was nonexistent until being the focus of so many critics. In 2005, Walmart created a so-called war room with some of the biggest names in the PR industry to preempt negative attacks from manufacturer to storefront. Walmart's most visible and concerted effort to give back to society has been its sustainability program, encompassing many of their initiatives in external communication and adopting the concept that sustainability goes beyond the environment and has broader economic and social components, including health care, economic opportunity, and the quality of life of the people who make the products they sell.

At the end of 2007, Walmart released the first Sustainability Progress to Date, 2007–2008, tracing their commitment to sustainability, from consumer to employee, from manufacturer to storefront. The report points out:

> We have found that there is no conflict between our business model of everyday low costs and everyday low prices and being a more sustainable business. To make sustainability sustainable at Walmart, we've made it live inside our business. Many of our environmental sustainability efforts, for example, mean cost savings for us, our suppliers and our customers.[5]

To make sustainability live inside their business—an aim that requires flawless execution—they created Sustainable Value Networks to integrate practices across the business, bringing together leaders from the company, suppliers, academia, government, and NGOs to explore challenges and to develop solutions to benefit business, as well as local and global communities. Each network has a sponsor at the level of senior vice president and is led by a network captain who has a sustainability team overseeing the activities. Walmart took the following steps to deal with a critical situation with many stakeholders involved:[6, 7]

- Created the war room to deal with the problem.
- Identified and analyzed all the stakeholders having an interest in the problem and desired outcome (both positive and negative).

- Planned how to engage the stakeholders by creating a sustainability program to promote change with many of the issues involved in their external communication.
- Developed a communication and reporting plan.
- Started executing the program, adjusting and improving it over the years and issuing a consolidated report every year.

The program approach using the sustainability flag was used by Walmart to ward off attacks by opposing groups. The fact that the company was under siege brings out a colloquial truism about the management of stakeholders: If stakeholders are not managed proactively, they will throw rocks at you. While the defensive program proved reasonably effective in dealing with Walmart's PR issues concerning the opposition stakeholders, proactive, preventive stakeholder management is a more effective way to go.

Who Are the Stakeholders Anyhow?

The first manned moon shot in 1969 had lots of stakeholders, including the president of the United States, the congressional leaders, the Soviets, the media, and, of course, NASA.

Certainly first-on-the-moon Neil Armstrong felt himself a major stakeholder in the Apollo project. Some people carry higher stakes than others, just as the proverbial pig's stake in a dish of ham and eggs is unquestionably greater than that of the chicken. Folklore has it that the original Apollo project objective was, "Before the end of this decade, we will land a man on the moon." It goes on to say that NASA astronauts added the words "and bring him safely back to Earth."

Here are some stakeholders who carry different stakes in projects:

- *Project Champions.* The champions are responsible for the project's existence. They initiate the movement and are ultimately interested in seeing the project get to its operational stage. They shape the way an organization perceives and manages its projects. These champions determine to what extent the company is prepared to manage multiple projects. Examples of those who champion the cause are investors, project sponsors, upper management overseers, clients (external or internal), and politicians (local, state, federal).

- *Project Participants.* This group performs the project work. From an Enterprise Project Management standpoint, these stakeholders merit special care because they are the ones who bring home the bacon. The role of the project team members is related to the project itself; they are usually not involved in the conceptual phases and likely will not follow into the operational phases. Some of these key players are project managers, team members, suppliers, contractors, specialists, regulatory agencies, and consultants.

- *External Stakeholders.* These parties, while theoretically uninvolved, may suffer from project fallout. In other words, they are affected by the project as it unfolds, or by the final results of the project once it is implemented. They also may influence the course of a project. Some of these external influences may not be manageable by the team assigned to a project; in such cases, support is required from elsewhere in the organization. Examples of external stakeholders are environmentalists, community leaders, social groups, the media (press, TV, etc.), project team family members, and opposition groups, as described in the Walmart case.

Exhibit 8-1 depicts some of the major stakeholders in the EPG arena.

How Does the Stakeholder Model Apply to Enterprise Project Governance?

For Enterprise Project Governance, principal stakeholders fall into the champion category. These champions have the power to initiate projects and shape their ultimate impact on the organization, and their decisions end up affecting all other internal and external stakeholders. In generic terms, the champions include investors, project sponsors, upper management overseers, clients (external or internal), and politicians (local, state, federal). A spotlight on EPG

Exhibit 8-1. Stakeholders in EPG Environment

itself, however, reveals a more detailed list of parties with stakes in the structuring and managing of projects across the organization. Here are some of them:

- *Board Members.* If the board has a strategic committee or something similar, then the committee chair exerts influence on EPG.
- *CEO, Executive Committee members, Chief Project Officer, or VP of Special Projects.* The CEO is ultimately responsible for EPG but is likely to delegate that responsibility to another C-level executive.
- *Strategic PMO, Corporate PMO, or Project Portfolio Manager.* In some cases, the responsibility may be delegated directly to high-level PMOs or portfolio managers.
- *Business Unit or Departmental PMOs.* Operational-level PMOs carry out a major role in ensuring that project management policies are implemented and followed.
- *Project Managers.* These are the hands-on players that transform the overall EPG policies into reality on each project.

What Are the Steps in Stakeholder Management?

The approach for managing stakeholders, outlined in this section, is fully applicable in the EPG arena.

While intuition is important when dealing with stakeholders, a step-by-step overview is recommended to ensure that all issues are taken into consideration.

- *Identify and gather preliminary information about stakeholders.* Make a list of all who lay claim, in any form, to a share of the project's outcome. In the case of the project to implement Enterprise Project Governance, who are the champions, the project participants, and the external stakeholders? Remember that stakeholders must be identified as individuals—with names and faces—as opposed to departments or groups. Be sure to include the following information:
  - Name
  - Background
  - Role of the individual
  - Special circumstances
  - Past experiences
- *Analyze each stakeholder's probable behavior and potential impact.* To what extent can stakeholders have an impact on a project? And to what extent can their behavior be influenced? Here is a simple way for classifying the stakeholders:
  - A = Stakeholders who can be influenced strongly
  - B = Stakeholders who can be influenced moderately
  - C = Stakeholders who can be influenced very little

  Stakeholders can also be classified by their degree of impact on the project. For instance:
  - D = Stakeholders who have a strong impact on the project
  - E = Stakeholders who have a medium impact on the project
  - F = Stakeholders who have a weak impact on the project
- *Develop stakeholder strategies.* Stakeholders are the way they are—except when they are different! Just as in team sports, it takes people with unique characteristics, each carrying out a differing role, to manage

a project-oriented organization. Professional teams, whether football, basketball, soccer, or cricket, all have on-field and off-field players. The off-field players include owners, managers, promoters, coaches, athletes, and support groups. Organizations that manage by project have a similar cast, and all parties have to do their parts for the organization's goals to be met. A plan needs to be developed to spell out how each stakeholder should be managed.

To understand how to handle stakeholders, these questions require responses:

- What are the stakeholders' stated objectives or position?
- What is the likely hidden agenda?
- What influences are exerted on the stakeholder?
- Who is the best person to approach this stakeholder?
- What tactics are best suited?
- What is the best timing?

- *Implement and maintain the strategies.* This phase calls for carrying out activities planned in the previous stage, via a stakeholder management implementation plan. This plan pinpoints actions, responsible parties, and completion dates for the actions. Then that plan is adjusted and reworked as needed. But, to begin, the stakeholder strategies are implemented in accordance with the relative importance of the stakeholders. For instance, there would be major emphasis on a small number of stakeholders who have a strong impact, normal efforts for an intermediate group, and moderate attention to stakeholders reckoned to have a lesser impact.

Influencing Stakeholders to Buy In: Not an Easy Task

A bank owned by a European automaker faced a stakeholder alignment challenge when several project management thrusts were taking place within the enterprise at the same time. The bank's Achilles' heel was a centralized credit approval project that was intended to speed up processing and eliminate bureaucracy at car dealerships, where credit applications were traditionally dealt with.

The project was a source of major conflict between the information technology people, who were managing the effort, and upper management, who exerted heavy-handed pressure to get it back on track. The head of training perceived a need for improved project performance and arranged for courses on the basics of project management. These courses did not take place, however, because the bank's quality group became convinced that the time was right to introduce a management-by-projects slant for running the organization, but they needed a go-ahead from upstairs to proceed. Upper management did not give the nod because the executives were not attuned to the need for a strategic approach to handling projects. The IT people, who were competent technically, had little or no training in how to run projects. No one, at any level, had taken into account the fact that the new structure would substantially shrink the functions of dozens of people and would play topsy-turvy with the power balance within the bank. This situation is a classic portrait of unaligned stakeholders. Each had a different perception of what the problems were and what needed to be done.

The responsibility for stakeholder management lies with the party who has the greatest awareness of the need for Enterprise Project Management. In the example of the bank, the quality group carried the burden of influencing stakeholders to rally around the management-by-projects philosophy. Once that commitment was received—and after an in-house awareness talk by a guest expert—the quality group began making headway toward changing the organization to a manage-by-projects format. This example illustrates the two principles given earlier: First, analyze who the stakeholders are and their stakes and, second, introduce your new approach to management in a way that is sensitive to the interests and concerns of all involved.

Promoting Project Management Among Company Stakeholders

Creating awareness is the first hurdle in implementing EPG in an organization. The change agents involved could be upper management, middle management, or organizational change agents or internal facilitators. No matter, the procedure for getting people to sign on is much the same. Since participation is needed for anything to work, several articulated moves, such as training programs, talks, and campaigns, can spread the spirit of project management throughout the company.

Another view is the evolution theory to promote a cause. Author Tom Peters looks at the issue like this: "How do you 'sell' this concept 'up' to your bosses? Don't!" Instead, he says, the positive results obtained through project management should filter up through the system and do their own marketing.[8] Third-party marketing, then, by way of the customer or internal client, is a way to let bosses know what a great job is being done via the diligent application of project management.

If Peters's approach sounds a bit simplistic, there are more proactive ways to promote project management among corporate stakeholders. One way is to compare performance with other companies or participate in benchmarking groups to see what practices are prevalent and effective. Numbers are another way to go; showing the potential savings of project management will surely move even the most resistant stakeholder.

Sponsors: Key Stakeholders in EPG

The figure of the sponsor provides the connection between the formal organization and the projects designed to carry company strategies. It's a crucial role that requires qualified people. As renowned international consultant Terence Cook-Davies points out, "This role is normally taken on by senior executives since only experienced top managers are likely to have credibility and knowledge of the permanent organization to interact effectively with other senior executives on the impact of projects with strategic and operational issues."[9] One of the roles of Enterprise Project Governance is to ensure that the organization has enough competent and well-trained sponsors to ensure that company projects stay on course.

This level of competence is particularly relevant in formal settings where the figure of the sponsor is institutionalized and specific responsibilities are associated with the role. From a practical standpoint, however, the sponsor role is not always formalized or fully understood by the sponsor or by those with whom the sponsor interacts. This creates an area of fuzziness in terms of organizational responsibility.

The formal institutionalized responsibilities of the sponsor are outlined next, along with comments for sponsors operating in less formalized settings.

Here are the roles that describe the essence of sponsors' contributions to EPG:

- Be responsible for the business case from start to finish (from proposal to benefits reaped).
- Act as a godfather figure to the project manager.
- Provide political support, and champion the cause.
- Govern the project.

These roles, properly carried out, are a near guarantee for success, whereas poor sponsorship tends to lay the groundwork for project failure.

The Business Case from Start to Finish

A vital role of the sponsor is to see that the project in question adheres to achieving the business objective. This requires a business case that provides the justification for committing resources to the project, based on the assumptions and objectives outlined in the project charter. The sponsor's role is then to ensure that the proposed facility, product, service, or improvement is duly delivered within the requirements and ultimately spawns the benefits desired as expressed in the business case.

The project sponsor is generally involved up front in the approval process of the business case, which outlines the desires of the organization's strategists. Sundry factors, however, influence the evolution of the project. So the sponsor is in fact a project guardian, charged with making sure the project does not sway off course and articulating adjustments as needed toward a happy project ending.[10]

The Sponsor as Godfather to the Project Manager

The sponsor's role as stakeholder manager with other senior executives is essential for the project manager to carry out his or her job. The sponsor provides a political shield to keep the project manager from being distracted from management duties. This role is necessary to meet challenges that can be resolved only at executive-suite levels. The sponsor takes on political roadblocks, such as reluctance by functional departments to provide resources or a lack of support by key players.

The godfather role involves providing political coverage as well as giving advice, counsel, and guidance to the project manager. Ultimately, the sponsor's success is tied directly to the success of the project manager, who deals with the daily issues and is charged with implementing the project. The sponsor may have to give some coaching and suggest directions on specific issues.

Even as the project is executed, the enterprise sponsoring it will be undergoing changes of its own. In this context, the sponsor is the one person best able to relate the overall enterprise risk, with its associated sustainability challenges, to the business case and to the uncertainty of the project itself.

Carrying Out Leadership Roles

How stakeholders in the organization see a project depends on the leadership of the sponsor. The challenges to the sponsor's leadership come from three different directions: project-related, interpersonal relationships, and sponsor self-management. All of these challenges are part of the sponsor's overarching responsibility as change agent because the desired business benefits are reaped only when the proposed change happens through implementing the project.

The *project-related* and *relationship* leadership issues are relatively intuitive for most sponsors. Yet the overall responsibility for sponsorship requires some reflection on sponsor self-management. This calls for internal assessment by the sponsor regarding the necessary allotment of time and effort required to do the job right.

The Sponsor as Governor of the Project

The sponsor, who invariably has other major responsibilities in the organization, is in fact responsible for governing the project. Of course, the project manager runs the project itself and is charged with the details of planning, implementation, and control. Yet overall governance of the project befalls the sponsor, who may or may not have deep knowledge of projects. Therefore, it's essential to establish and monitor major checkpoints and gain responses to specific questions in each phase, such as:

- *Preproject.* Is the business plan coherent with the organization's strategy?
- *Concept.* Does the project charter provide full definitions of objectives, benefits, resources, and time-cost parameters?
- *Planning.* Does the project plan include sufficient detail to carry out the project effectively, including topics such as quality, risk, documentation, scope packages, and communications management?
- *Implementation.* Is the formal reporting timely, and are regular meetings carried out to ensure effective implementation?
- *Closeout.* Are subcontracts being closed out appropriately, and is there a transition plan for the operational phase?
- *Postproject.* Are lessons learned fully documented? What postproject actions need to be made to optimize the benefits desired?

In some cases, the sponsor may be supported by a formal governance body, such as a project control board, steering group, or development committee.

Conclusions

Successful stakeholder management calls for a structured approach to deal with the parties who have vested interests in the project, and it is essential for effective Enterprise Project Governance. This means that all players (champions, participants, and external stakeholders) require proactive management; therefore, stakeholder management comes into play in two distinct ways. First, to implement the Enterprise Project Governance project, the stakeholders have to be managed during the implementation phase. Second, once the concept is put into place, company executives must ensure that the stakeholder concept becomes a part of the company culture. The sponsor's role is critical to the success or failure of projects and to the effectiveness of Enterprise Project Governance. The role is multifaceted, ranging from caring for the business case from start to finish, acting as a godfather figure to the project manager, carrying out leadership roles, and governing the project.

9

EPG Performance: Beyond Time, Cost, and Quality

When driving a car, a glance at the dashboard provides feedback data on the vehicle's performance. Speed, fuel levels, and engine temperature are shown on the gauges, and a GPS gives directions for the most convenient and efficient route. The input destination to the GPS corresponds to an organization's strategy because the strategy defines where an organization wants to go. To get there, companies require guidance and gauges to help measure the progress along the way. The importance of performance measurement is summed up by Peter Drucker: "What gets measured gets done, what gets measured and fed back gets done well, what gets rewarded gets repeated."

Once a specific strategy is determined, it's time for the performance measurement criteria to be selected. With appropriate feedback and reward criteria in place, a good strategy stands an excellent chance of achieving the desired results. Since EPG is based on the principle of doing the right projects right, performance management is the key component for ensuring that strategic projects are done right.

The Pizza Chain

A large pizza chain had more than a hundred stores across the country offering restaurant service and delivered pizzas. They sold 100,000 pizzas a day with an average income of US$1.5 million per day. The financial department proposed to cut 10 percent of the cheese in the pizza in order to save 5 cents per pizza, or US$150,000 per month, since customers would not notice it. The marketing department tendered an opposing tack, suggesting that an additional 5 cents' worth of cheese ("Our pizza has more cheese!") could increase sales to 120,000 pizzas a day, increasing income to US$1.8 million per day and thus generating more value to the company. This meant that management could leave things how they are, follow the financial proposal, or follow the marketing proposal. This is how opposing forces interact in an organization. These forces are good if not allowed to run unchecked. Performance measurement is the way to track forces and movements in a company as a support to decision making.[1]

Measuring EPG Performance

Performance measurement promotes accountability to stakeholders by facilitating informed decision making and reliable monitoring, as well as by analyzing and communicating the degree to which organizations meet key goals. Here are the five steps to achieve effective performance measurement:

1. *Establish the fundamental performance topics.* The process is initiated considering the business strategy in order to find the crucial performance topics. The correct representation of these topics—that is, what needs to be evaluated in relation to performance—will drive what ultimately gets done in alignment with the proposed strategy. The focus is on making performance topics out of the gap between where the company is today and where it wants to go.

The second source for choosing performance topics is the stakeholders. This process starts with understanding what the stakeholders' value for EPG success and then translating expectations into performance topics. Commonly, this process reveals conflicting interests and performance factors in tension with one another, which must be balanced.

Two more sources to analyze are the critical processes and the capabilities that need to be enhanced in order to leverage future results.

2. *Identify key performance factors.* Once the performance topics are established, one or more key performance factors (KPFs) must be set for each. KPFs are used to identify whether performance is on target (meeting desired standards) or requires improvement.

3. *Create performance indicators associated with the KPFs.* Performance indicators measure the activities carried out in execution and are often compared with recommended practices. To track each KPF, one or more performance indicators must be established.

4. *Assign accountabilities related to KPFs and performance indicators.* An organization is made of collections of people who are brought together to serve common purposes but who frequently create opposing forces. For this reason, assigning responsibilities for performance measurement is the way of forcing the necessary alignment.

5. *Report performance.* After assigning accountabilities and setting goals with areas and individuals, results must be tracked, performance reviewed, the pace and direction adjusted, and rewards provided. For this, periodic progress review for monitoring implementation and execution must be determined.

Executives and management teams are responsible for mapping out which projects, initiatives, KPFs, and measurement indicators are best to speed the organization to the strategic destination. A particularly striking example of the positive influence of KPFs took place at the drugstore chain Walgreens.

Founded in 1901 as a neighborhood drugstore, Walgreens is a premier pharmacy in the United States with an extensive store network nationwide. In the 1990s, the company undertook a project to determine strategic KPFs with the aim of improving profitability. This resulted in the definition of a single central metric for the business: profit per customer visit. Walgreens wanted to have conveniently located stores, but that sometimes implied expensive locations. If profit per store were used as an indicator, cheaper locations might be preferred, but that would run against the convenience concept. After analysis, Walgreens switched its focus from profit per store to profit per customer visit. Every strategy, every initiative, every department strived to maximize this core metric. Even though management was using other metrics as well, having one that enabled a unified understanding of how to evaluate the organization as a whole, from C-level down to the ground floor, was essential for success. Although finding such a single key performance factor may not be possible, just having such a dialogue yields valuable insights and helps narrow the selection of the truly key indicators.

The Meaning of Success

While good project management cannot save an organization from a bad strategy, bad project management can harm a good strategy. Troubled projects are bad news to shareholders and CEOs. Bad project management may have lasting impacts on customer perception, client relationship, and potential future sales. And overbudget projects impact profit margin. Troubled projects increase working capital needs. Delays on getting client acceptance pile on additional financial burdens and saddle cash flow with negative impacts. Late launches of new products represent the loss of inflow from sales. Schedule problems in the implementation of solutions such as ERP (enterprise resource planning) sabotage expected cost benefits. And fines and litigation fees due to flawed execution can cause profits to flounder.

In June 2004, the National Offender Management Service (NOMS) in the United Kingdom initiated the National Offender Management Information System project, designed to track offenders in a single system covering offenders both during their prison stay and during probation time. The project, denominated C-NOMIS, proposed an integrated way to manage offenders, replacing separate records for prison inmates and for offenders on probation and allowing prison and probation officers to access shared records in real time. The objective of the project was to create a single database allowing prison authorities to track and manage offenders while in custody and after their release. The implementation of the project was scheduled for January 2008 and was to have an approved lifetime cost of £234 million to 2020. With less than six months remaining to delivery date, £155 million had already been spent on the project, it was two years behind schedule, and the estimated lifetime project costs had spiraled upward by a factor of 2.5. After additional delays and cost overruns, authorities abandoned the single database concept and rescoped the program. In January 2008, work began on the revised program with an estimated lifetime cost of £513 million.

The National Audit Office (NAO) in the United Kingdom, an organization that scrutinizes public spending on behalf of Parliament, analyzed the C-NOMIS and concluded that:[2]

> Overall the C-NOMIS project was handled badly and the value for money achieved by the project was poor. Many of the causes of the delays and cost overruns could have been avoided with better management of well known issues. The project's failure at the start to appreciate the product customization and business change required, its inadequate oversight and weak relationships with suppliers led to a doubling in program costs, a three year delay in program roll-out and reductions in scope and benefits. In particular the core aim of a shared database to provide a single offender record accessible by all service providers will not be met.

The NAO's summary findings describe a broad set of project management and governance problems leading to this failure and enumerates the following key reasons for delays and cost increases:

- *There was inadequate oversight by senior management.* While the project board met at least once every two months, it did not actively monitor delivery of the project and was unaware of the full extent of delays or the implications of its decisions on project cost. It was three years after project initiation that senior officials discovered that it was running two years late and that costs had more than doubled.
- *Appropriate resources and structures were not put in place to deliver such a complex project.* The overall governance and resources applied were not adequate given the scale of the task. Roles and responsibilities were

blurred. In particular, financial accountability was unclear, and insufficient skilled resources were applied to the project.

- *Program management was poor in key aspects, including planning, financial monitoring, and change.* Initial planning was overly optimistic in terms of both cost and timescales. For example, there was no contingency, despite some recognition that the project carried a high level of risk. Budget monitoring was absent, with cost control focusing on monitoring the spending against the annual budget rather than matching cost against project deliverables. Change control was weak, and no process was in place for assessing the cumulative impact of individual change requests on the project budget or delivery timetable.

- *Technical complexity of the project was significantly underestimated.* A single offender database is technically realizable, but other potential solutions were not adequately explored, and the cost of customizing the software selected for the Prison Service was underestimated. The estimated cost of developing the application rose from £99 million when the full business case was approved in June 2005 to £254 million by July 2007, primarily because of customization.

- *The need to invest in business change was underestimated.* No sustained effort was made to simplify and standardize business processes across prisons and probation areas around the country.

- *Contractual arrangements with its key suppliers were weak, and its supplier management poor.* Instead of tendering key project contracts, NOMS opted to use its current suppliers under existing framework agreements to develop and deliver the application. NOMS allowed these contracts to go forward on a time and materials basis for longer than it should, which meant that there was insufficient pressure on suppliers to deliver to time and cost.

NAO and the Office of Government Commerce (OGC) have identified eight common causes of project failure. It is an NAO routine to evaluate the projects they analyze against the eight causes. Using the NAO OGC list as reference and the lessons learned from projects, programs, and portfolios, the authors have indicated the following top 10 causes of failures for EPG:

1. *Lack of Alignment with the Organization's Key Strategic Priorities.* The alignment issue is critical when the project's goals are not in step with the organization's basic vision.

   Hurdles:
   - Team members and other resources are pulled for higher-priority "strategic" projects.
   - Management's time commitment is limited.
   - Management is slow to respond to critical issues and risks.

   Action Items:
   - Identify which items on the strategic plan your project supports.
   - Understand the priority of the strategic plan.
   - Clarify the value that the project and programs bring to the business.
   - Establish key success factors.

2. *Lack of Clear Governance and Ownership.* Time and effort are needed, sometimes at the highest levels in an organization, for the governance arrangements to function correctly and to provide stakeholders with confidence in the arrangements. Any initiative will suffer immensely if project managers are unable to develop a cohesive strategy and supervise the direction of the effort.

   Hurdles:
   - The right level of support is absent when needed.
   - Issue resolutions are slow to arrive, sometimes causing stoppages or delays.
   - There is a lack of focus.
   - Leadership is missing.

   Action items:
   - Identify the sponsors.
   - Determine the sponsors' roles and responsibilities.
   - Elicit sponsorship from the C-level executives who will receive the greatest value from the project.

3. *Lack of Engagement with Stakeholders.* Successful EPG delivers in large part because of engaged stakeholders. Whether they are business unit executives, sponsors, or executive management, the chain of command is generally an active participant in the successful project.

   Hurdles:

   - Products developed do not meet customer needs.
   - Product design takes longer than expected.
   - The product is not accepted by the customers.
   - The products developed do not provide a return on investment or add value to the business.
   - Benefits are not achieved.

   Action items:

   - Establish a stakeholder management plan.
   - Have a common understanding and agreement of the stakeholder requirements secured.
   - Consistently communicate to stakeholders.

4. *Lack of Proven Approach.* There must be a coherent approach to EPG that guides the teams in the application of best practice, providing guidance on the actions required to be undertaken and the information necessary to make sound decisions, and that ensures that progress is reported correctly.

   Hurdles:

   - Unknown conflicts and timing issues delay projects and programs.
   - Unexpected staffing needs crop up.
   - Unexpected equipment and supply needs occur, increasing cost of project.

   Action items:

   - Perform a detailed plan before the start of projects and programs.
   - Allocate sufficient resources.
   - Review and adjust the plan frequently.

5. *Scope Creep.* Modifying products is risky and the most common form of scope creep. The best practice is to implement and get the benefit

quickly, then modify later. For complex, expensive issues containing many unknowns and volatile risks, institute a scope investigation phase in advance of approval and execution.

Hurdles:

- Development never ends; product changes frequently.
- Modifications to product during initial development drastically increase your risk of failure.
- Cost, effort, and duration increase unexpectedly.

Action items:

- Modify products only if they are business critical.
- Test the change in scope against the business case.
- Evaluate the impact on cost, schedule, and risks.
- Implement scope changes in the next release.
- Set up a change management committee.

6. *No Consideration in the Business Case of the Long-Term Value of Money and Securing Delivery of Business Benefits.* Project and program justification is based on a combination of intangible and quantitative factors. In many organizations, that is the last time anyone ever looks at the business case in any detail to analyze the delivery of the expected benefits.

Hurdles:

- Commitment from top management is lacking.
- There is a desperate need for resources.

Action items:

- Explain thoroughly why the project or program must be taken.
- Consider the full implications of external forces—competitive, environmental, regulatory.
- Take into account business criticality and affordability.

7. *Lack of Understanding of and Contact with the Supply Chain at Senior Levels in the Organization.* The supply chain provides a real opportunity to innovate and implement strategies to increase efficiencies, which in turn can deliver significant cost savings.

Hurdles:

- Suppliers have no understanding of the project's desired outcomes and deadlines.
- Increasing performance and efficiency is difficult.
- There is fragmentation and no collaboration.

Action items:

- Establish a strategy for engaging with suppliers.
- Create the time to understand the needs and potential solutions to unlocking efficiency improvements.
- Establish arrangements for sharing efficiency gains with suppliers.

8. *Ineffective Team Integration and Development.* Although the payoff is potentially great, the forging of a team is complicated. It requires dedication and persistence to transition a group of professionals with a high degree of interdependence from being focused on the achievement of a goal to becoming a team working in harmony and effectiveness.

Hurdles:

- Communication is fragile.
- The team is in conflict.
- Team meetings are unproductive.
- Individual development targets are absent.

Action items:

- Clarify expectations, roles, and responsibilities.
- Define communication channels.
- Establish arrangements for sharing efficiency gains with the project team.
- Consider integration with the supplier team.
- Establish individual development plans.

9. *Inattention to Risk.* One of the underreported areas of project failure is risk management. In many cases, when risk is an active part of the execution process, the rigor devoted to this area is negligible. Too often, problems are addressed reactively.

Hurdles:

- Nobody likes discussing risks.
- Teams are not prepared for disaster.
- The view of status is unrealistic.
- There are unexpected delays and cost overruns.

Action items:

- Identify the risks of EPG's processes.
- Continually revise risk mitigation and contingency plans.
- Educate teams on the benefits of performing risk management.
- Decide whether the risks are too high to continue.

10. *Underestimating Change to the Business.* Change management calls for changes in business processes. When implementing EPG, failure usually occurs when sponsors do not understand that they must either change the business to work with EPG or change EPG to work like the business. An important element of change management is training.

Hurdles:

- EPG and business processes are not aligned.
- Business process changes are not considered.
- Drastic process or EPG changes required at the last minute cause overages and delays.
- Costs increase during operations and maintenance.
- Customer acceptance is low.

Action items:

- Clarify the expected benefits.
- Understand the business process impact of the product.
- Establish a change management plan with training included.
- Set up a change management committee.

EPG Performance and the Eye of the Beholder

As just shown, the causes of failure can be various. But how can the success or failure of EPG be determined? On the one hand, some failures are clear:

- Nothing was delivered, and all the money and time spent have been wasted.
- The wrong benefits, products, or services were delivered.
- The delivery was so late as to make the benefits, products, or services useless.
- The quality was so poor as to make EPG useless.
- EPG costs too much, making it financially not viable.

On the other hand, some successes are indisputable:

- The delivery surpassed all the expectations on cost and time.
- Quality and functionality are acclaimed by the market.

EPG performance depends on the eye of the beholder. It therefore requires evaluation across a spectrum between failure and success, based on performance measurement that balances strategy alignment, stakeholder satisfaction, critical processes, and capabilities, as illustrated in Exhibit 9-1.

Exhibit 9-1. Evaluating the EPG Performance Spectrum

Taken together, the four performance factors yield a comprehensive view of EPG success or failure.[3] Once these dimensions of performance are detailed and monitored, the chances of project success will be higher, especially in consideration of its four crucial milestones: startup, recovery, termination, and closeout.

The Olympic Games

On July 2005, London was chosen to host the 2012 Olympics with a bid's estimate that the games would cost £2.4 billion. The estimate was described as "robust" by the Greater London Authority and London Development Authority and "well supported and documented" by the International Olympic Committee Evaluation.[4] However, according to the United Kingdom's Taxpayer Alliance, the 2012 Olympics budget, between July 2005 and March 2007, increased nearly fourfold, from £2.4 billion to £9.35 billion.

On March 5, 2007, the Public Accounts Committee (PAC) revealed widespread problems with the Olympics project, including a flawed management structure with no single individual in charge, the lack of a proper budget before bidding, and government funding guarantees that failed to limit the cost of the project. PAC Chairman Edward Leigh concluded that "there is no single person in overall control which will be a recipe for arguments and delay."[5] Ten days later, amid widespread criticism, Culture, Media and Sport Secretary Tessa Jowell announced the revised budget of £9.35 billion, indicating serious problems such as a lack of tax costs and contingency margins in the original bid and the failure to include significant elements of the security operation. Also, the original bid estimated that private sector funding would reach £738 million, a quarter of the total costs, although there was now little prospect of significant private sector funding.[6]

Considering the dimensions of project performance, the London Olympics were slated for success from the point of view of time and operation but at a substantial cost overrun and amid much accumulated criticism from stakeholders.

Lessons from the Arabian Gulf

Revisiting the performance dimensions throughout the project life cycle determines actions for project recovery or termination. Project recovery is composed of the effort and activities related to addressing troubled projects, followed by the decision on whether to save it. One example is the Saudi Peace Shield Program. In 1985, Saudi Arabia, supported by the United States Air Force, started developing a system of radars, computers, and command centers to serve as an electronic blanket over the country's air borders. The objectives were to defend the economic installations and the widely scattered population centers of Saudi Arabia against attack and particularly to repel air attacks or amphibious assaults against the country's highly vulnerable oil pumping stations, processing and loading facilities, and oil platforms in the Persian Gulf.

To implement the program, the Saudis contracted with a consortium headed by Boeing. In 1991, it was announced that Hughes Aircraft Corporation, later acquired by Raytheon, would assume management of the project, which had been subject to successive delays. The Saudis placed their $1 billion order for Hughes just after the Gulf War and at a time when Saudi military leaders felt vulnerable to air attack from Iran or Iraq. They wanted the product as soon as possible, so the contract included a heavy incentive: Deliver Peace Shield three months early and get a $50 million bonus. Deliver it late and lose the bonus. In this case, project recovery was done by changing the contracted party and offering a bonus for early completion. The project was concluded three months early, and Raytheon cashed in on the bonus. Time and overall stakeholder dissatisfaction were determinant to drive the project recovery.

While the Saudi project was successfully turned around, a better choice for other projects might be termination. This is not an easy task because such a decision to abort a project causes frustration for stakeholders who believed the project could produce the results expected and because the project manager and team members will feel that they personally failed.

Also, some projects take on such a life of their own that it becomes virtually impossible to stop them, even though all signs point to ultimate failure. How do projects create this kind of momentum, and why is it so difficult to pull the plug on a clear loser? Isabelle Royer, in *Why Bad Projects Are So Hard to Kill*,[7] blames an irrational optimism that blinds everyone involved to reality. This collective belief is a strong conviction based on feeling rather than on evidence that the project will eventually succeed. This conviction is shared by most of the decision makers, who minimize negative feedback. Moreover, even when they are able to spot problems, this mind-set leads them to increase their commitment and pursue the project more ardently. They are too enthusiastic and emotionally attached to the project to envision a failure. The project champion plays a key role in building and sustaining the collective belief. He or she is usually the original true believer who will spread the cause to others using his or her credibility. When problems are identified, the project champion participates to sustain the belief enthusiastically.

In 1970, RCA Corporation, a major electronics company in existence from 1919 to 1986, developed the first prototype of the SelectaVision videodisk player. Many experts believed phonograph-like technology was obsolete and questioned why RCA based its new product on such a platform. Seven years later, all of RCA's competitors had abandoned videodisk research in the face of the improved quality and popularity of the VCR. RCA remained convinced that its SelectaVision product was going to be a hit. In 1981, even when all the signs pointed to nearly certain failure, RCA introduced the product. The public was completely underwhelmed. Finally, in 1984, after investing $580 million and 14 years of research effort, RCA realized that the product was going nowhere and terminated the project. In the case of SelectaVision, the dimension of stakeholder satisfaction—in reality, stakeholder optimism—obliged all other participants to continue the project.

In these crucial cases, where momentum exists for pursuing a project headed toward doomed results, a high-level, project-based structure, as suggested in EPG, is fundamental for providing the political and corporate-level support for making the right decision.

Performance Management and Closeout

Closeout, the last phase of a project, finalizes the project and guarantees the acceptance of the project, product, service, or facility. It addresses transferring the responsibility of operations, maintenance, and support to the performing organization, and it calls for postproject evaluation, documenting the lessons learned and recommendations to support success of future projects, and communicating results. From an EPG standpoint, project closeout finalizes the performance management part of the project implementation, yet maintains a focus on postproject performance issues.

Closeout is a concern to project managers across diverse industries and organizations because it is frequently underfunded, understaffed, and poorly planned and performed. The literature, in addition to anecdotal accounts from industry professionals, indicates that the problem of project closeout is prevalent and has serious consequences. In the construction industry, for instance, closeout delays can cost administrative time for owners, tension between project parties, and cash flow problems.

The Channel Tunnel project, undertaken to create an underground tunnel between England and France, is an example of the issues arising during a closeout and how they can contribute to project failure or success. In 1986, the project was awarded to Eurotunnel to construct a 51.5-kilometer tunnel, the longest of its type in the world, at a bid price of US$5.5 billion and a concession agreement that gave them the sole right to operate the tunnel for a period of 55 years.[8]

The project involved the cooperation of two governments, 700,000 shareholders, 220 lending banks, numerous construction companies and suppliers, and several regulatory agencies. Due to unexpected conditions and changes required by interested parties, the project required significant changes. When the implementation phase was completed, the project was 19 months late, and cost overruns of US$3 billion made the total cost US$7.1 billion.

By closeout, a great part of the effort was focused on analyzing the sources of cost overruns and attempting to assign blame to one or more participant organizations and minimize the amount of claims. The delivery delay and the corresponding impact on the beginning of operations left the financial backers with the challenge of minimizing their losses and refusing to accept negotiated arrangements for settling key contract disputes. Several arbitration bodies were involved to bring the competing sides to negotiations.

The success of a closeout phase is closely connected to the effectiveness of change management. However, most of the changes in the Channel Tunnel project resulting in significant cost overruns were a consequence of slow decision making associated with the ability of the Health and Safety Commission to demand changes without the authority to provide additional funding. According to Colin Kirkland, technical director of Eurotunnel from 1985 to 1991:

> We should seek to advise future generations contemplating the creation of very large infrastructure developments not to get carried away by the excitement of the design and construction process before they have clearly established the rationale, the relationships among key players, and the means by which the totality of the process is to be managed.

Conclusions

Businesses continue to expand the number of projects even with constrained resources. As projects become more complex, enterprises are tasked to deal with conflicting objectives resulting from increased complexity and shorter delivery times. In this environment, executing projects and programs successfully and keeping them aligned to strategy throughout the organization's portfolio are key business requirements. This chapter includes the dimensions of EPG performance and causes of poor performance. Five steps are necessary for the project performance criteria corporations to perform successfully, navigate the inevitable challenges, and be better positioned for success.

10

EPG in Mega Projects, Joint Ventures, and Alliances

In 1962, President John F. Kennedy justified going to the moon this way:

> We choose to go to the moon in this decade, not because it is easy, but because it is hard, because that goal will serve to organize and measure the best of our energies and skills, because that challenge is one that we are willing to accept, one we are unwilling to postpone, and one which we intend to win.[1]

Despite all the barriers and difficulties, humans took that small step on the moon, representing a giant leap for humankind.

The challenging situation faced in the sixties was doing business as usual. In the twenty-first century, projects are bigger, more complex, and more ambiguous, and they require a closer focus on integration to deal with countless interfaces. Great flexibility and a tenacity to deliver in the face of unknown obstacles and difficulties are also required, along with skills to manage the growth of interconnections and interdependencies. IBM's 2010 Global CEO Study, for example, highlights that 79 percent of the CEOs researched indicated that the degree of complexity is expected only to rise and that more than half of them doubt their ability to manage it.[2]

This suggests that traditional project management tools and techniques, while still necessary, are insufficient to manage highly complex projects to successful delivery on time and within costs and performance targets. The magnitude of potential benefits and savings gained by improving the management of complex projects is enormous and stands to contribute significantly to the effective and sustainable development of the global community.

Putting Mega Projects into Perspective

Mega projects are colossal by nature and made up of proportionally gigantic pieces. These projects use huge amounts of manpower, involve multiple stakeholders, include governmental players, require multibillion-dollar financing, and are exceedingly complex. The list goes on: the volume of services, equipment, and materials is gargantuan; communications involve multicultural issues; risks range from conventional accidents to compliance with regulatory agencies. And to top it all off, project success depends strongly on the collaborative effort of the major stakeholders through a partnering arrangement.

On mega projects, partnering is a given because no one entity has the funding, political leverage, managerial competence, technology, and labor force to make such mammoth enterprises happen. This partnering happens at two distinct levels:

1. *Ownership.* This level usually involves governments or governmental agencies. In this setting, formal partnering agreements are established. These agreements fix the basis for governance among the parties and include basic premises for the agreement, how decisions are to be made, and how disputes are to be settled. Such was the case in the bilateral agreements between England and France for Eurotunnel, constructed under the English Channel and completed in 1994.[3] Brazil and Paraguay formed a bilateral organization called Itaipu Binacional to implement

and manage what was at the time the largest hydroelectric project in the world, harnessing the power of the mighty Paraná River, with the 18 initial generating units completed in 1991. In this case, Argentina was also included in the agreement because changes in the river flow affect Argentina downstream from the dam.[4] Multiparty agreements are also common, as in the case of CERN, the European organization for nuclear research, where governance policies applicable to the 20 countries were developed, as described later in this chapter.[5] Aside from the government-spawned mega projects, private companies also partner at the ownership level. Major oil companies typically share risks in exploration and subsequent operations, and have partnering agreements that fix the governance policies.

2. *Implementation.* Mega project owners generally do not perform the services required to implement a project. They contract third parties to take care of the design, procurement, construction, and related functions to carry out the job. Once again, the term *mega* carries over to the implementation phase. The magnitude of the tasks moves the participating vendors and contractors to partner with other companies so that the monumental demands and targets can be met. This means making agreements that establish the policies for governing the relationships among the parties. Two types of partnering arrangements are commonly used in the implementation phase of mega projects:

   • *Joint Ventures.* This form of partnering joins two or more contracting parties to perform given services for the major client/owner. The relationships and responsibilities of the parts are defined in the contract documents.

   • *Alliance Contracts.* This form of contracting assumes that the implementation party partners with the client/owner in a collaborative agreement, in search of the best possible outcome for the project and a limited amount of risk.

In all forms of partnering, clear principles of governance are fundamental for the parties to work synergistically. This is true for the owners, as well as for the parties charged with execution. A list follows of the essential items to be included in partnering agreements with respect to governance of mega projects:

- The structure of governance (designation of committees)
- Rules for meetings and management of the partnership
- Rules for decision making and the resolution of disputes
- Policies with respect to auditing and risk management
- Rules for hiring and firing the principle executive of the mega project

The relevance of clear governance policies is demonstrated in the following cases.

A Saga of Atom Smashers

Two multibillion-dollar science projects were undertaken with markedly different governance structures and with dramatically different results. The superconducting collider projects, sometimes referred to as atom smashers, were in fact designed to construct a high-energy accelerator to study the physics of subatomic particles in the hopes of, among other things, gaining glimpses into the origins of the universe. Both projects involved a high degree of complexity and included numerous governmental, scientific, and private stakeholders. Here are the stories of these projects, which had the same objective and ended up with strikingly different aftereffects.

Superconducting Super Collider

The U.S. Department of Energy's multibillion-dollar (US$10 billion plus) Superconducting Super Collider (SSC) project was set to be the most powerful scientific instrument in the world. The intended result was a state-of-the-art, high-tech facility to be used for basic research in physics, including the quest to unveil the origins of the universe. Noted as being the world's largest such collider of its day, the SSC project was well underway near Waxahaxie, Texas, when terminated by the U.S. Congress in 1993.[6]

Logistically, the project involved a 90-kilometer tunnel, ranging from 15 to 76 meters below ground, requiring over 16,000 acres of land to accommodate the necessary facilities, including nearly two million square feet of office and laboratory space. The project was estimated to take from 10 to 12 years to complete.

In January 1989, although the SSC was primarily a construction project, the Department of Energy (DOE) contracted with Universities Research Association (URA), a conglomerate of universities, to serve as the prime contractor. Perhaps the schools were skilled in technical and scientific matters, but they had limited experience in construction. Later on, major stakeholders—the subcontractors, the DOE, the various audit agencies—recognized that this was a serious mistake.

The mega project status of the SSC project called for comprehensive oversight and a unique management structure. The project structure established determined that the project manager reported both to the headquarters program director and to the secretary of energy, in theory to facilitate day-to-day activities and to ensure that the secretary had direct oversight on the project. This peculiar reporting relationship spawned a situation that shielded the project from the standard DOE governance function, allowing room for ambiguity in the oversight.

The URA project manager also admitted that SSC was a hundred times larger than any construction project with which he had been involved. He acknowledged that many of the problems he encountered were new to him and that it had been difficult for him to manage hundreds of subcontractors in a complex cost and schedule system. He also admitted that he had ordered that work on new cost estimates at the SSC be stopped because URA management did not want them to be done.[7]

There were also serious leadership and management issues. Most of SSC leaders and managers had limited experience in leadership and teamwork. Team morale quickly deteriorated. URA failed in dealing with the stakeholders and was unable to communicate to society the project benefits. As a result, public support for the project spiraled downward.

The downfall of the SSC project signaled a major breakdown in the overall project governance and consequently set off a reform in U.S. scientific policy. In 1993, the president of the United States created the National Science and Technology Council (NSTC), which was given cabinet status. The President's Committee of Advisors on Science and Technology was also created, intended to help NSTC to coordinate relations with the private sector, thus creating a governance structure to support future scientific efforts.

Causes for the multibillion-dollar fiasco can be traced in part to a lack of emphasis on risk management. Although the technological risks were identified and tracked, other risks were not sufficiently sized up and managed. These included risks related to the cost of the gigantic undertaking, as well as those associated with the politics and the public image of the project. The need for early involvement for international funding and stakeholder participation in this large-scale science and technology project was another point that was not given sufficient forethought.

Another cause was the underestimation by major stakeholders of the complexity of managing a mega project. The URA consortium had successfully managed smaller projects and perhaps assumed that the same approaches would work for a project a hundred times the size of their success. Finally, the function of overall governance of the enterprise comes into question. Was it adequately designed for the setting involved? And did it cover the involvement of the multiplicity of players and the overall complexity of the project?

CERN

The European Organization for Nuclear Research known as CERN (originally for *Conseil Européen pour la Recherche Nucléaire*) was established in 1954 as a joint European research center located just north of Geneva on the Swiss-French border. The Large Hadron Collider (LHC) is a 2-kilometer-diameter circle through the Switzerland and France countryside in a tunnel about 100 meters underground (Exhibit 10-1).

The construction of LHC was approved in 1995 with a budget of SFr2.6 billion, with another SFr210 million toward the experiments. However, cost

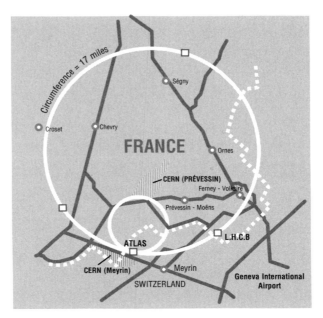

Exhibit 10-1. The Large Hadron Collider

overruns, estimated in a major review in 2001 at around SFr480 million for the accelerator and SFr50 million for the experiments, along with a reduction in CERN's budget, pushed the completion date from 2005 to 2007.[8]

In comparison with the failed U.S.-based SSC, the CERN accelerator is smaller, with a circumference of about 27 kilometers, roughly one-third the size of the SSC undertaking. The convention establishing CERN was ratified in 1954 by 12 countries in Western Europe, later expanded to 20 members. Because the research center is a joint venture among governmental stakeholders, formal governance was imperative from the founding.

The primary topics of the LHC Convention included the establishment of the organization; purposes; the conditions of membership; organs; the council; the directors-general and staff; financial contributions; cooperation with UNESCO and with other organizations; legal status; disputes; withdrawal; nonfulfillment of obligations; and dissolution. Complementary governance was added in 1963 with the foundation of the European Committee for Future

Accelerators (ECFA), which was set up to peer into the future by establishing working groups for related activities, including oversight.

Effective governance policies were key to the success of the Large Hadron Collider project, which formally began conducting experiments in September 2008 and quickly became the focus of the worldwide physics scientific community.

Like Day and Night

The SSC project in Texas was flawed from the beginning due to the lack of appropriate governance structure and insufficient evaluation of risks. Whereas studies indicate that the principal cause was "inadequate project management structure," the deficiency stemmed from poor governance policies and underestimated challenges peculiar to such a mega project. To further complicate matters, many of the presumed international stakeholders had not bought into the project. On the other hand, CERN was born out of the European culture, which by nature requires formal governance conventions to provide order to the governmental relationships.

Although the SSC project had its qualities in terms of design and management, and the CERN accelerator project had some shortcomings along the way, the success of projects is ultimately measured by end results. In the case of the SSC and CERN, the contrast is like night and day. Even though many factors contributed to the respective failure and success of the two projects, governance deserves to be at the head of the list.

The International Linear Collider

A consultative group on high-energy physics was created in 2000 by the OECD Global Science Forum with the objective of evaluating future trends in high-energy physics, the study of interaction among the smallest components of matter. This area has developed consistently over the last 50 years, but many gaps remain before we have an in-depth understanding of the mysteries of the universe.

There was complete agreement in the group that the next large accelerator-based facility had to be an electron-positron linear collider, the International

Linear Collider (ILC), operating concurrently with the Large Hadron Collider at CERN. Based on the input from the communities, the group constructed a road map identifying the major scientific questions expected to define the frontiers of elementary particle physics during the next 20 to 30 years and related them to potential new major accelerator facilities.[9] The agreement among physicists on the linear collider as the next step suggested to the group that there was a powerful argument for the communities to establish global scientific and technical coordination mechanisms.

A major consensus existed among the interested parties regarding a common scientific quest: to discover the composition of matter down to its most miniscule elements. This objective requires having subatomic particles collide with one another at nearly the speed of light and then examine the results. The purpose of the ILC is to obtain measurements of the collision of accelerated electrons and positrons with great accuracy through the use of detectors. The scientific network participating on the conception effort consists of about 1,000 scientists and engineers from 100 countries.

The project organization should be designed so that all participants consider themselves integral parts of the common project, as having a strong stake in its success and appropriate influence on its decision-making processes and the selection of members of its various bodies. The structure should be robust, with clear lines of authority and responsibility, covering technical and administrative aspects of the project activities. The International Committee for Future Accelerators (ICFA), created in 1976 to facilitate international collaboration in the construction and use of accelerators for high-energy physics, was put in charge of this initial step to formulate a robust business case. An ILC steering committee was formed with the role of defining the scope and primary parameters for the accelerator and detectors, monitoring the R&D activities, making recommendations on coordination, and sharing information. The steering committee established a Program Advisory Committee (PAC) to assist with the oversight of the detectors. The Global Design Effort (GDE) team, headed by Barry Barish, was responsible for setting the strategy, priorities, and coordination of the work of hundreds of scientists and engineers at universities and laboratories around the world in order to deliver a technical design report by the end of 2012.

In 2009, the Nobel Prize–winning physicist U.S. Secretary of Energy Steven Chu estimated the total cost of ILC at $25 billion. Given the amount involved, a group of Funding Agencies for the Large Collider (FALC) was created to help develop international funding mechanisms. FALC meets on a regular basis with members of the Global Design Effort to establish a dialogue between the funding agencies, governments, and the ILC scientific community.

During the project justification phase, many of the basics of EPG outlined in Chapter 2 were taken into account. Initially, there was a need for organization, and ICFA was designated as the owner of the program. A steering committee was formed, assisted by PAC, in charge of the oversight of the GDE and detector teams. With regard to strategy, PAC has recommended the need for a post-2012 strategy, after the accelerator and detector teams complete their work. This is to ensure that a clear direction is in place, the participating parties are aligned, and the importance of the project is demonstrated to the participating governments. Stakeholder management is another fundamental issue. The funding agencies were identified as critical, and FALC was created to help deal with those issues. However, many more stakeholder issues need to be managed in such a globally funded project.[10] For instance, the governments involved might interrupt funding depending on economic conditions. In the beginning of 2010, for example, support for the initial phase was fairly stable but not for the construction project, which subsequently required the development of a solid case clearly stating costs and benefits in a language comprehensible outside the physicists' community.

On July 2010, a proposal document, *Governance of the International Linear Collider Project*,[11] was released during the 35th International Conference on High Energy Physics to facilitate a structured discussion of governance issues in the construction and operation stages. The purpose was to produce a document containing comments from the international community and to integrate it into the project implementation plan. The project will require complex governance across different national systems and traditions that will not be easy to forge. The recommendations, based on similar international projects, address the project's future organization and performance.

1. *Organization.* To take advantage of taxation benefits, the document proposes the formation of an international treaty organization and establishing agreements with the participating governments and organizations. The ultimate governing body is a council composed of delegates of the supporting countries. The CEO responds to the council and manages a team of directors in charge of the project.

2. *Project Performance.* One of the guidelines is to promote competitive bids from member countries to own parts of the endeavor. Also, a total centralized contingency fund of 10 percent is proposed and is to be allocated, as needed, during the course of the project. The total use of the fund before the end of the project should lead to appropriate project descoping. The document also addresses how the different organizations will charge their operational costs. This is always a problem in large organizations, and it will be not different in such a project.

The structuring of ILC has similarities to risk-sharing partnerships. As explained later in this chapter, such partnerships were successfully used in the construction of the Embraer 170-190 and resulted in many problems in the case of the Boeing 787. Nevertheless, the approach to dealing with so many suppliers from the funding governments involved should be carefully organized from the very beginning.

Large and complex programs involving intergovernmental consultations and negotiations are lengthy and complex. The issues on which agreement has to be reached lie within the sphere of competence of national administrations and are, to a large extent, independent of and complementary to the technological goals, governance requirements, and parameters of the project. Sufficient time is needed for appropriate discussions at national, regional, and international levels well before any financial, time, or other commitments are expected.

As Barry Barish, the Global Design Effort director for the proposed International Linear Collider, mentioned on his January 20, 2011, newsletter:

> The ILC is still very much a dream and the path to a real project remains highly uncertain, even though the scientific case is as strong as ever and we continue to meet all our highest priority goals. Let's just hope that exciting early Large Hadron Collider results and an improved world economic situation will combine to enable the changing of our dream to a reality.[12]

The atom smasher's saga is just one example of many demonstrating the need for new contract models, the growing requirements for governance frameworks, the importance of dealing with transformation, and innovative approaches to creating value.

Project Alliancing

Successful major capital projects involve risks that are managed by an effective contracting strategy. The traditional approach entails project owners' shifting as much risk as possible to others: designers, constructors, suppliers, and insurance companies. This avenue stimulates adversarial postures: The owner transfers risks to contracted third parties; consequently, contractors accept what is imposed and later take advantage of contract loopholes and file compensation claims for performance of out-of-scope services.

Conflicts of interest are inherent in the theaters of construction, defense, and infrastructure projects. The owner/client wants a quality project delivered on time at minimal cost, and contracted parties want to perform services so as to maximize their own profit. As a result, competitive-bidding contracting practices are not conducive to forming honest, open, transparent engagements among the stakeholders. Such flexible agreements, based on mutual trust, are contrary to the mind-set expressed as, "You show me yours, and I'll show you mine—but you have to show me yours first." Contracts that emphasize punitive measures for the contractor's nonperformance and that rarely contain equally weighted sanctions for the owner's nonperformance have proven counterproductive.

Oil exploration in the North Sea became uneconomical in the early 1990s because of dwindling reserves. British Petroleum, a major player in the arena, concluded that a substantial reduction in capital expenditures for project implementation could render the oil fields feasible. To strive for significant economies, BP decided to make a major departure from traditional contracting practices. As opposed to the previously prevalent competitive bidding, BP chose to adopt a collaborative approach on the Andrew field. John Martin, BP's project manager, argued against the traditional adversarial relationships among oil companies, contractors, and suppliers:

> We believed that only by working in close alignment with our contractors could we hope to make Andrew a success. To this end, behavior was identified as the essential partner for technology; the twin building blocks which if brought together could be capable of producing extraordinary results.[13]

BP recognized that a new approach would be required to reduce the costs generated by the conflictive relationships characteristic of the then prevalent lump sum or fixed price contracting practice. This called for a radical switch by all the contracted parties players to relate to one another based on teamwork and trust, working toward the best interests of the project. This contracting approach became known as Project Alliancing.

The original £450 million estimate for the Andrew field far exceeded the limit for project feasibility. With the new mind-set, it was decided to target project completion at £373 million. The collaborative efforts among the players quickly spawned additional benefits. The alliance revised the estimate down to £320 million within three months after project initiation, and the team felt the project could finish three months earlier than scheduled. The project ended up at £290 million and produced oil six months before originally scheduled. Savings were shared among the alliance partners, as foreseen in the alliance contracts. BP attributed the extraordinary success to the commitment of professionals who were liberated from the constraints of traditional adversarial behavior.

Shortly after the BP alliance success, Australia vigorously embraced the approach, with the Wandoo Project, an oil field project started in April 1994, and the East Spar Project, a gas field project that began in July 1994.[14]

Alliancing is a method of procuring and managing major capital assets in which the owner—or owners—and one or more service providers work collaboratively as an integrated team to deliver a project. The contractual framework is such that the participants' commercial interests are aligned with the best interests for the project.

Alliance contracting is characterized by key features that require the parties to work together in good faith, act with integrity, and make best-for-project decisions. The alliance participants work as an integrated, collaborative team and make unanimous decisions on all key delivery matters. Under alliance contracts, risks are jointly managed by the parties through mutually agreed-on risk-reward arrangements, as opposed to legal liability.

What follows are the key features for Project Alliancing.

Alliance Development

- *Establishing the Alliance.* In this early phase, the project owner selects the other participants. Selection is based on noncost criteria. Once the alliance participants are selected, the primary commercial parameters are established.
- *Project Development Phase.* The second phase is the development of the scope of services and the project targets. Participants work as a team to develop and agree on project performance targets. When the alliance partners agree on the targets, implementation takes place.
- *Implementation Phase.* Participants work together to deliver the project. The alliance management team formulates a plan that incorporates policies, procedures, and the supporting framework. In this phase, good governance and control over the project are key. Commercial incentives by way of the gain-share/pain-share regime also help ensure that participants strive to deliver peak performances.
- *Practical and Final Completion.* After practical completion of the project, all participants remain responsible during the defects correction period stipulated in the contract.

Risk Sharing Versus Risk Transfer

Project Alliancing uses risk sharing as opposed to allocating risk among project participants (risk transfer), a practice that tends to set off adversarial relationships and litigious battles. In Alliancing, all uninsurable risk is shared among the contracting parties with the assumption that collective responsibility leads to improved overall project outcomes. The project team and thus the alliance partners either wins or loses collectively.

Compensation Structure

Alliance contracting's gain-share/pain-share compensation model is 100 percent open-book and consists of three tiers. The first encompasses all direct project costs, including rework, and project overhead incurred by the alliance team members. The second tier refers to corporate overhead and contractors' margins. Tier three involves predetermined gain-share/pain-share arrangements.

The most critical component of Project Alliancing is the development of the target cost. If the actual cost of the project comes in under the target, then the alliance as a whole wins, and the partners share in the savings. If the actual cost of the project ends up greater than the predetermined target cost, then the alliance partners suffer the losses.

Culture and Communication

The project team works together within a best-for-project culture. The driving force is a commitment to meet the project objectives. The participants work together on the project in an environment of trust, with open and honest communication. All transactions are transparent. The participants agree to no-blame/no-dispute behavior where disputes and conflict are handled internally under predetermined governance procedures.

To achieve outstanding results and benefits, effective alliance teams implement strategies aimed at peak performance. An internal or external alliance facilitator develops an alliance culture and creates a flexible, innovative project delivery environment. Successful alliance strategies include establishing a clear vision and purpose for the alliance, ensuring that all team members understand

and commit to the alliance principles and objectives, developing and nurturing innovation and breakthrough thinking, and monitoring and continuously improving the effectiveness of the strategy. Effective alliance communications go beyond basic information flow and include alliance identity that applies to internal marketing and promotional materials including advertisements, signage, newsletters, stationery, and clothing.

Governance

The project alliance is led by a joint body typically called the project alliance board. This body is comprised of senior members of the owner and of the non-owner participants. The members have a peer relationship and equal say in the decision making. The players in the alliance, partner-owner and partner-contractor, typically reach agreement on strategic and project levels in formal documents, as shown in Exhibit 10-2. The strategic alliance agreement (known as Sala) defines generic understandings that govern the alliance. Each project conducted under the alliance concept then becomes the object of a complementary agreement called Pala (project alliance agreement).

Pala = Project alliance agreement

Exhibit 10-2. Structure of Alliance Agreements

Water Corporation

Water Corporation is a state-owned company with the purpose of providing the sustainable management of water services to Western Australia in order to make it a great place to live and invest. Their services, projects, and activities span an area of 2.5 million square kilometers, about one-third of the Australian continent, making it one of the world's broadest operating areas for this industry.

To ensure enough water for all, there is a need to address the challenges of Australia's drying climate and increasing population; an additional challenge is minimizing the environmental impact by using less water. Their strategic plan, *Water Forever*, provides a portfolio of options to manage demand and supply balance to 2060 by reducing water use by 25 percent, increasing wastewater recycling to 60 percent, and developing new sources. *Water Forever* has become a catalyst for change in how the company provides sustainable water services across the nation.[15]

The corporation has a five-year-plan capital program of $1 billion Australian. A significant component of the program is being delivered using various forms of relationship contracts.

Water Corporation has used alliance contracts as one of its capital, operational, and maintenance delivery methods since the mid-1990s. The company defines governance as "a framework of rules, relationships, systems and processes by which authority is exercised and controlled in alliances. It encompasses the mechanisms by which alliances, and those in control, are held to account." It articulates the objectives, power, functions, obligations, limitations, and relationships of the alliance.[16]

A Capital *Alliance Governance Manual*, constructed in accordance with their corporate governance framework, contains the following:

- *Rules.* The alliance agreement provides the primary rules within which the alliance will operate.
- *Relationships.* Relationships are both internal (lead team, management team, nonowner participants, Water Corporation) and external (regulators, community, shareholder, contractors, and suppliers), and the alliance will be required to manage them.

- *Systems and Processes.* Each alliance will have its own systems and processes, which will be captured in the governance plan and will include accountabilities, responsibilities, duties, procedures, and reporting.
- *Audits and Compliance.* The audit is a good governance practice and assists in providing assurance that controls are operating as intended. Audits can be undertaken by any of the participants. When the alliance has many participants, it may be more efficient to procure an internal audit service.

From Battlefield to Board Room: The Mega Project War Room

The term *war room* became known during World War II. Winston Churchill and his cabinet rooms in London were designed for running government affairs and directing the British armed forces. What Churchill liked about the cabinet rooms was the close proximity of all essential functions, including an enciphered hotline to the U.S. president, facilitating the decision-making processes.[17]

In the project context, a war room is a focused, intense effort to organize the complexities of business decision making in large programs and projects. The war room enables a collaborative team to break down complex programs and information processes into comprehensible parts, to promote structured dialogue and brainstorming, and to comprehend program intricacies and the impacts of the interfaces involved.

Critical questions in large projects are how to exercise leadership, establish the right amount of communication, monitor and control progress, and have a timely decision-making process. The NASA approach, similar to the war room concept, embraces mission control rooms to organize the top of a hierarchical organization in its purest form. Once the interdependencies and complexities of how decisions affect the interested parties are understood, continuous information flows into one room to support strategic dialogue.

Essentially, a mega project war room has four reasons for being: (1) creation of a common information framework, (2) effective information supply, (3) management collaboration, and (4) timely decision making. The war room requires planning, design, and implementation to ensure that the best solution is achieved in a cost-effective way. The planning process is as important as the final product because substantial benefits are reaped in terms of strategic focus, decision-making coherence, and senior management integration. The checklist for the smooth and successful implementation of a new war room normally includes:

- The identification of control functions and their interrelationships
- The development of job descriptions/operational specifications
- Feasibility studies with cost estimates
- Operations policy documentation and user manuals
- The determination of space requirements
- Interior design advice, including lighting and environmental control
- Equipment and software selection
- Physical and electronic security measures
- Staff training

Production Integration Center

In the mid-1990s, the global aircraft industry began to establish risk-sharing partnerships with its suppliers, in an attempt to reduce costs and consequentially to focus on core competence areas. This was the case for Embraer, a Brazilian aircraft manufacturer, when it decided to develop a US$900 million ERJ-170/190 program aimed at dominating the 70–110-seat airplane market, a market segment smaller than that dominated by Boeing and Airbus. According to Embraer, the operating cost of the Embraer 190 is 10 percent less than that of the Boeing 717 or the Airbus A318, the two smallest models of the two major manufacturers. The program achieved success. December 2010, the company had delivered 699 Embraer 170/190 models and had a firm order backlog of 248 aircraft.

In a risk-sharing partnership, partners rely on the commercial success of the project to receive the total or part of its share for the activities or products delivered. As such, the project owner coordinates a three-level network of partners. On the first level are those who take financial risks in the projects, participate jointly in the project design, and add technological value. The second level consists of suppliers who provide the systems, parts, components, and services according to the specifications given. This group may make significant investments in development and also participate in the last part of the joint definition phase. The third group is responsible for less complex and less expensive components.[18]

In the development of the new 787 airplane, Boeing decided to adopt risk-sharing partnerships deviating from their established method of designing the parts, sending the designs to their suppliers, the suppliers building the parts to Boeing's specifications and shipping them to Boeing, who then put the parts together. In their new approach, about 70 percent of the 787 is built by companies other than Boeing. Final assembly occurs at the company's Everett factory.[19]

With this change, Boeing could cull ideas from the many supplier company engineers, who have specific expertise and who create the best designs. However, the result was governance problems that plagued Boeing and its suppliers and that contributed significantly to the 787 delays. Stock analysts estimated that the company initially planned to invest $8–10 billion in developing the project but could end up spending $20 billion, including the penalties it will owe to airlines and to the partners for delivery delays.

The company established a Production Integration Center in December 2008, aimed at minimizing potential problems caused by outsourcing design and development functions. In practice, this constitutes a war room focused on monitoring the global vendor network and synchronizing overall production activities. This modern war room overlooks the final assembly area of the 787 and features giant color screens that provide information on component production as well as full aircraft assembly. Other tracking information includes international parts shipments, pending technical matters, and weather or natural disaster phenomena that might affect the schedule. Slippages are tightly tracked using a red-yellow-green convention.

The center is able to field overseas calls from suppliers to clear up questions or to troubleshoot issues. High-definition video cameras facilitate communications, allowing interested parties to zoom in on any component under discussion. The objective is to speedily resolve each issue so that the program stays on schedule. The center also controls the shipping schedules, including those of four 747s specially adapted to bring parts to the assembly line in Everett, Washington. Boeing benchmarked similar war room facilities at NASA, Disneyworld, emergency operations centers, and Los Angeles traffic control.[20]

Robert Noble, Boeing's vice president of supplier management who runs the 24-hour center, says, "immediate, multimedia communications have eliminated the problem of often unclear email exchanges between distant engineers who work on opposite ends of the clock."[21]

The war room concept has also been adopted by software development companies, using agile approaches to expedite projects. It's an evolution of a concept long used in the automobile industry called *concurrent engineering*, where all the related stakeholders are housed in one setting to facilitate constant and immediate communication. In the case of software development companies, project managers, software developers, business analysts, and quality experts share common space so that they can generate synergy and jointly work through pressing issues. Although sophisticated communications technology is increasingly effective for dealing with project issues, the potential synergies spawned by shared space and face-to-face encounters create possibilities for making quantum leaps in project productivity.

From War Room to Crisis Center to Operations Center

The governance of cities presents a major challenge, both in terms of projects and day-to-day operations. In 2010, Rio de Janeiro, Brazil (with a greater metropolitan population of 11 million), faced overflowing urban sprawl, a skyrocketing crime rate, and frequent flooding, as well as long-range undertakings, such as preparation for the 2014 Soccer World Cup and the Olympic Games of 2016, as well as the upgrading of the transportation grid. Although these undertakings are not fully under the city's control, they strongly affect the workings of the ever evolving metropolis.[22]

After a major storm flooded the city's key arteries in April 2010, Mayor Eduardo Paes entertained a proposal to install a so-called crisis center to deal with such events. Although he found the idea appealing, he observed that an operations center would be more appropriate—to deal with preventive measures, not just postdisaster mop-ups.

From a governance standpoint, there was growing concern early on, both in Brazil and globally, about the city's ability to deal with emergencies that might occur during the international events. Mayor Paes articulated an approach that included a contract with IBM under their Smarter Cities program, as well as partnering arrangements with suppliers such as Samsung for the dozens of monitors for a giant wall display. The operations center project was built at breakneck speed, beginning construction in September 2010 and completed in time for a successful test run at the New Year's celebration on December 31, 2010. The operations center includes representatives from primary city services, such as light and power, gas, water, traffic, sanitation, health, meteorology, and special events. The Rio de Janeiro Operations Center thus represents a major piece of the overall governance structure needed for the city to deal with the demands of the international games and expanding economy.[23]

Conclusions

Different approaches for Enterprise Project Governance are applicable for different stages in project life cycles. Because of their size and complexity, specific governance practices are required for each mega project. Mega projects are colossal by nature and made up of proportionally gigantic pieces. They use huge amounts of manpower, involve multiple stakeholders, include governmental players, require multibillion-dollar financing, and are exceedingly complex. The list goes on: the volume of services, equipments, and materials is gigantic; communications involve multicultural issues; and risks range from accidents to compliance with regulatory agencies. And to top it all off, project success strongly depends on the collaborative effort of the major stakeholders through some sort of partnering arrangement. On the SSC project, hindsight spotlights a lack of an effective governance framework from the outset. In the CERN project, more governance elements were established due to the European experience of dealing with multiple cultures, resulting in a favorable outcome. The third superconducting collider, the ILC, under development with a governance approach at its inception, stands to gain from the experiences of the SSC and CERN endeavors. Project Alliancing, often used in managing mega projects, is a form of collaborative contracting based on the concepts of collaboration, transparency, and mutual trust between the owner and contracting parties. First used effectively in the 1990s, the concept has spread and is widely used on major capital projects. War rooms are also commonly used for major undertakings. A war room is a focused, intense effort to organize the complexities of decision making in the running of large programs and projects.

CHAPTER

11

EPG for Different Types of Projects

The governance of projects is required in all types of organizations. The applicable EPG concepts have been explained in earlier chapters, and the case of partnering contracts has been addressed in detail in Chapter 10. Because industries have peculiarities, this chapter focuses on projects whose approaches differ from the conventional ones used in capital expenditure ventures: information technology (IT), research and development (R&D), and organizational change.

Information Technology

Governance in information technology projects came into focus in the early 1990s, when executives identified the need to align IT projects with corporate direction. This was dramatically illustrated in 1994 when the Standish Group published its first *Chaos Report*, which documented gigantic investment wastes on software development projects that were never completed. The report unveiled the shocking result that 53 percent of the projects surveyed were considered failures when measured against the classic criteria of completion on time, on budget, and with required functions (i.e., meets user requirements).[1] The growing interest in IT governance is also due to stricter twenty-first-century government compliance requirements, spurred by the Sarbanes-Oxley Act in the United States and by Basel II in Europe. Principally, however, the aim is to make better decisions about the use of IT in the best interest of the organization and its stakeholders.

The objective of IT governance is to ensure that the investments in information technology are directly related to top management directives and that they generate long-term benefits for stakeholders. Effective IT governance guarantees buy-in by all stakeholders, including the board, executives, clients, and staff, and it fixes clear accountability for decisions affecting IT. So information technology governance aims to (1) ensure that investments in IT generate real value and (2) mitigate risks and potential losses inherent in IT. Exhibit 11-1 shows the relationship between EPG and governance for IT projects in Water Corporation.

How does IT governance relate to EPG? The enterprise view of IT governance is an integral part of corporate governance and focuses on the processes, structures, and interfaces that create synergy in support of alignment between business and IT. Enterprise Project Governance, focused on IT, establishes the policies that ensure that the projects are compatible and consistent with corporate strategies. This means that the IT governance structure must conform both to business strategies and to information technology industry best practices.

Vast literature exists on IT governance. Three references provide an overview and include references for structuring and implementing the governance.

- COBIT (Control Objectives for Information and Related Technology) is a leading governance and control framework for the IT industry. COBIT presents a model of IT processes typically found in an organization and includes major areas, such as planning and organization, acquisition and implementation, delivery and support, and monitoring and evaluation. COBIT provides managers with a basis for IT-related

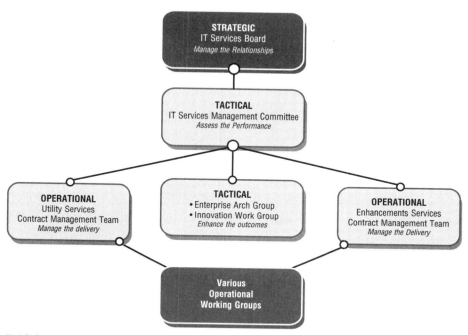

Exhibit 11-1. Framework for Governing Water Corporation IT Services Providers

decisions. Of particular relevance to Enterprise Project Governance are items targeting governance and control framework, control objectives, management guidelines, and an implementation guide. Originally created by ISACA (Information Systems Audit and Control Association), COBIT is the responsibility of ITGI (IT Governance Institute).[2]

- The ISO/IEC 38500 standard for corporate governance of information technology aims to provide executives with the understanding they need to meet legal, regulatory, and ethical obligations with respect to IT, thus providing guidance for the governance of organizations. The standard applies to organizations of all sizes and types, providing guidelines for executives on the effective use of information technology.[3]

- ITIL (IT Infrastructure Library), while not aimed at projects, is a high-level framework focused on the successful operational service management of IT. It is therefore one of the foundations for overall IT governance. It is maintained by the Office of Government Commerce of the United Kingdom in conjunction with the IT Service Management. Although not specifically focused on IT governance, the related information is a reference source for IT function improvement projects.

Others references are ISO 27001, with a focus on IT security; CMM (Capability Maturity Model), aimed at software engineering; and TickIT, a quality-management certification program for software development. ISO 31.000 focuses on risk management and exerts a strong influence on IT governance. A specific certification exists for governance in information technology. CGEIT (Certified in the Governance of Enterprise Information Technology) was created by the ISACA. Experienced professionals, with a minimum of five years of experience in a managing or advisory role in the governance and control of IT at an enterprise level, are eligible to obtain certification, provided they pass the four-hour exam and demonstrate adequate understanding of enterprise IT management.[4]

Success stories in the implementation of governance instruments in IT abound in the literature. Two international cases follow.

Banco Superville S.A.

In 2009, Banco Superville S.A., one of the main private banks of the Argentine Republic, launched an IT governance project, using COBIT as the reference framework. The CEO assumed sponsorship, and the CIO was the primary IT leader. The process started by measuring the maturity level of the ongoing processes by using COBIT, ITIL, and local norms. Once the current level was measured, the proposed goals were discussed and agreed on with top management.

Here's how COBIT was applied at the bank. To raise awareness and overall knowledge, all systems and technology managers and staff underwent COBIT-based training. IT internal processes were also regrouped and brought into alignment with those established by COBIT. Specifically with respect to projects, the COBIT governance undertaking redefined roles and responsibilities and reinforced initiatives aimed at achieving project goals. The project control area was also beefed up, and an IT risk governance area was established. A control dashboard was put into place based on COBIT's main metrics. The implementation of COBIT's framework strengthened the bank's overall IT governance policies and upgraded processes related to the management of its projects.[5]

Water Corporation

Western Australia's Water Corporation, as explained in Chapter 10, is the main supplier of water, wastewater, and drainage services for homes, businesses, and farms. Its Information Services Branch manages over a hundred outsourced IT service contracts. In 2004, a specific governance project was chartered to develop the best service delivery model and sourcing strategy for future information support services. The scope included infrastructure support and projects, applications support and projects, and consulting and business change.[6]

A solid governance framework, based on partnering principles, was considered essential to deal effectively with the multitude of contracts. The governance structure is outlined in Exhibit 11-2. The example illustrates the need for setting up a specific project to design and implement a governance framework.

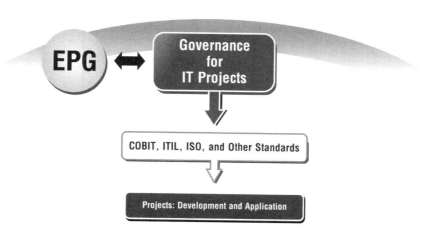

Exhibit 11-2. EPG and IT: A Special Case

Governance of Research and Development Projects

R&D projects have points in common with IT endeavors. The final product for both types of projects is rarely crystal clear, and the pathway for arriving at a final result invariably contains twists and turns. This contrasts sharply with a conventional project, such as a building, where the target result can be designed and the work program outlined in a detailed schedule.[7]

These fuzzy characteristics affect the governance of R&D projects. The range of uncertainty strongly impacts the type of governance applicable. Research projects may span from "Let's see what we can discover," found in some academic and scientific settings, to "Let's develop an innovative children's toy product to be launched by the third quarter of next year." Investments in R&D range from about 3.5 percent of revenues for industrial companies to as much as 15 percent for some pharmaceutical firms. Governance policies, often embedded in the culture of an organization, ultimately affect the productivity and creativity of R&D projects. A striking example is the search, during the first decade of the twenty-first century, to find the balance between productivity and creativity at the Minnesota-based 3M Company, long noted for its innovative products (see Exhibit 11-3).

Exhibit 11-3. EPG and R&D: A Critical Issue

Efficiency Versus Creativity at 3M

In 2001, James McNerney, an ex-GE executive, became the first outsider to lead 3M, the company noted for innovative products including masking tape and Post-it notes. During his four and a half years at the company before leaving for a top job at Boeing, McNerney brought with him efficiency programs such as Six Sigma, designed to identify problems in processes and detailed measurement requirements to reduce variation and errors. This policy, which was highly effective and publicized at GE under Jack Welch, was soon imposed by McNerney on the until then relatively laid-back R&D culture at 3M. The company's sluggish results in the late 1990s contributed to the 3M board's yearn for a more aggressive approach aimed at producing an improved bottom line. This implicitly placed 3M's R&D projects under new governance principles that required rigorous tracking and compliance and that were tied to targeted results.

Under McNerney, R&D at 3M became structured in ways totally contrary to the prevailing work atmosphere. Some employees reacted to what they perceived as excessive bureaucracy. Researchers were required to fill in a so-called red book with pages of charts aimed at analyzing the market potential, commercial applications, and manufacturing considerations. The challenge of conciliating productivity with creativity became exacerbated by the inherent nature of *process excellence*, which requires discipline, consistency, and repetition, as opposed to *innovation*, which calls for experimentation, alternative approaches, failure, and luck.

George Buckley, who succeeded McNerney as CEO, moved toward a middle-of-the-road policy, as the number of creative products that 3M launched began to wane. He commented about the application of rigorous controls to R&D: "You can't put a Six Sigma process into that area and say, well, I'm getting behind on invention, so I'm going to schedule myself for three good ideas on Wednesday and two on Friday. That's not how creativity works."

The policies that govern R&D projects at 3M thus shifted from a focus purely on profitability and process toward an emphasis on growth and innovation. Finding the middle ground that conciliates business interests with the need for researchers to dream is the crux of the challenge for policy makers striving to develop effective R&D governance criteria. This barrier faces all organizations whose futures depend on synergy between creativity and productivity. Says Vijay Govindarajan, a management professor at Dartmouth's Tuck School of Business: "The mindset that is needed, the capabilities that are needed, the metrics that are needed, the whole culture that is needed for discontinuous innovation, are fundamentally different."[8] So governance policies must take into account not only the conflict inherent in creative growth, but also the cost/benefit of radically changing a legacy culture.

Governance of Collaborative R&D Efforts: FP7

When various institutions tackle R&D projects collaboratively, governance is a key success factor. In this collaborative arrangement, parties enter into a pact and agree to combine their knowledge to create innovative products. The European Union's Seventh Framework Program (FP7) is such a case. It involves dozens of European academic institutions and other entities, collaborating to keep pace with modern trends and to analyze the needs, demands, and desires of an ever changing marketplace.

The collaborative effort to ensure that the European Union becomes the "most dynamic competitive knowledge-based economy in the world" is at the base of FP7. For that end, the R&D efforts were grouped into four categories: cooperation, ideas, people, and capacities. For each type of objective, specific programs relate to the four main areas of EU research policy. All the programs work collectively to promote the creation of European poles of scientific development.[9]

Organizational Change

Organizational change programs are a matter of survival. Either companies change and adapt, or they become susceptible to tsunami-like waves of external market pressure, quantum leaps in technology, and internal dissatisfaction. The needed changes may loom in the form of mutations in organization structure, implementations of new systems, or transformations of organizational culture. Well-orchestrated change makes it possible to transition to a new state that ensures both organizational survival and renewed hope for prosperity.

These change programs take place in scenarios that set them apart from conventional programs or projects. Organizational change generally involves several projects coordinated under a program designed to produce desired results. For instance, the program may involve technological upgrades, cultural change, and structural change in varying geographical locations. Such a program is articulated from the center of power yet ultimately affects multiple levels and multiple stakeholders. Here are examples:

- A top-down lean program involving fewer employees with advanced technology operating from home offices
- A new quality management approach using Six Sigma techniques in a research setting
- Adopting a different form for contracting major construction projects using a partnering philosophy that requires forming a culture of mutual trust

Upper management players are accustomed to general management principles, internal politics, and a variety of organizational challenges. But, by definition, their view is one of broad scope concerned with the overall health of the organization. For a desired change to take place, a structured, planned, and sharply focused approach is required. That approach needs direction and nurturing over the duration of the program and thus the skills and techniques found in project management. Items like program scope definition and attention to cost and schedule are a must.

Although commonality exists between the general management and change-focused project management communities, in fact, a conceptual mismatch is often the case. Troubling issues tend to arise throughout the life of change projects because sponsorship challenges and vested interests appear, and key players begin jockeying for positions in the new organization. Even though reasonable alignment is possible among the stakeholders involved in change initiatives, a politically charged atmosphere is inevitable at various stages of the program.

Because of differing mind-sets between general management approaches and a projectized view, Enterprise Project Governance is of particular importance. When EPG is in place, the classic general management versus project management mismatch is partially mitigated. An EPG setting implies having a general awareness of the broad role of project management throughout the enterprise. The key to success depends on the ability of change leadership to transform perceived mismatches into complementary strategies and actions.

From a general management viewpoint, here are some of the problems perceived in implementing change programs, based on analysis of influential articles from the *Harvard Business Review* and summarized in the book *The Right Project Done Right.*[10]

- *Defining Project Scope.* Successful business change projects depend on appropriate dimensioning and focus of scope. Some culprits of failed change projects are the lack of a strong tie to business results, over-ambitious and diffuse intent, and an unhealthy influence of executive personal agendas. Organizational change projects also fail because of a lack of methodology and structure to make the change happen and in some cases because of a lack of a decisive, power-packed approach.

- *Lack of Understanding of the People Factor.* The human factor of resistance to change ranks high on causes for failed organizational change programs. When the factor is underestimated, emotions are ruffled. When emotions spin out of control, the change effort is susceptible to sandbagging by concerned stakeholders who did not buy into the program in the first place. When the winds of change begin to blow, defensive thinking and turf standoffs are common reactions of insecure executives.

- *Poor Sponsorship from the Top.* Leadership and sponsorship from the top are essential for successful change management programs. Not having firm sponsorship in place for organizational change is akin to having a weak foundation in a building. In both cases, heavy winds can cause structural fractures and bring the house tumbling down. The lack of individual commitment by executives and insufficient management coalition are other causes for downfall.

- *Inadequate Communication.* Shoddy communication is the root evil for most organizations' ills, particularly for change management initiatives. A lack of persistence, overoptimism, and inadequate communication outside the change program team are common causes for program breakdown. Successful change depends in part on a finely tuned communications project supporting the program.
- *Inadequate Metrics.* As in any program, metrics are required to measure progress. This requires planting milestones along the way and firmly fixing the finish line. Problems related to metrics include a poor tie of the program to business results, measuring only time elapsed as opposed to actual progress, and using insignificant measurements like the volume of participants in training courses.
- *Inadequate Program Organization.* It takes a project management logic and team approach to conduct successful change programs. When that isn't the case, challenges arise. Some typical problems are poor leadership and mediocre players on the team, a closed-door approach with poor communications within the organization, and a lack of adequate planning and connection with the business objective.
- *Insufficient Involvement and Empowerment.* Two keys for success in the quest for organizational transformation are the involvement and empowerment of the right people in the program at the right time in the program life cycle.

Special Approaches for Managing Change

The literature and authors' observations indicate that business change projects perform significantly worse against schedule than other types of projects. On average, these so-called soft projects overrun schedules by 20 percent and in some cases by as much as 40 percent.

Some practices from the arsenal of project management are particularly applicable to organizational change and other soft projects. While hard projects involving physical construction of facilities may thrive on predominantly technical approaches, change programs call for a broader scope and a full enterprise-wide view. Practices that boost performance on change programs are program management, stakeholder management, portfolio management, and benefits management.

Where Enterprise Project Governance is in place, the probability for successful change increases because EPG by nature is designed to encompass a big-picture view of organizational dynamics. When such a change effort is articulated under well-positioned and competent sponsorship in an EPG setting, favorable results are probable, particularly when special attention is given to the following avenues to managing change.

Change Through Program Management

A program vision for change makes sense. Because complementary initiatives comprise such an undertaking, each can take on a project status. This program-wide view paints a change panorama and provides a framework for defining the roles and responsibilities for subordinate projects across the enterprise.

The big pharma companies, as described in Chapter 6, represent an industry in dramatic flux, with a clear need for change management programs. A leading pharmaceutical organization introduced a framework for business change that includes the following four program elements:

- *Purpose.* This defines the overall scope and ensures that the vision is documented along with the business case and desired results.
- *Interactions.* The relationships among people and processes are outlined here. Governance relationships and stakeholders are identified and managed, as well as the changes needed to meet the business needs.
- *Operation.* Program operation encompasses ensuring that a program structure and governance model are in place, along with defined roles and responsibilities, and the allocation of resources within budget and cost restraints.
- *Processes.* These processes are comprised of an effective project office that manages the program's needs for information and of communications and change management. Processes are also required for benefits realization, issues resolution, and risk management.

Stakeholder Management and Politics

Troubling governance and management issues arise throughout the life of change projects because vested interests become visible as key players begin to protect their turfs from undesired changes. So politics and stakeholder management are particularly crucial to the successful management of change. Change is fundamentally about getting people to buy into and adapt to a different way of doing things. Managing stakeholders goes way beyond establishing new tools, techniques, and processes; it is essentially about dealing with the soft principles of project management. In the case of a merger between major organizations, the issues to be resolved can be put into two categories: technical and behavioral. Technical challenges consist of choosing the best processes or melding existing complementary processes. Fixing and adjusting the best organizational structure can also be seen as a technical issue. Behavioral challenges in a merger setting involve people and politics, and these factors can strongly influence the final technical decisions. Organizational change programs call for heavy emphasis on stakeholder management, as outlined in Chapter 8, to ensure smooth sailing even in troubled waters.

Portfolio Management

Organizational change undertakings are packaged in the form of programs because they involve the complementary initiatives of projects subordinated directly to the change program: program communications, process review, organizational restructuring, and training. Aside from these directly related projects, organizations conduct other projects that may impact change programs, such as plant expansion, marketing, and career planning programs.

Change programs in organizations implementing Enterprise Project Governance involve policies for managing multiple projects. Good project portfolio management makes a difference in the results achieved in companies, as outlined in detail in Chapter 5. Change programs must be highly prioritized in the overall portfolio of projects and programs. Since good portfolio management involves more than simple project prioritization, major attention is required for the effective implementation of the portfolio. This requires separating the governance of portfolios from the management of individual projects, where the governance is concerned with prioritization and portfolio balance and the project management with getting each job done as planned.

Benefits Realization

To be effective, change programs require a strong connection with the business objectives. The programs are initiated on the premise that they help implement strategies, in turn generating benefits to the organization and principal stakeholders, as shown in Exhibit 11-4. This requires monitoring projects proactively during implementation as well as tracking and adjusting postproject results. Quality-related techniques such as Six Sigma, widely applied at GE, are sharply focused on guaranteeing the benefit as initially envisioned, even if this means making midproject and postproject adjustments. A systematic approach of benefits mapping used by a major U.K. corporation proved helpful in showing the relationship between the organization's capacity to change and the ability to reap benefits. A high-level benefits governance committee was established to oversee the business units and to assess the program change and how it impacts operational results.

Managing the Change

As in any project-related endeavor, every change program is unique. The settings and stakeholders are surely different from previous efforts; the times are not the same, and the program objectives will differ. So what worked last time in a different and unique scenario might spell disaster this time around. And other previously ineffective approaches may prove invaluable in a new situation. So a

Exhibit 11-4. Organizational Change Program

design-to-fit policy is fundamental when planning change programs, starting out with a solid situation size-up, followed by a customization of the program in accordance with the objectives, the stakeholders, the setting, and the times.

Involvement of the business-as-usual people in organizational change programs is essential in all situations. Since these are the people who will live with (and hopefully benefit from) the implemented changes, their participation is crucial. Although the management of change programs is normally led by a group separate from line and operational personnel, the business-as-usual people deserve to be heard, involved, and informed as the program evolves.

Changeover projects are special cases. In projects like the implementation of enterprise resource planning (ERP), where new systems take over from the old, line personnel are intrinsically involved from start to finish. The new processes require input from outside consultants but also from line people who know the business. As the new processes evolve, line management has to prepare itself for operating two systems simultaneously—the old and the new—until such time as the new is fully adopted. This is the flip-of-the-switch moment where the process change happens instantaneously, at the same time setting off corresponding echoes in organizational behavior. For that reason, these flip-of-the-switch projects must also be couched in an overall change program to ensure success.

Leadership plays a big-time role in change programs because all tiers of management are obliged to work toward changing the corporate culture, and this also means making adjustments in their own behaviors. Massive downsizing, delayering, and change programs do not always yield the results planned by the strategists because the impact of behavioral issues is often underestimated.

The skills set required for an effective leader of change management is not easily found in a single person. Thus effective change leaders rely on the complementary capabilities of the project team to deal with all the issues that come up in change management. Business strategy knowledge and skills are required to ensure that the change project stays on the beam toward improving business results. Effective change also hinges on traditional project management leadership skills to inspire the project team and workforce toward fulfilling the proposed goals. At the sponsorship level, leadership encompasses choosing the right project leaders for each arm of the program, as well as navigating internal politics and conflicting personal agendas.

Due to the magnitude of the program and the corresponding leadership challenge, outside consultants are often hired to provide the external expertise and steadfast focus. Another option for supporting change projects is to use internal consultants when professionals of sufficient stature are available. These internal consultants may also act as a project office to coordinate the various projects comprising the change program, or they may serve as a liaison between outside consultants and ongoing activities within the organization.

Change at Samsung to Compete in a New World Order

The magnitude of the leadership challenge for change projects is demonstrated by the major transformation made by Samsung Electronics over the past few decades. Samsung's objective was to convert from a leading manufacturer in a developing country to a major player in the global marketplace. This objective meant competing on a worldwide basis, where the practices and cultures of other successful global players varied considerably from the Korean sociocultural environment.

When Lee Kun-hee inherited the Samsung chairmanship in 1987, the group was content with the status of number one firm in a developing country. To make the change, he was faced with the question of how to provide the momentum for the quantum leap from the developing country model to that of an advanced country. The model chosen took the form of successive waves, with the aim toward making the needed changes in norms, values, culture, and mind-sets to consolidate an aggregate Samsung core competency.

- *The First Wave.* In 1973, Samsung started the semiconductor industry at the persistence of Lee Kun-hee, who, in effect, started the IT industry in Korea.
- *The Second Wave.* Mr. Lee Kun-hee announced in 1987, "Let us divorce from the tradition of quantity-oriented management (economic scale as a source of global competition) and move on to the

quality-oriented management (knowledge-based and hi-tech-based global leadership)."

- *The Third Wave.* In March 1993, Lee perceived the need for increased marketing and merchandising to be successful globally.
- *The Fourth Wave.* In 1993, in a technological advancement staff meeting for Samsung Electronics in a Tokyo hotel, Lee emphasized the need to attain greater maturity in core competencies as well as bettering brand image and overall design.
- *The Fifth Wave.* In early July 1993, Lee started the 7-to-4 system, adjusting over 200,000 employees' work hours from 7 A.M. till 4 P.M. Lee wanted to instill behavioral shock from previous practices as a tangible symbol of change for all Samsung employees who were reluctant to change, despite the successive waves of communication.
- *The Sixth Wave.* On March 9, 1995, 2,000 managers and employees were assembled from the Koomi Factory, where 10 employees with large hammers suddenly broke down and destroyed boxes full of freshly made cellular phones amounting to 150,000 sets. This was another shock message aimed at boosting quality at the factory.
- *The Seventh Wave.* Samsung Electronics benchmarked GE, Sony, and other electronic giants but was hesitant to apply restructuring because of the Far East culture of lifelong employment. However, the International Monetary Fund crisis in December 1997 provided justification for drastic measures, which resulted in laying off 20 percent of Samsung's 30,000 employees.[11]

The complexities of leadership in change management are shown in the Samsung odyssey toward cultural transformation. Studies show that the second-generation Korean owner and CEO Lee Kun-hee combined behavioral and persuasive leadership. He also employed seven instruments of goal accomplishment, approaches of power relationships, and transformational leadership—all aimed at achieving the desired goals. His process included behavioral approaches in (waves 1, 3, 5, 6, 7) and persuasive approaches in (waves

2 and 4). In the process, Mr. Lee built core competence of technological capability, brand and design, and a high level of quality by applying multiple theories over waves of effective change management.

Conclusions

Governance in different types of industries takes on different characteristics, particularly when high degrees of uncertainty are involved. Such is the case for projects in the arenas of IT, R&D, and organizational change. In the information technology area, several governance frameworks are available to help govern both IT projects and operations. R&D initiatives vary widely and range from process improvement to new product development to breakthrough discoveries. Such projects are challenging because, by definition, researchers do not know in advance how to achieve the desired results. The governance of R&D products therefore requires customized policies designed to conciliate the need to create with down-to-earth business interests. Organizational change programs present both technical challenges and softer behavioral issues. Of particular relevance in change endeavors are four topics drawn from the field of project management. These include expertise related to the management of programs, portfolios, stakeholders, and benefits.

12

The EPG Plan: A Roadmap to Transformation and Success

An EPG plan maps out a journey between a point of departure, with defined tollgates along the way, to a destination, which is a vision of future success where a transformed state is expected. The plan outlines steps for implementing an overall governance of portfolios, programs, and projects through direction, control, assurance, and support by people across the organization's strategic, tactical, and operational layers. The resulting deliverables of this plan become a guide to consolidating the policies, standards, and lessons learned resulting from the implementation of the actions involving the EPG framework. An example of such a plan follows.

The Fish & Wildlife Compensation Program

In 1995, the Fish & Wildlife Compensation Program of Canada was established. Its goal was to restore the fish and wildlife resources adversely affected by the original development footprint of hydroelectric facilities owned by the provincial company BC Hydro in the Canadian portion of the Columbia Basin. These footprint impacts included historical effects on fish and wildlife that occurred as a result of reservoir creation, watercourse diversions, and the construction of dam structures. Viewed as one of the largest successful lake restoration programs in the world, it rebuilds the food web in the respective water bodies impacted by upstream dams that trap nutrients.

The program is a joint initiative of the government of British Columbia (Ministry of Environment), the federal government (Fisheries and Oceans—DFO), and BC Hydro. Since its formation, it has identified, funded, and delivered over 700 conservation and enhancement projects and has invested Can$60 million.[1, 2] Funding applications go through a review and decision-making process to determine which projects will be blessed with funding. The program operates on a governance model, which is analyzed here using the EPG governance framework presented in Chapter 2.

Strategy

The basin was divided into four regions that were subdivided into 15 areas, each having a strategic plan to reduce adverse impacts on fish and wildlife or to recover losses in fish and wildlife diversity and production created by hydroelectric development. Plans outlined the direction and approach to restoration within the watersheds, with a focus on addressing historical losses of fish and wildlife habitat. They described the type and scale of impacts from hydroelectric development and proposed strategies to achieve improvement in the diversity and production of fish and wildlife within the constraints imposed by biophysical conditions and hydroelectric operations. These plans constituted the basis for aligning project selection and prioritization.

Risk

The program spreads risk through delegation. An overall formal risk management plan was not established; instead, the responsibility for aligning projects with strategy was delegated to the specific areas.

Portfolio

Project applications are reviewed to ensure that they are cost-effective, achievable, biologically appropriate, and socially desirable. Once accepted, projects are ranked and submitted to the board. After preselection, projects are subject to the following four stages:

- *Acceptability Criteria.* Any project submitted must meet certain criteria before receiving further consideration: It must be aligned with strategic plans, consistent with program objectives, compatible with other resource management, and based on sound biological principles.
- *Ranking Project Proposals.* Fish tasks are to be ranked based on ratings and weightings for a series of criteria. Criteria ratings are then weighted according to their relative importance. Wildlife tasks are ranked based on their raw scores.
- *Board Considerations.* Projects are submitted to the board, which adds qualitative criteria to the selection such as socioeconomic and geographic values.
- *Portfolio Organization.* The selected projects are organized and presented in a project handbook. Each selected project is identified by name; objectives; leaders; how it is to be developed, implemented, and monitored; duration; and associated partners.

Organization

The program structure establishes clearly defined roles, responsibilities, and opportunities for participation:

- *Board.* The board leads the generation of the program and inspires others by their commitment to program outcomes and integrity. The board is expected to bring partner perspectives to set conflict-of-interest policy, to shape funding allocation policy, to select nontechnical criteria for project evaluation, to decide which projects will be funded, and to evolve and maintain the governance framework, including the performance measurement framework. The board is composed of nine representatives from the participating partners.

Their meetings may incorporate a variety of decision processes benefiting from the exploration of a range of interests and options. It is intended that principles of consensus building and conflict resolution will be applied in all key policy decisions. In awarding funding, they have flexibility to select from among technically sound, eligible projects as defined by strategic plans, but they will not necessarily fund projects in a sequence based solely on technical priorities.

- *Planning Committee.* This committee is responsible for and signs off on key technical elements of the governance framework. Specifically, it signs off on strategic plans that determine project eligibility for funding, sets technical criteria for project evaluation, signs off on the technical review process, and develops the performance measurement framework to be applied.

- *Technical Review Committees.* These appointed committees are composed of up to five persons who conduct technical evaluations of projects submitted for funding, based on criteria provided by the planning committee. Members must have scientific or academic qualifications or analytical expertise. All parties are encouraged to work as a team and ensure that roles are complementary. If conflicts in roles arise, parties are encouraged to work with the program manager to resolve them.

- *Program Sponsor.* The program sponsor performs the necessary checking and administrative functions, ensures the control of monies and assets, hires program staff, ensures that tax and reporting are handled, and ratifies the compliance of board decisions on program awards and appointments.

- *Program Manager.* The program manager facilitates and coordinates the program work. It is accountable to the board for implementing board directions within its mandate and to the program sponsor for ensuring that administrative functions are appropriately carried out. Key roles include supporting the board, facilitation of the work of the planning and technical review committees, communications, administrative budgeting and planning, financial controls, project administration and evaluation, coordination of other program activities, and maintenance of program records.

- *Decision-Making Processes.* The main program processes are outlined in Exhibit 12-1.

Stakeholders

The program considers the input of First Nations (a term of ethnicity that refers to the aboriginal peoples in Canada) and of the public in the decisions,

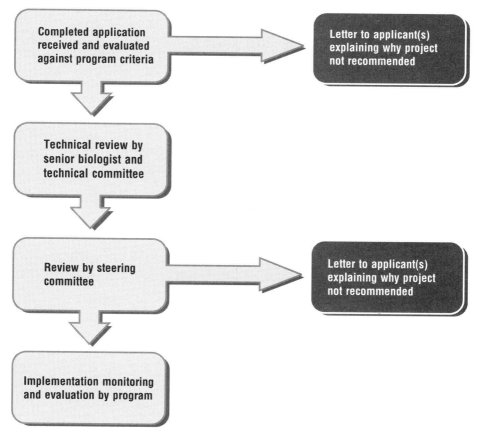

Exhibit 12-1. Fish & Wildlife Decision Processes

although how this is done is not explicit. With the project decentralization policy, it would be possible to have a stakeholder management plan for each project, yet an overall consolidated one is still lacking.

Performance

The monitoring and reporting is done project by project, but an overall performance management plan was not identified. However, one of the board's responsibilities is to establish a performance measurement framework.

Transformation

To cope with transformation, change management plans are put into place to deal with the impacts and benefits resulting from projects. Each project is responsible for monitoring change, although plans for tracking overall program results are not identified.

We used the EPG framework to analyze the Fish & Wildlife Compensation Program. Now this framework will be detailed in the form of a generic plan that may be customized and applied to the characteristics of each organization.

Enterprise Project Governance Plan

The elaboration of an EPG plan may ultimately develop into a basis for a manual for maintaining the concept in place. Such a manual becomes a register for definitions, approaches, processes, and lessons learned from execution—a legacy for new entrants to review as an introduction to EPG. As time goes on, the document will be subject to adaptation, review, change, and improvement, creating an organizational learning cycle. The topics to be considered for inclusion depend on each organization, but the following ones are typical.

Context and Culture

Understand the internal and external business contexts and current culture in which the organization operates, so that the EPG system can address current realities and identify opportunities to enable change to better achieve desired outcomes.

Exhibit 12-2. The EPG Plan

- *External Business Context.* Analyze the external context and key issues impacting the organization.
- *Internal Business Context.* Understand the organizational structure and key assets that drive organizational value.
- *Culture.* Analyze the existing culture, including the organizational climate and attitudes toward projects and compliance; analyze the characteristics of the culture that may impact the EPG system.

Directing

Promote and motivate expected behaviors by organizing the regulatory environment, policies, methodologies, standards, and guidelines.

- *Mandatory Compliance.* Make explicit all the necessary compliances. A section on SOX compliance is included in Annex A for organizations that need to consider it.
- *Policies.* Develop and implement policies that address portfolio, program, and project development. These policies must include software recommendations.
- *Methodologies.* Describe all the methodologies that must be adopted for the portfolio, programs, and projects.
- *Standards and Guidelines.* Describe all the standards and guidelines available.

Strategy Alignment

Investment activities are subject to a governance process to be resourced and financed adequately. For mandatory projects, the decision is not whether to undertake the project but how to manage it using the appropriate methodologies in order to meet the performance requirements. For successful program and project selection, attention is focused on alignment with strategic objectives and on the go/no-go decision with respect to best value.

- *Explicit EPG Mission, Vision, and Values.* Make explicit the foundations on which the EPG system is developed.
- *Strategic Referential.* Establish the referential by which projects and programs will be selected. A strategy map is always a useful tool.
- *Value Creation Referential.* Make explicit the benefits expected from the strategic referential.

Risk Management

Ideally, managing risk in an integrated way allows for effective responses to rapid changes in the organizational environment, to natural disasters, and to political instability. For such events, the overall organizational risk management approach, the critical organizational risks, and how to analyze risks in portfolio, program, and project management must all be explicit.

- *Risk Processes.* Describe the processes used in portfolio, program, and risk management.
- *Risk Integration.* Describe how the approach to the portfolio, programs, and projects is integrated with the overall risk approach to the organization.
- *Crisis Response, Continuity, and Recovery.* Describe how to respond to crisis issues and business disruption.

Portfolio Management

A single project inventory can be constructed containing all of the organization's ongoing and proposed projects. Alternatively, multiple project inventories can be created representing project portfolios for different departments, programs, or businesses. Since project portfolio management can be conducted at any level, the choice of one portfolio versus many depends on the size of the organization, its structure, and the nature and interrelationships among the projects being conducted.

- *Portfolio Proposals.* Describe how to select projects and programs that represent the best value to the firm and that are aligned with strategy.
- *Portfolio Processes.* Describe how the portfolio will be managed.
- *Portfolio Integration.* For companies with portfolios across business units or geographical areas, describe their integration processes.

Structure, Roles, and Responsibilities

To be effective, the individuals who direct and those who oversee governance activities must be organized. Their contributions must be modeled to ensure that authority and decision making has a clear source, that the work of management and oversight is efficient, and that the needs for direction and decisions are all addressed.

- *Goals and Expected Outcomes of the EPG System.* Define the scope of the EPG system, what it will achieve, and how it relates to the business objectives.
- *Key Roles and Accountabilities.* Define and enable oversight roles and accountability.
- *Board Roles and Accountabilities.* The board has oversight of the system and ultimately is the active monitor for shareholder and stakeholder benefit. The board must:
  - Address long-term issues.
  - Direct the purpose and desired outcomes of the organization.
  - Set a charter for its involvement.
  - Set business objectives and ensure they are congruent with values and risks.
  - Obtain regular assurance that the system is effective.
- *Committees Roles and Accountabilities.* For the EPG system to operate effectively, it may be necessary to create many committees to support the board's decision-making processes. Most of EPG work is carried out by committees and, for many organizations, multiple committees work at different levels. The actual committees depend on the organization.
- *The Role of Management.* Management must:
  - Design, implement, and operate an effective EPG system.
  - Provide regular assurance about the effectiveness of the system.
  - Communicate with key stakeholders about issues as they arise.
  - Evaluate and optimize the performance of the system.
- *The Role of Assurance.* Management should obtain and provide regular assurances about the effectiveness and performance of the EPG system. An independent expert can reveal weaknesses in design or operation, opportunities for integration, and exchanges of best practices. For its part, the board is required to obtain regular assurance about the effectiveness of the system. Internal or external independent reviews can be used. Those providing assurance, whether internal or external, should:

- Provide assurance that risks are appropriately identified, evaluated, managed, and monitored.
- Provide regular assurance to the board and management of the effectiveness of the EPG system in light of the organization's culture and objectives.
- *Decision-Making Processes.* A set of processes must be established as authoritative, within which portfolios, programs, and projects are initiated, planned, and executed in order to ensure that goals and benefits are met.
- *Project Identification.* This describes the processes for proposing a program or a project, including whether it is mandatory or aligned with business objectives.
- *Project Selection.* This describes how projects and programs are selected and how to decide for go/no-go.
- *Why-How Framework.* This describes how to develop a why-how framework for each project or program.
- *Project Start-Up.* This describes how to initiate a project or a program.
- *Project Reviews.* This describes the approach for programs and project reviews.
- *Risk Processes.* This is described in Chapter 4.
- *Portfolio Processes.* This is described in Chapter 5.

Stakeholder Management

All people have expectations that drive how they interact. Expectations are their vision of a future state or action, many of which are unstated but critical to EPG success. Understanding and responding to these expectations comprise an art, and expectation management is useful in any area in which human beings must collaborate effectively to achieve a shared result. Failure to recognize that people are bound to have positive and negative reactions only results in disaster.

Stakeholder analysis reveals the performance factors that must be considered. Sometimes stakeholders' interests will be aligned and support one another, but, more commonly, conflicting interests will emerge. Most stakeholders will not be effective in supporting the EPG's delivery unless they are accurately and currently informed about the progress and consulted on the challenges ahead. One of the aims of Enterprise Project Governance is to build a common sense of ownership by informing, listening, and creating an environment of trust. Here's the process:

- *Who are the critical stakeholders?* The critical stakeholders must be identified.
- *What do they care about?* Stakeholders must be carefully examined to find out what's important to them.
- *Implement the stakeholders' management plan.* Interact with stakeholders to manage expectations.

Performance Evaluation

To be effective, EPG has to be measured and its performance monitored on a periodic and ongoing basis to ensure that it contributes to business objectives while being effective and responsive to the changing environment. The five steps presented in Chapter 9 must be used.

Transformation

All effective business transformation is continuous. Continuous transformation is essential to any organization in implementing its business strategy and achieving its vision. It is an ongoing requirement because vision and strategy will always need adapting and refining as changing economic influences impact. Business agility—the ability to achieve business transformation—is therefore a true measure of both management and corporate success and, as such, part of the EPG structure. Developing the internal capability for change management is an essential step in assuring the successful implementation of any change project. Establishing change capability enables clients to continue optimizing performance in response to changing service demands and new strategic drivers.

- *Change Management Approach.* Define an approach to prepare the organization for the changes brought by the implementation of programs and projects.

- *Awareness and Education.* Educate the board, management, and workforce about expected conduct and policies, and develop necessary skills and motivation.

- *Human Capital Incentives.* Implement incentive and compensation plans that motivate and reward desired conduct.

- *Provide a Helpline.* Establish ways for the teams to seek guidance on the reporting of noncompliance or unethical conduct.

- *Inquiry and Survey.* Periodically seek input.

- *Organizational Learning.* This ensures the development of organizational learning as a result of program and project portfolio's implementation.

Information

Capture, document, and manage EPG information so that it efficiently and accurately flows up, down, and across the extended enterprise, as well as to external stakeholders.

- *Information Management and Documentation.* Implement and manage a way to guarantee that the information is relevant, reliable, timely, secure, and available.

- *Reporting and Disclosure.* Describe the flow of reporting and disclosure. For upward flow, consider the status, progress, and issues for resolution; for downward flow, consider the policies, guidelines, directions, and decisions made.

- *Technology and Infrastructure.* Enable technology support where appropriate.

- *Internal and External Communication.* Deliver information to the right audiences as required by mandates or as needed to perform and shape attitudes.

Ericsson: a Case of EPG Evolution

In practice, many organizations evolve over time toward a broad enterprise-wide approach for managing projects. Such is the case of Ericsson, a global telecommunications manufacturer headquartered in Sweden, which spent decades developing project management expertise. Known as PROPS (*project for project steering*), the framework's objective is to enable project managers anywhere in the world to complete their projects successfully. In the late 1980s, the company developed the first PROPS version to support the development of digital telecom switches. The introduction of mobile telecom networks sparked the need to develop a more generic model that was uncoupled from specific product lines. Later, generic versions were developed with focuses on (1) customer projects, (2) market-based R&D, and (3) internal company projects. This broadened the focus to general project management practices and encompassed the business context of projects.[3]

Ultimately, this led to the company's projectization, where projects became the way of working at Ericsson, since as much as 80 percent of the company's employees work on projects. The PROPS framework has gone through multiple versions and become a framework for Enterprise Project Management aimed at all project-related areas, including project management, program management, portfolio management, and project offices. The focus is on the enterprise as a whole and on multiple projects of sundry natures. The key points of the PROPS framework are:

- Business perspective
- Human perspective
- Project life cycle model
- Project organization model

In essence, the framework contains the basics for Enterprise Project Governance and is used as a basis for similar programs at Volvo, Saab, and other international companies.

The creation and evolution of PROPS was sponsored and supported by top management. A small unit responsible for project management support was given the assignment to host the framework and act as an internal consultancy team. A group of technical writers was brought in to ensure that PROPS was documented and launched in a way that would be reader friendly and attractive to potential users. Later, an internal center of excellence became responsible for the development of PROPS, as well as for project management training and support. This focused group of people dedicated to PROPS was a key factor in its success.

Ericsson gradually developed a fully projectized culture from top to bottom and did so by continuously upgrading its basic project management framework, with the full involvement and support of top managers. According to Ericsson's Inger Bergman, "Changing a company from a traditional hierarchical, functional manufacturing industry to an agile player in the IT area is not easy and takes time and effort. Project management is now seen as an important asset for the company and a competitive advantage in R&D and sales delivery." Ericsson is an example of the evolution of project governance capabilities.

Creating Enhanced IT Governance Capability in New York State

Enterprise IT governance is defined as the effort toward the coordinated, enterprise-wide use of IT resources. A subset of EPG, it specifically targets goal attainment, assessing and minimizing risk, and providing oversight of IT investments. A case of enterprise IT governance is examined next.

The State of New York has made huge investments in information technology over the years, involving more than a hundred agencies. Officials began to ask about the current enterprise IT governance capabilities and to question what additional value could be created for the state through enhancements. As a result, a project was launched to elicit the best strategies to make existing practices more effective and to identify what kinds of changes to the existing structures and processes were needed.

The project culminated in a set of recommendations made in 2009 about New York State's enterprise IT governance structure design and implementation:[4]

1. *Reduce redundancy and establish prioritization mechanisms.* The diversity of agencies, organization structures, and levels in New York State government can result in redundancy and conflict over priorities. There is a need, therefore, for collaboration to solve common business problems through IT solutions, with effective prioritization providing a foundation for coordinated enterprise-level strategies and initiatives.

2. *Reduce political directions and swings.* A well-designed governance structure cannot eradicate political swings, but it can provide a continuity plan to span political leadership changes and create consistency of vision for IT projects, which are often multiyear endeavors that span more than one administration.

3. *Establish standards.* Technology and information standards are a foundation for the interagency collaboration necessary for interoperability to become an achievable goal for many of the state's departments and units. Enhanced enterprise IT governance for New York State should set out clear rules for developing statewide standards.

4. *Foster the sharing of services and information through agency collaboration.* With clear standards in place, New York State government has the potential for expanded shared services offerings and innovative collaborations. Enhanced enterprise IT governance should provide a space for greater coordination and collaboration among agencies, authorities, and localities.

5. *Align IT with the business of the state government.* Alignment of IT with business needs is a commonly accepted goal of IT governance, yet it is very difficult to achieve. Enhanced enterprise IT governance for state and local government should provide mechanisms for alignment between IT investments and program priorities.

These recommendations aim at collectively creating the governance capability that the state needs by outlining new structures related to three primary areas of decision making: (1) IT investments, (2) ensuring alignment of IT investments with the overall strategic plan of the state, and (3) setting policies and standards.

To achieve the recommendations in the three primary areas of decision making, a four-entity model was proposed for enhanced IT governance of the state:

- *Executive Enterprise Governance Board.* This board fills one of the gaps in the current governance structure by providing a robust mechanism for ensuring the alignment of IT investments with state plans and priorities. It is also tasked with periodically reviewing the existing governance procedures and proposing changes if necessary.

- *Information Technology Investment Board.* The primary responsibility is to review and make final decisions about state agency IT investment requests, with special attention paid to the identification and deployment of enterprise-level investment and projects. The board will also provide transparency and openness to a process that has previously been more closed.

- *Council of CIOs (Chief Information Officers).* This council is an advisory body to the state CIO on matters of information technology policy, management, and operations. It provides a forum for the state agencies' CIOs to address issues of mutual concern, make recommendations on IT issues, share information, and promote cooperation.

- *State CIO.* This leads the development of statewide policies and standards.

A temporary Enterprise IT Governance Implementation Committee was also suggested to ensure the implementation of the new structure and to provide accountability to the key stakeholders by making the governance development process transparent. This case shows how to initiate a process by leveraging the various stakeholders involved.

Conclusions

An EPG plan is a roadmap that identifies the steps required to reach strategic goals by implementing Enterprise Project Governance. Three cases were presented. The Fish & Wildlife Compensation Program shows the adequacy of the framework presented in Chapter 2. The Ericsson case demonstrates that results may not be immediate and that evolution is key to successful implementation. The New York State example shows how an Enterprise Project Governance process can be initiated. EPG deals with people and the changing culture of an organization; therefore, patience and perseverance are called for. The examples outlined are suitable to an array of companies and organizations and may be used as a basis for new EGP plans.

CHAPTER

13

Challenges and Roadblocks

The implementation of EPG is bound to face bumps in the road and, in some cases, major roadblocks. The reasons vary, but any one may be sufficient to scuttle a well-intentioned EPG initiative. Perhaps there is a lack of awareness about the topic at various levels in the organization, not enough *buy-in* to the concept by the right stakeholders, or insufficient resources and structure. Here is a breakdown of the challenges and suggested responses to mitigate negative effects.

The Why Factor

"We've never needed EPG before. Why now?"

This reaction stems from a lack of awareness. As a new twist on organizing project efforts on a holistic basis, stakeholders have not been exposed to the EPG concept. Executives and other related stakeholders are constantly bombarded by new trends in management and organizational fixes, ranging from Six Sigma to balanced scorecard to agile management approaches. EPG may therefore not be greeted with immediate applause until benefits are apparent to the interested parties.

"How about ROI of EPG? Can it be measured?"

When the implementation of EGP is articulated with portfolio management and an effective corporate-level PMO, concrete results are highly probable. Measurable benefit is produced when seamless relationships tie together project governance policies with portfolio, program, and project management at multiple levels in the organization. This measured benefit depends on the availability and accuracy of information generated and funneled through an organization's systems. Since a primary objective of EPG is to produce a positive balance when comparing overall performance of projects against planned performances, then the quality of the project information systems becomes a vital link for making a case for improved ROI.

By pooling the positive results from numerous projects, the surplus resources generated (investment, personnel, installations) can be reutilized in other ventures, thus boosting ROI. This is called the *throughput approach* because it involves gathering surplus resources and putting them through to other beneficial undertakings, as illustrated in Exhibit 13-1. Theories on effective PMOs propose that use of the throughput approach may generate as much as a 10 percent contribution to ROI on related projects. Presumably, if the project management umbrella is broadened beyond PMOs to include an enterprise-wide view encompassing all portfolios and programs, that contribution could be even greater.[1]

Involvement and Motivation

"Everybody is already overloaded. We don't have time for this."

Perhaps everybody is busy because of lack of an approach that puts order to projects. The *busy-ness* may be due to rework spawned by subpar performance or from fuzzy priorities that make people squander time on less noble causes. Behavioral issues caused by a poor organizational climate can also sandbag potential synergies. Other culprits are inadequate processes that require

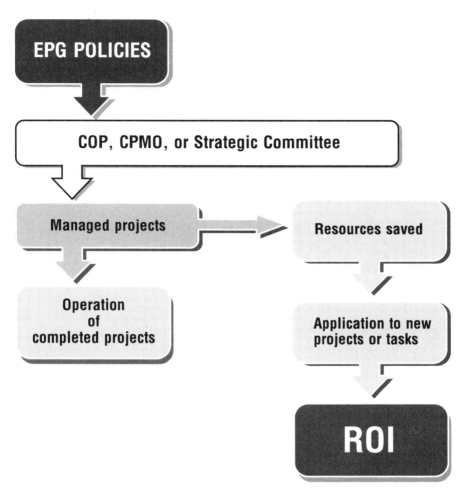

Exhibit 13-1 Improving ROI by the Throughput Method

unnecessary efforts and poor time management practices by professionals. All these issues can be targeted and put under the umbrella of Enterprise Project Management.

"How do we get people to buy into this?"

Stakeholders are particularly moved when they get a satisfactory response to the question that underlies most human motivation: What's in it for me?

People crave to be shown the benefit of implementing EPG; otherwise it probably won't happen. That benefit might be recognition, less work, fewer problems, greater productivity, or greater synergy. If the concept doesn't garner enthusiasm, then a boost is required to get stakeholders to buy into the program. When that benefit isn't fully obvious, a change management approach is called for, encompassing the following steps:

- A change project is mapped out with an action plan and schedule.
- Leadership is assigned to a change agent, who articulates informative campaigns, workshops, and detailed planning sessions designed to make the project happen.
- The identification and management of stakeholders are also a major part of getting the buy-in.

Organization and People

"We're already top heavy in the organization. We don't need more overhead!"

Issues like head count and overhead costs are high on the radar in all organizations. How, then, to show that the eventual costs of EPG will be far surpassed by the resulting benefits? First, EPG need not add significant costs to the organization. By shifting focus and using existing resources, benefits can be reaped without adding extra ballast. For instance, if there is no position corresponding to the CPO (chief project office), then another C-level or vice-presidential-level executive could absorb the EPG initiative until the movement gains momentum. Also, an existing PMO can be beefed up and upgraded to take on EPG-related functions. Overall competency in project management also creates synergy in the organization and holds down costs.

"We don't have people trained in this type of approach."

Building competency within an organization begins with training professionals in the knowledge, skills, and approaches required. While training involves an investment in time and money, payback may be manifold when the investment results in a team of professionals working competently and synergistically toward company goals. The training of the stakeholders for optimum enterprise project performance includes these types of target audiences:

- Project management awareness for top-level executives and project sponsors
- Project management basics for all directly or indirectly related to projects
- Project management certification for project team members
- Advanced training and coaching for project leaders

To Overcome Roadblocks, Forget the Facts!

In business endeavors, decisions are made based on numerous factors, some of which are related to the facts. Fact-based decisions predominate in settings where the facts are undisputable, as in fields of science. In business, other influences—such as assumptions, opinions, politics, previous experiences, and prevailing culture—tend to tilt scales heavily. So overcoming challenges and roadblocks on the pathway to implementing EGP goes far beyond pulling data together. It means sizing up the real reasons behind the eventual lack of support and launching a program to overcome resistance. Approaches for dealing with the challenges fall into two categories: the proactive preventive school and the corrective, fix-it tack. Both views are required to overcome the roadblocks.

Preventing Challenges and Roadblocks

Here are ways to mitigate problems en route to EPG:

- Show what the competition is doing with regard to project management.
- Demonstrate studies from professional associations, such as PMI and IPMA, regarding the impact of an organizational approach to project management.
- Benchmark with other companies with known expertise in high-level project management.
- Do a risk analysis of the implementation project, including factors such as probable challenges, likelihood of occurrence, and stakeholder influences.

Getting Around Challenges and Roadblocks

Here are some corrective approaches to unexpected barriers:

- Put the program temporarily on pause. Sometimes time itself will sort out an issue.
- Reevaluate the situation. What has changed? What new factors have come into play?
- Replan. If a plausible plan B is on standby, then put it into play. If not, then develop a modified plan.

Challenges and Roadblocks in Implementing EPG Components

Major organizational components of EPG are portfolio management, program management, support for project management (PMOs), and the managing of projects themselves. Since EPG is not necessarily implemented as an integrated program from the outset, the components are often not articulated along a coordinated time frame. In fact, the components are usually implemented as the need arises within the organization, independently from a global EPG movement. The implementation of each of these components may meet with its own set of peculiar roadblocks. Next are some challenges for implementing the major organizational components.

Challenges in Implementing Project Portfolio Management

Project portfolio management takes place at a level in the organization that involves major alignment among stakeholders. The complexity of managing the demands for projects, in addition to dealing with the multiple stakeholders, constitutes a complex scenario, complete with potential challenges. The challenges in dealing with project portfolios are numerous, but the major pitfalls are five:

1. *The Lack of Alignment with Strategic Goals.* This may be due to poor initial alignment when strategic projects are originally defined or due to projects having strayed from the initial intent and without realignment.

2. *Excess Active Projects with Not Enough Resources to Handle Them.* Having too many projects and not enough resources boils down to a lack

of prioritization, which is perhaps the most common of all portfolio challenges.

3. *Projects with Insufficient Value to the Organization.* This portfolio defect stems from poor prioritization of the strategic projects, when undue emphasis is given to less strategic projects for internal political reasons.

4. *The Lack of Structure and Focus on Portfolio Issues.* When structure and organization are lacking in project portfolios, dealing with issues, such as accelerating or aborting, becomes a challenge. The lack of structured support for project implementation is also a potential hazard.

5. *Unbalanced Portfolio.* Lopsided portfolios with too much weight on, say, production as opposed to sales or on short term versus long term may prove disastrous. Portfolios require equilibrium.

Effective portfolio management depends on an organization's ability to deal with these five hurdles, all of which stem from lack of definition by upper management. Issues such as return on investment, executive sponsorship, prioritization, resource allocation, formal portfolio processes, proper documentation, and project interrelationships are all under the control of upper management. If these types of issues are properly defined, then the role of the portfolio manager is greatly facilitated. If not, the portfolio manager is required to help facilitate these issues and strive to obtain the needed definitions by interacting with the appropriate decision-making parties.

Program Management

Programs also encounter barriers. Since they involve multiple projects, the number of challenges is naturally greater. Here are the potential roadblocks for managing programs:

1. *The Lack of Sufficient Stakeholder Management.* Stakeholders abound in programs. They range from upper-level decision makers—involving financing institutions, corporate executives, and government officials—to interorganizational relationships between players from business units, departments, and individual projects. This array of interested parties

presents a major challenge because each stakeholder has individual interests, opinions, and biases. So stakeholder management, involving mapping, planning, and action items, is fundamental for the success of programs.

2. *Insufficient Interfacing Among Projects.* Since a program is a group of related projects managed in a coordinated manner to obtain benefits and control not available from managing them individually, effective interfacing between projects becomes particularly crucial. Projects managed under a program umbrella are designed to benefit from synergy, and that synergy depends on the artful management of the relationships among projects. Effective interfacing depends on having in place the basics of program communication, including a steering committee, program governance, and communications matrix with scheduled meetings.

3. *Inadequate Leadership.* Leadership at the program level calls for talents and abilities that extend beyond the requirements of wrangling a single project. The responsibilities are broader in nature and require a powerful component of political savvy. Therefore, while great project managers might perform well at the program level, if they have a tendency to dwell on project details, they will ultimately be rightly accused of micromanagement, which is definitely not an admirable quality for program managers. The choice of the right leader for the program—one with political, organizational, and communications skills—greatly increases the chances for the success of the program as a whole.

4. *Poor Allocation of Resources Across the Program.* Part of the logic behind herding related projects into programs is to economize on resources. This results in savings in cost, manpower, and infrastructure, and it boosts the chances of the program's meeting its goals. Program-wide resource planning is the key to making sure that the individual project needs are met and that at the same time valuable resources are not squandered unnecessarily.

Upper management is ultimately responsible for making sure the program is properly led, managed, and controlled and that it stays the course in delivering the originally envisioned benefits. When a group is responsible for project portfolio management, that group can also influence the destiny of programs. Likewise, a corporate-level PMO is also positioned to exercise positive influence on program management.

Support for Project Management

The implementation of PMOs presents challenges from both an organizational and a political standpoint. Project offices range from slightly supportive at one extreme to the all-powerful on the other end. The names vary greatly, reflecting the myriad versions in practice, as described in Chapter 7. In spite of the diverse types of PMOs, the challenges relating to their implementation have points in common and fall under these categories: context, organization and people, support functions, and project execution responsibility.

1. *Ambiguous Context.* When the relationship of the PMO to the overall context of the enterprise is unclear, the PMO finds itself adrift in an organization of shifting winds. This fuzzy situation tends to spawn insecurity and conflicts, and ultimately it undermines the effectiveness of the PMO.

2. *Organization and People.* How the PMO is structured has a strong impact on its effectiveness, as well as on the formal relationship of the PMO with other parts of the organization. Another challenge encompasses stakeholder management, which calls for mapping and managing all the parties with a stake in the activities and results produced by the PMO, as discussed in Chapter 8.

3. *Poor Alignment of Support Functions.* Although PMOs provide support and control, they do not manage projects. Each project team does that. The PMO acts more as an interface between the organization's interests and each project's needs. The alignment of what the PMO does in support of projects versus what the project team itself is to do is crucial for the successful implementation of the PMO.

4. *Unclear Project Execution Responsibility.* While some PMOs may have a predominant hands-on responsibility, others are strictly strategic in nature. Independently of the scope, however, the ultimate challenge of a PMO is to see that the projects under its umbrella are performed on time, under budget, and to the satisfaction of the client. So a responsibility matrix, showing the roles of key players, is particularly important.

Each of the four categories contains potential pitfalls. To avoid negative consequences, what is needed is a proactive stance that takes into account the context for the PMO, organization and people, support functions, and project execution responsibility.

Managing Projects

Here's another view of potential challenges and roadblocks, this time from the vantage point of individual projects. In some cases, when EPG or its components are in place, the potential challenges are partially mitigated.

1. *Poor Link Between the Project and the Organization's Priorities.* A serious disconnect between a project's and company priorities may result in a successful project but little or no contribution to the company cause. In its most extreme case, this corresponds to the medical pronouncement: "The operation was a success, but the patient died." Here's how to avoid such a disaster:
   - Identify which items of the strategic plan the project supports.
   - Understand the priority of this strategic plan item.
   - Clarify the value that the project brings to the business.
   - Establish critical success factors (CSFs) for the project, and obtain agreement with stakeholders.

2. *Unclear Sponsorship and Ownership of Project.* This pitfall can have a devastating affect on a project. Even though the project itself may start out on course, the lack of clear sponsorship and governance policies is

a minefield as the project moves on through changing contexts and scenarios. To avert potential roadblocks, here are questions for clarification:

- Does the project management team have a clear view of the interdependencies among the projects, the benefits, and the criteria against which success will be judged?
- If the project traverses organizational boundaries, are there clear governance arrangements to ensure sustainable alignment with the business objectives of all the organizations involved?
- Are decisions taken early and decisively, and are they followed in order to facilitate successful delivery?
- Does the project have the necessary formal approval to proceed?
- Does the sponsor have the ability, responsibility, and authority to ensure that the business change and business benefits are delivered?
- Does the sponsor have a suitable track record of delivery? When necessary, is this being optimized through training?
- Are the governance arrangements robust enough to ensure that bad news is not filtered out of progress reports to senior managers?

3. *Lack of Engagement with Stakeholders.* Since projects are carried out by people, stakeholder management deserves to be put at the forefront of any project. The challenge on individual projects is to ensure that this managerial focus is maintained. Here are checklist questions to help ensure a strong stakeholder focus:

- Have the stakeholders been identified and prioritized?
- Have a common understanding and agreement of stakeholder requirements been secured?
- Does the business case take into account the views of all stakeholders?
- Is a stakeholder management plan in place to ensure buy-in, overcome resistance to change, and allocate risk to the party best able to manage it?
- Has sufficient account been taken of the existing organizational culture?

4. *Inadequate Project Management and Related Skills.* No project can be

expected to be successful if the basics of project management are absent. A lack of methodologies, planning techniques, and implementation approaches are enough to derail any project initiative. For a project to avoid these dangers, the following questions beg for a positive response:

- Is there a skilled and experienced project team with clearly defined roles and responsibilities?
- Have sufficient resources been allocated to the project?
- Are there adequate approaches for estimating, monitoring, and controlling the total expenditure?
- Are there effective systems for measuring and tracking the benefits proposed in the business case?
- Is the project founded on realistic timescales, taking account of statutory lead times and showing critical dependencies so that delays can be handled?
- Are the lessons learned from relevant projects being applied?
- Have enough review points been built in so that the project can be stopped, if changing circumstances mean that the business benefits are no longer achievable?

5. *Scope Creepage, Change, and Risk.* Change happens to some degree, all day and every day. And certainly during the life of projects, changes of various degrees are bound to happen for better and for worse. The challenge in all projects is to keep change from jerking the project off course and swerving away from delivering the desired benefits. Risk is also related to change and requires preventive management. Here are the critical questions regarding change, risk, and their potential for affecting project scope:

- Is scope management part of the project plan?
- Is a change management committee in place?
- Are the changes being reviewed against the business case?
- What is the long-term plan beyond this implementation? Are the next steps defined?

- How will the upcoming changes impact the end users and other involved parties?
- Have the processes been analyzed and a plan established to align with the upcoming changes?
- Are the major risks identified, weighted, and treated?
- Has a shared risk register been established?

6. *Team Integration.* Lack of synergy among team members is potentially one of the most damaging of challenges to the success of projects. The barriers include breakdowns in communications, interpersonal conflicts, and poor group dynamics. The following questions help size up the readiness of the project team:

- Have the needs for behavioral development been assessed?
- Is there a project team development plan?
- Have integration events been planned to ensure that all stakeholders are aligned?
- Is there early supplier involvement to determine and validate what outputs and outcomes are sought for the project?

Conclusions

Challenges are bound to appear along the path to EPG. Challenges to overcome include justification, motivation for change, and how to organize and prepare people. To get around roadblocks, displaying the facts is not enough because organizational change is strongly affected by factors such as tradition, opinions, and politics. Ways to prevent potential challenges involve situational analysis, planning, and carrying through with a change program. Corrective approaches to unexpected roadblocks include backtracking, reanalysis, and replanning. The individual components of EPG, such as project portfolio management (PPM), program management, PMOs, and management of individual projects, are often implemented separately. These independent implementations also present challenges and roadblocks that ultimately may have a major impact on the overall effort to institute project management seamlessly across the enterprise.

Sarbanes-Oxley Compliant Projects

Sarbanes-Oxley (SOX) legislation centers on ensuring the accuracy, consistency, transparency, and timeliness of financial results and reports. Its section 302 mandates that CEOs and CFOs attest to the accuracy of their company's quarterly and annual reports. Section 404 is the most demanding for demonstrating compliance. This section involves establishing, maintaining, and assessing an effective internal control structure for public corporations. It requires a statement in the annual report on the adequacy of internal controls and that management has the responsibility to institute and sustain an internal control structure.

The added challenge of section 404 is the auditor's attestation report. Not only must organizations ensure that appropriate controls are in place, they must also provide their independent auditors with documentation supporting management's assessment of internal controls, including project and program controls. This means that auditors are required to review projects and programs to ensure that all established control processes are being followed.

The Stock and Exchange Commission in the United States (SEC) has recognized Committee of Sponsoring Organizations (COSO) as the preferred framework for SOX compliance. COSO is a voluntary, private sector organization dedicated to improving the quality of financial reporting through business ethics, effective internal control, and corporate governance. According to the COSO framework, internal controls consist of five interrelated components:

1. *Control Environment.* The control environment sets the tone of an organization by establishing attitude standardization. It is the foundation for all other components of internal control, providing discipline and structure. Control environment factors include the integrity, ethical values, and competence of the corporation's people, management philosophy, and operating style.

2. *Risk Assessment.* Every entity faces a variety of risks from external and internal sources, and those risks must be assessed. Because economic, industry, regulatory, and operating conditions will continue to change, mechanisms are needed to identify and deal with the special risks associated with that change.

3. *Control Activities.* Control activities are the policies and procedures that help ensure that management directives are carried out—that the necessary actions are taken to address risks during the achievement of company objectives. They also ensure that control activities occur throughout the organization, at all levels and in all functions. They include a range of activities as diverse as approvals, authorizations, verifications, reconciliations, reviews of operating performance, security of assets, and segregation of duties.

4. *Information and Communication.* Pertinent information must be identified, captured, and communicated in a form and time frame that enables people to carry out their responsibilities. Information systems produce reports containing financial-related information that make it possible to control the reliability of financial reporting.

5. *Monitoring.* Internal control systems need to be monitored. This is accomplished through ongoing monitoring activities, separate evaluations, or a combination of the two. Internal control deficiencies should

be reported upstream, with serious matters reported to top management and the board.

The failure to properly disclose information and the failure to properly scope major projects are as much a failure of the performing organization's corporate governance systems as they are a failure of the organization's project management systems. From the evidence, it would appear that the majority of boards still have to deal with the issues surrounding the effective governance of projects within their organizations.

What can project-based organizations do to ensure compliance with the Sarbanes-Oxley Act? If there is no properly defined internal process for project management, then, according to section 404 of the Sarbanes-Oxley Act, one has to be implemented. Legal accountability for poor project management does not rest only on the shoulders of CEOs and CFOs. Project managers may also find themselves liable. The financial mismanagement of a company's projects may leave project managers and senior management legally exposed. If a cost overrun is not foreseen and anticipated in financial forecasts, the effects may seriously impact the project profit for a given period.

Forecasting cost and revenue on all projects or project portfolios, analyzing and measuring financial risk, maintaining real-time data about where a project is against budget, having traceability of the data, and documenting and standardizing core processes and best practices are all examples of how project managers reinforce the decision making of their financial executives and comply with Sarbanes-Oxley.

Projects and programs are under the umbrella of SOX compliance if they are classified as financially significant. And once they are considered financially significant:

1. It is vital for the project manager to understand the Sarbanes-Oxley Act and its impact on the project.
2. Record retention is vital for SOX compliance. The project manager is responsible for retaining project-related documents.
3. Working with the SOX steering committee is vital for effectively managing these projects. These committees are in existence to ensure that

all SOX compliance projects are following the methodology necessary to successfully manage these types of projects.

4. For companies with a corporate PMO, these offices should incorporate SOX compliance within their project management methodology.

The changes to corporate governance have in turn mandated the need to establish formal internal controls with regard to IT project management. In addition, because the auditors must certify that all internal controls are being followed during their annual audit of the company, the need to document each control process is also required. Operational executives (such as the CTO, CIO, COO, and the director of PMO) and project managers need to know about the potential threats that can cause poor governance. These executives must evaluate whether their company is suffering from the following material weaknesses:

- *Financial Threat.* Ineffective budget, cost, and revenue tracking, in addition to the lack of chargebacks and cost allocations to business units.
- *Process Threat.* Loosely defined inconsistent business processes for project control.
- *Governance Threat.* Material weaknesses of internal controls that result in internal or external governance audit failure.
- *Compliance Threat.* The violation of various industry and government regulations, such as employment wage laws, fair labor laws, and generally accepted accounting principles.

An IT internal control framework is needed to create an environment that is prepared for the audits now mandated by SOX. Several IT internal control frameworks exist, but the IT control objectives known as COBIT are considered particularly useful and aligned with the spirit of SOX requirements.

Notes and Sources

Preface

1. Dinsmore, Paul, and J. Cabanis-Brewin. *AMA Handbook of Project Management*, 3rd ed. New York: AMACOM, 2010.
2. Dinsmore, Paul. *Human Factors in Project Management*. New York: AMACOM, 1984.
3. Dinsmore, Paul. *Winning in Business with Enterprise Project Management*. New York: AMACOM, 1999.
4. Englung, Graham, and Paul Dinsmore. *Creating the Project Office*. San Francisco: Jossey-Bass, 2003.
5. Dinsmore, Paul, and Terry Cooke-Davies. *Right Projects Done Right: From Business Strategy to Successful Project Implementation*. San Francisco: Jossey-Bass, 2006.

Chapter 1: Introduction to Enterprise Project Governance

1. *OECD Principles of Corporate Governance*, rev. ed. Paris: OECD, 2004. http://www.oecd.org/daf/corporate/principles.
2. Bumiller, Elisabeth. "Bush Signs Bill Aimed at Fraud in Corporations."

New York Times, July 31, 2002. http://query.nytimes.com/gst/fullpage. html?res=9C01E0D91E38F932A05754C0A9649C8B63.

3. Higgs, Derek. "Review of the Role and Effectiveness of Non-Executive Directors." Department for Business, Enterprise and Regulatory Reform, January 20, 2003. http://www.berr.gov.uk/files/file23012.pdf.

4. During 10 years as president of the World Bank, James D. Wolfensohn implemented a range of significant reforms to help achieve its mission and broke ground in several major areas, including corruption, debt relief, disabilities, the environment, and gender. http://www. worldbank.org/wolfensohn.

Chapter 2: The Essence of Enterprise Project Governance

1. Association for Project Management (APM). *Directing Change: A Guide to Governance of Project Management.* High Wycombe, UK: APM, 2004. http://www.apm.org.uk/Directingchange.asp.

2. Project Management Institute. *PMBOK, Organizational Project Management Maturity Model (OPM3)*, 2nd ed. Newtown Square, Penn.: PMI, 2008.

3. Office of Government Commerce. *Portfolio, Programme and Project Management Maturity Model (P3M3)*, v 2.1. London: OGC, 2010.

4. International Organization for Standardization. *Standard ISO 21500 Guidance on Project Management.* Geneva: ISO, 2012.

5. Airways. *Vision 2015: A Strategic Vision of Air Traffic Management in New Zealand to 2015 and Beyond.* Christchurch, New Zealand: 2009. www.airways.co.nz/documents/Vision_2015_Strategic_Document.pdf.

6. NAO. *The Failure of Metronet.* London: Stationery Office, 2009.

Chapter 3: Linking Strategy to Portfolio

1. Unilever. *Unilever Annual Review 1999.* London: 2000. http:// www.unilever.com/images/1999%20Previous%20Years%20EN%20 Sterling_tcm13-5374.pdf.

2. Cescau, Patrick, and Richard Rivers. *Unilever Investors Seminar.* London: 2007. http://www.unilever.com/images/ir_1.2_growth_ strategy_rivers_speech_tcm13-86705.pdf and http://www.unilever. com/images/ir_1.2_growth_strategy_slides_rivers_1303_ppt_tcm13-86707.pdf.

3. Unilever. *Unilever Annual Review 2004.* London: 2004. http://www. unilever.com/images/2004%20Annual%20Review%20%20-%20 English_tcm13-11991.pdf.

4. Unilever Press Release. "Unilever Streamlines Its Leadership Structure." London: October 2, 2005. http://www.unilever.com/mediacentre/ pressreleases/2005/Unileverstreamlinesitsleadershipstructure.aspx.

5. Unilever Press Release. "Unilever CEO Succession." London: April 9, 2008. http://www.unilever.com/mediacentre/pressreleases/2008/ announcement040908.aspx.

6. Polman, Paul. "Unilever Investor Seminar, Setting the Scene." Singapore: Unilever, 2010. http://www.unilever.com/images/ppirsingaporefinal_ tcm13-241474.pdf.

7. Markoff, John. "Michael Dell Should Eat His Words, Apple Chief Suggests." *New York Times*, January 1, 2006. http://www.nytimes. com/2006/01/16/technology/16apple.html.

8. Helft, Miguel, and Ashlee Vance. "Apple Passes Microsoft as Number 1 in Tech." *New York Times*, May 26, 2010. http://www.nytimes. com/2010/05/27/technology/27apple.html.

9. Lashinsky, Adam. "How Jobs Transformed Apple." *CNN Money*, May 11, 2010. http://money.cnn.com/2009/11/04/technology/steve_jobs_ ceo_decade.fortune/index2.htm.

10. Grossman, Lev. "How Apple Does It." *Time*, October, 16, 2005. http:// www.time.com/time/magazine/article/0,9171,1118384-1,00.html.

11. Morris, Betsy. "Steve Jobs Speaks Out." *Fortune*. March 2008. http:// money.cnn.com/galleries/2008/fortune/0803/gallery.jobsqna. fortune/.

12. Associated Press. "Incoming Nokia CEO Stephen Elop." *Bloomberg*

BusinessWeek, September 10, 2010. http://www.businessweek.com/ap/financialnews/D9I54Q0G0.htm.

13. TOI Tech. "Nokia's CEO Letter to Employees." *Times of India,* February 9, 2011. http://articles.timesofindia.indiatimes.com/2011-02-09/telecom/28546254_1_oil-platform-strategy-and-financial-briefing-nokia-ceo.

14. Wong, Grace. "JetBlue Fiasco: $30M Price Tag." *CNN Money,* February 20, 2007. http://money.cnn.com/2007/02/20/news/companies/jet_blue/index.htm.

15. Barger, Mike. "A Framework for the Development of an Effective Learning Function and a Mechanism for Evaluating Learning Function Performance." University of Pennsylvania, January 1, 2009. http://repository.upenn.edu/dissertations/AAI3374192.

16. Harries, Sarah. "The 'Grandfather of Benefits Management' Perhaps ...." *Benefits Management SIG Newsletter.* London: APM, January 25, 2010. http://apm5dimensions.com/sites/default/files/newsletter%201_0.html.

17. World Bank. *The LogFrame Handbook. A Logical Framework to Project Cycle Management.* Washington, D.C.: World Bank, 2005.

18. Australian National Audit Office. *Performance Information in Portfolio Budget Statements.* Canberra, Australia: ANAO, 2001.

Chapter 4: Risk Management: Dealing with Uncertainty

1. Rumsfeld, Donald. "DOD News Briefing—Secretary Rumsfeld and Gen. Myers, News Transcript." U.S. Department of Defense. Washington, D.C.: February 12, 2002. http://www.defense.gov/transcripts/transcript.aspx?transcriptid=2636.

2. Clausewitz, Carl von. *On War.* Ed. and trans. Michael Howard and Peter Paret. Princeton, N.J.: Princeton University Press, 1976, p. 101.

3. "Loss of the Shuttle; Excerpts from the Report of the Columbia Investigation Board." *New York Times,* August 27, 2003. The quote can

be found in the Board Statement, and the full report can be retrieved from NASA's investigation Web site (http://caib.nasa.gov). http://www.nytimes.com/2003/08/27/us/loss-shuttle-excerpts-report-columbia-accident-investigation-board.html.

4. NASA. "2000. Enhancing Mission Success—A Framework for the Future." http://history.nasa.gov/niat.pdf. Also, NASA risk management archives: http://www.hq.nasa.gov/office/codeq/risk/risk_archive.htm.

5. Deepwater Horizon Investigation Report. http://www.bp.com/liveassets/bp_internet/globalbp/globalbp_uk_english/incident_response/STAGING/local_assets/downloads_pdfs/Deepwater_Horizon_Accident_Investigation_Report.pdf.

6. FT Reports. "Backlash Greets BP's Internal Report." *Financial Times*, September 8, 2010. http://www.ft.com/cms/s/0/e76e6e68-bb36-11df-b3f4-00144feab49a.html#axzz1OoSi10ot.

7. Commission Final Report on the BP Deepwater Horizon Oil Spill. http://www.oilspillcommission.gov/.

8. COSO definition of internal control can be retrieved at http://www.coso.org/IC-IntegratedFramework-summary.htm. COSO reference for internal control is the publication *Internal Control—Integrated Framework*.

9. It is worth checking the BHP Billiton Web site (http://www.bhpbilliton.com/bb/aboutUs/governance.jsp) to analyze how their corporate governance is structured, especially the terms of reference for the audit and risk committee.

10. Tilley, Kate. "Risk Management in Practice: Keeping Your Risks Close." *Risk Management*, December 6, 2011. http://www.riskmanagementmagazine.com.au/articles/93/0C052193.asp?Type=125&Category=1239.

11. Aabo, Tom, John R. S. Fraser, and Betty J. Simkins. "The Rise and Evolution of the Chief Risk Officer: Enterprise Risk Management at Hydro One." *Journal of Applied Corporate Finance*, Vol. 17, No. 3, October 6, 2011.

12. Beasley, Mark, Bruce Branson, and Bonnie Hancock. "Current State of Enterprise Risk Oversight and Market Perceptions of COSO's ERM Framework." COSO, 2010. http://www.coso.org/documents/COSOSurveyReportFULL-Web-R6FINALforWEBPOSTING111710.pdf.

13. "ISO Risk Management—Principles and Guidelines, ISO 31000." Geneva: 2009.

14. Basel II. www.basel-ii-accord.com/Basel_ii_719_to_817_Supervisory_Review_Process.htm.

Chapter 5: Project Portfolio Management: The Right Combination of the Right Projects

1. Levine, H. A. *Project Portfolio Management: A Practical Guide to Selecting Projects, Managing Portfolios and Maximizing Benefits.* San Francisco: Jossey-Bass, 2005.

2. Dinsmore, Paul C., and Terry Cooke-Davies. *Right Projects Done Right: From Business Strategy to Successful Project Implementation.* San Francisco: Jossey-Bass, 2006.

3. Dinsmore, Paul. *Winning in Business with Enterprise Project Management.* New York: AMACOM, 1999.

4. Project Management Institute. *The Standard for Portfolio Management*, 2nd ed. Newtown Square, Penn.: PMI, 2008.

5. da Silva, Amanda C. Simões, Mischel Carmen N. Belderrain, and Francisco Carlos M. Pantoja. "Prioritization of R&D Projects in the Aerospace Sector: AHP Method with Ratings." *Journal Aerospace Technology Magazine*, Vol. 2, No. 3, September–December, 2010. pp. 339–348.

6. Kendall, Gerald, and Steven Rollins. *Advanced Project Portfolio Management and the PMO.* Fort Lauderdale, Fla.: J. Ross Publishing, 2005.

7. Dye, Lowell, and James S. Pennypacker. *Project Portfolio Management.* Glen Mills, Penn.: Center for Business Practices, 1999.

Chapter 6: Turning Strategy into Reality

1. Economist Intelligence Unit. "Strategy Execution: Achieving Operational Excellence, The Benefits of Management Transparency." *Economist*, November 2004.

2. American Management Institute and Human Resource Institute. *Keys to Strategy Execution, A Global Study of Current Trends and Future Possibilities*. New York: AMACOM, 2007.

3. Conference Board. *CEO Challenges 2007: Top Ten Challenges*. New York: Conference Board, 2007. http://www.conference-board.org/publications/publicationdetail.cfm?publicationid=1362.

4. Bossidy, L., and R. Charan. *Execution: The Discipline of Getting Things Done*. London: Random House, 2002.

5. "Cures for an Industry in Crisis: Big Pharma Scrambles to Find New Ways to Develop Drugs Faster." Knowledge at Wharton, February 10, 2011. http://knowledge.wharton.upenn.edu/article.cfm?articleid=2709.

6. Roland Berger. "Fight or Flight? Diversification Versus Rx—Focus in Big Pharma's Quest for Sustainable Growth. Press Briefing." Germany: Roland Berger, 2010.

7. Redfern, David. "JP Morgan Health Care Conference." San Francisco: GSK, January 12, 2011. http://www.gsk.com/investors/presentations/2011/JPMorgan-Jan11.pdf.

8. Dinsmore, Paul. *Winning in Business with Enterprise Project Management*. New York: AMACOM, 1999.

9. Project Management Institute. *PMBOK, A Guide to the Project Management Book of Knowledge*, 4th ed. Newtown Square, Penn.: PMI, 2008.

10. International Project Management Association. *IPMA Competence Baseline*, v. 3. Netherlands: IPMA, 2008.

11. "A Closer Look: Virginia Department of Transportation." *PM Network Magazine*. Newtown Square, Penn.: Project Management Institute, April 2009, pp. 48–51.

Chapter 7: Organizing for Enterprise Project Governance

1. One of six Global Fund Board committees is the Portfolio and Implementation Committee. http://www.theglobalfund.org/en/board/committees/.

2. L'Oreal Strategy and Implementation Committee clarifies the strategic orientations submitted to the board. http://www.loreal-finance.com/eng/corporate-governance-3#.

3. Dinsmore, Paul. *Winning in Business with Enterprise Project Management.* New York: AMACOM, 1999.

4. Parts of this chapter adapted from Chapter 4 of Randall L. Englung, Robert Graham, and Paul C. Dinsmore. *Creating the Project Office.* San Francisco: Jossey-Bass, 2003.

5. Campos, Roberto. "PMO Estratégico em Contexto Regional." Presented at 7 Forum Nacional de Benchmarking em Gerenciamento de Projetos: PMI-RJ, 2010.

Chapter 8: Stakeholder Management and the Pivotal Role of the Sponsor

1. PM Network. *Double the Stakeholders.* Newtown Square, Penn.: Project Management Institute, 2011, p. 44.

2. De Avila, Joseph. "Why Wal-mart Needs Help." *BNET Business Network,* August 8, 2007. http://www.bnet.com/article/why-wal-mart-needs-help/158177.

3. Walmart Watch. This site contains a lot of information about Walmart from the point of view of Walmart Watch, 2011. http://walmartwatch.org/.

4. Wake Up Walmart is a campaign group founded by the United Food and Commercial Workers Union and is often critical of the business practices of Walmart. http://www.wakeupwalmart.com.

5. Walmart. "Sustainability Progress to Date, 2007–2008." http://

walmartstores.com/sites/sustainabilityreport/2007/documents/SustainabilityProgressToDate2007-2008.pdf.

6. Walmart. "Global Sustainability Report," 2009. http://walmartstores.com/sites/sustainabilityreport/2009/index.html.

7. Walmart. "Global Responsibility Report," 2011. http://walmartstores.com/sustainability/7951.aspx.

8. Dinsmore, Paul. "Tom Peters Is Behind the Times." Dallas, Tex.: Dinsmore Associates, 2009. http://www.dinsmorecorp.com/us/articles/id140/Tom_Peters_is_Behind_the_Times.

9. Dinsmore, Paul. Parts of this chapter adapted from Chapter 6 of *Winning in Business with Enterprise Project Management*. New York: AMACOM, 1999.

10. Parts of this chapter adapted from Paul C. Dinsmore and Terry Cooke-Davies, *Right Projects Done Right: From Business Strategy to Successful Project Implementation*. San Francisco: Jossey-Bass, 2006.

Chapter 9: EPG Performance: Beyond Time, Cost, and Quality

1. Frost, Bob. *Measuring Performance*. Dallas, Tex.: Measurement International, 2000.

2. National Audit Office. *The National Offender Management Information System*. London: Stationery Office, 2009.

3. Ryan, Nelson. "Project Retrospectives Evaluating Project Success, Failures and Everything Between." *MIS Quarterly Executive*, Vol. 4, No. 3, pp. 361–372.

4. National Audit Office. *The Budget for the London 2012 Olympic and Paralympic Games*. London: Stationery Office, 2007, pp. 21–24.

5. Public Accounts Committee. *Preparations for the London 2012 Olympic and Paralympic Games—Risk Assessment and Management*. London: Stationery Office, 2007, pp. 5–6.

6. Jowell, T. "Oral Statement by Tessa Jowell on Costs and Funding

for the 2012 Olympic & Paralympic Games." National Archives. March 2007. http://www.culture.gov.uk/Reference_library/Minister_Speeches/Ministers_Speech_Archive/Tessa_Jowell/oral_statement_funding_2012games.htm.

7. Royer, Isabelle. "Why Bad Projects Are so Hard to Kill." *Harvard Business Review*, February 2003.

8. Anbari, Frank T., et al. *The Chunnel Project, PMI Case Studies in Project Management*. Washington, D.C.: George Washington University, 2004. http://www.pmiteach.org/UploadedDocuments/Faculty_Resources/Chunnel_Project_FTA_Final.pdf.

Chapter 10: EPG in Mega Projects, Joint Ventures, and Alliances

1. John F. Kennedy's Moon Speech at Rice. Houston, Tex.: 1962. http://er.jsc.nasa.gov/seh/ricetalk.htm.

2. IBM. "Capitalizing on Complexity, Insights from the Global Chief Executive Officer Study." IBM: 2010. http://www-935.ibm.com/services/c-suite/series-download.html.

3. National Audit Office. *The Channel Tunnel Rail Link*. London: Stationery Office, 2001.

4. Schreiner, David. "Brazil and Paraguay's Dam Deal." Council of the Americas, July 28, 2009. http://www.americas-society.org/article.php?id=1818&nav=res&subid=54#.

5. CERN. *The Governance of CERN*. Geneva: CERN: 1971. http://council.web.cern.ch/council/en/Governance/Convention.html#5.

6. Anbari, Frank, et al. "Superconducting Super Collider Project." PMI Case Studies in Project Management. Washington, DC: George Washington University, PMI, 2005.

7. Willard, E. "The Demise of the Superconducting Collider: Strong Politics or Weak Management?" PMI Seminar Proceedings, 1994, pp. 1–7.

8. Information about the Large Hadron Collider. http://public.web.cern.ch/public/en/lhc/lhc-en.html.

9. OECD. "Report of the Consultative Group on High-Energy Physics, Global Science Forum." Paris: Organisation for Economic Co-operation and Development, June 2002. http://www.oecd.org/dataoecd/2/32/1944269.pdf.

10. The planning, designing, and funding for the proposed International Linear Collider (ILC) will require global participation and global organization. http://www.linearcollider.org/about/What-is-the-ILC/Status-of-the-project.

11. *Proceedings of Science, Governance of the International Linear Collider Project. 35th International Conference on High-Energy Physics.* Paris: ILC, July 2010. http://ilcdoc.linearcollider.org/record/29465/files/ICHEP_Paris_writeup.pdf.

12. Barish, Barry. "What Did We Accomplish Last Year?" *ILC Newsline*, Director's Corner, January 20, 2011. http://www.newsline.linearcollider.org/2011/01/20/what-did-we-accomplish-last-year/.

13. Sakal, Matthew. "Project Alliancing: A Relational Contracting Mechanism for Dynamic Projects." *Lean Construction Journal*, Vol. 2, 2005, pp. 67–79.

14. Australia is a leading country in Project Alliancing. Information can be found at the site of the Department of Treasure & Finance from the State Government of Victoria. http://www.dtf.vic.gov.au/project-alliancing.

15. Water Corporation. *Water Forever, Options for Our Water Future.* Australia: Water Corporation, April 2008. http://www.watercorporation.com.au/_files/PublicationsRegister/22/Water_Forever_Options_Report.pdf.

16. The present status of Alliancing contracts from Water Corporation. http://www.watercorporation.com.au/_files/InfrastructureProjects/Bundle_Slides_2009.pdf.

17. Daum, J. H. "Management Cockpit War Room: Objectives, Concept and Function, and Futures Prospects of a Still Unusual, but Highly Effective Management Tool." *Controlling—Zeitschrift für die erfolgsorientierte Untemehmensführungs*, Vol. 18, June 2006, pp. 311–318. http://www.iioe.eu/fileadmin/files/publications/MC_Controlling_Daum_e.pdf.

18. Figueiredo, Paulo, et al. "Risk Sharing Partnerships with Suppliers: The Case of Embraer." *Journal of Technology, Management and Innovation*, Vol. 3, No. 1, 2008, pp. 27–37.

19. Drew, Christopher. "A Dream Interrupted at Boeing." *New York Times*, September 5, 2009. http://www.nytimes.com/2009/09/06/business/06boeing.html?pagewanted=all.

20. James, Andrea. "Boeing's 787 Production Is Mission-Controlled." *Seattle.Com*, April 30, 2009. http://www.seattlepi.com/default/article/Boeing-s-787-production-is-mission-controlled-1303651.php.

21. Michaels, D., and P. Sanders. "Dreamliner Production Gets Closer Monitoring." *Wall Street Journal*, October 8, 2009.

22. IBM. *Smarter Cities for Smarter Growth*. New York: IBM Global Services, 2010. http:// www.ibm.com/smarterplanet/us/en/smarter_cities/overview/index.html.

23. "GE, Intel/IBM/Care Innovations, Rio Operations Center." *Contagious Magazine*, January 4, 2011. http://www.contagiousmagazine.com/2011/01/ge_intel_ibm.php.

Chapter 11: EPG for Different Types of Projects

1. D. Hartmann. "Interview with Jim Johnson of the Standish Group." *InfoQ*, 2006. http://www.infoq.com/articles/Interview-Johnson-Standish-CHAOS.

2. IT Governance Institute. *Cobit 4.1 Excerpt and Executive Summary*. Rolling Meadows, IL: ITGI, 2007. http://www.isaca.org/Knowledge-Center/cobit/Documents/COBIT4.pdf.

3. ISO. "Corporate Governance of Information Technologies, ISO IEC 38500." Geneva: ISO, 2008.

4. Bon, J., and T. Verheijen. *Frameworks for IT Management.* Norwich, Netherlands: Van Haren Publishing, 2006.

5. ISACA. *COBIT Case Study: Banco Superville S.A Implements COBIT as it Pursues Expansion.* Rolling Meadows, IL: ISACA, 2011. http://www.isaca.org/Knowledge-Center/cobit/Pages/COBIT-Case-Study-Banco-Supervielle-SA-Implements-COBIT-as-It-Pursues-Expansion.aspx.

6. Water Corporation. "Setting Up Governance for IT Contracts." *Connections Newsletter,* story 4, 2007. http://www.watercorporation.com.au/_files/PublicationsRegister/6/Connections_April_2007.pdf.

7. Cassiman, Bruno, Chiara Di Guardo, and Giovanni Valentini. "Organizing for Innovation: R&D Projects, Activities and Partners." Working Paper, IESE, July 2005. http://www.iese.edu/research/pdfs/DI-0597-E.pdf.

8. "At 3M a Struggle Between Efficiency and Creativity." *Bloomberg BusinessWeek,* June 11, 2007. http://www.businessweek.com/magazine/content/07_24/b4038406.htm.

9. Information about FP7 can be found at the European Commission Cordis Web site. http://cordis.europa.eu/fp7/understand_en.html.

10. Parts of this chapter adapted from Chapter 11 of Paul C. Dinsmore and Terence J. Cooke-Davies. *Right Projects Done Right: From Business Strategy to Successful Project Implementation.* San Francisco: Jossey-Bass, 2006.

11. Chul-boo, Hur. "Samsung Electronics Competes in the New World Order." *Korea IT Times,* April 13, 2010. http://www.koreaittimes.com/story/8315/samsung-electronics-competes-new-world-order.

Chapter 12: The EPG Plan: A Roadmap to Transformation and Success

1. The Fish & Wildlife Compensation Program has delivered more than 700 projects that conserve and enhance fish, wildlife, and their supporting habitats. www.bchydro.com/bcrp/index.html.

2. FWCP, "Backgrounder, An Introduction to the Fish & Wildlife Compensation Program," British Columbia, Canada: FWCP. http://www.fwcpcolumbia.ca/version2/info/media/fwcp-backgrounder.pdf.

3. The Ericsson Props and quote from Inger Bergman in Paul C. Dinsmore and Terence J. Cooke-Davies. *Right Projects Done Right: From Business Strategy to Successful Project Implementation*. San Francisco: Jossey-Bass, 2006, pp. 111–117, 275–280.

4. Pardo, T., et al. *Creating Enhanced Enterprise Information Technology Governance for New York State: A Set of Recommendations for Value-Generating Change*. Albany, NY: Center for Technology in Government, 2009.

Chapter 13: Challenges and Roadblocks

1. Kendall, Gerald I., and Steven C. Rolling. *Advanced Project Portfolio Management and the PMO*, Chap. 2. San Francisco: J. Ross Publishing, 2003.

Glossary

1. Office of Government Commerce. *OGC PPM Portfolio, Glossary of Terms and Definitions*. London: Stationery Office, 2010.

Glossary

accountability—The obligation to answer for a responsibility conferred. It is a relationship based on the obligation to demonstrate and take responsibility for performance in light of agreed expectations, whether or not those actions were within your direct control.

alignment—The purposeful development of sound processes, practices, and evolving human relationships that embrace mutual understandings of goals, values, culture, and capabilities that leverage the development of strategies, and that can ultimately facilitate coadaptation to changing situations and the creation of value for the organization. With alignment, a company's ability to react to increasingly uncertain and dynamic markets is significantly enhanced; companies can define entirely new markets or set the standard of excellence in their industry.

assumptions—Hypotheses regarding the conditions necessary for the realization of strategies over which the organization has no control. Assumptions represent the risks that you may not achieve desired outcomes. Any change to an assumption during the execution cycle should force a revision.

assurance—All the systematic actions necessary to have the confidence that the target (process, program, project, outcome, benefit, capability, product output, deliverable) is appropriate. Assurance must be independent from what is being assured.

benefit—The improvement resulting from outcomes perceived and expressed in terms of advantages for the organization, such as decreases in operating costs or product failures and increases in profit or productivity.

business case—The justification for a project or program, against which performance is compared throughout the life cycle. Typically, the business case contains costs, benefits, risks, and timescales.

compliance—The ability to operate in the way defined by a regulation. Many organizations are introduced to governance concepts as they begin the process of complying with business regulations, such as Sarbanes-Oxley or Basel II. These regulations are enforced by audits that determine whether business decisions were made by the appropriate staff according to appropriate policies. To pass these audits, organizations must document their decision rights, policies, and records, specifically that each of the decisions was in fact made by the appropriate person according to policy.

conformance—The ability to operate in the way defined by a certain standard established to comply with a regulation.

constraint—The restriction or limitation that the project is bound by.

contingency—Something that is held in reserve, typically to handle time and cost variances or risks.

corporate governance—Essentially, decision making and communications. The need for good governance stems from the need of organizations to make good decisions and to communicate them effectively. Often, when faced with poor outcomes, the organization needs to review how the decisions were made and then put into place structures that support better future decisions. It can be considered to encompass relationships among a company's management, its board (or management team), its shareholders, and other stakeholders and to provide the structure through which the objectives of the company are set, as well as the means of attaining those objectives and monitoring performance.[1]

corporate PMO—The structure that serves as the critical link between executive vision and the work of the enterprise in managing the program and project portfolio that result from the strategies to achieve that vision. It provides the organizational home for taking the strategy document and converting it into a portfolio of programs and projects that carry out the strategies. It is a value-adding structure that provides coordination and that has the broad perspective needed to select, prioritize, and monitor projects and programs that contribute to the attainment of corporate strategy.

dashboard—A technique to represent vast amounts of decision-support information at an amalgamated level using tabular and graphic representation, such as graphs and traffic lights.

empowering—The ability to help others achieve their individual potential in order to obtain more effective organizational behavior. Empowering requires the capacity to facilitate conditions that allow people to express themselves better, recognizing the value of their work and stimulating personal and professional growth as well as self-esteem. Empowering is necessary to achieve results and to develop people.

enterprise—A large corporation or government agency. Depending on context, it may also refer to a company of any size with many systems and users to manage. The terms *enterprise, company, corporation,* and *organization* are used synonymously.

enterprise project governance—Project governance initiated under the umbrella of corporate governance. It is about ensuring that projects succeed by establishing a well-defined approach that all parties understand and agree on, that the approach is followed throughout the life cycle of portfolios, programs, and projects, and that progress is measured and actions are proactively taken to confirm that everything stays on track and that the agreed-on benefits, products, or services are delivered.

enterprise project management—A form of project management based on the concept that most managerial energy is expended on the development, planning, and implementation of an organization's portfolio of projects, as opposed to the running of repetitive operations.

escalation—The process by which issues are drawn to the attention of decision levels above the project, program, or portfolio manager.

goal—A statement that qualifies desired results. It is the end toward which efforts are directed. It is normally general and timeless, yet attainable.

governance framework—A set of processes established as authoritative and within which portfolios, programs, and projects are initiated, planned, and executed in order to ensure that goals and benefits are met.

internal control—A process that is affected by an entity's board of directors, management, and other personnel and that is designed to provide reasonable assurance regarding the achievement of objectives in various categories. It comprises the measures to safeguard the organization's assets, check the accuracy of and reliability of data, promote operational efficiency, and encourage adherence to regulations, standards, and norms.

issue—Any concern, query, request for change, suggestion, or off-specification raised during a project. Project issues can be about anything to do with the project.

key performance factor (KPF)—Essential measure of success for the organization, project, program, or portfolio that ensures progress toward a successful conclusion, adding value to the organization.

milestone—A significant event in a plan's schedule, such as the completion of key work packages, a technical stage, or a management stage (OGC[1]).

monitoring—The recording, analyzing, and reporting of performance, as compared to the plan, in order to identify deviations.

objective—The goal broken down into manageable tasks so that you can carry them out and measure for success. It is more precise and capable of both attainment and measurement.

outcome—The result of change, normally affecting real-world behavior and/or circumstances. It is the manifestation of part or all of the new state conceived. Outcomes are desired when a change is conceived. They are achieved as a result of the activities undertaken to effect the change.

output—The tangible or intangible product resulting from planned activity. It enables a new outcome in operations.

performance—The quality of outputs, outcomes, benefits, and results achieved.

performance indicator—The measurement of the execution of activities. A performance indicator is often compared to recommended practices. It is a quantifiable target for achieving the adopted key performance factors. *Metric* is the unit of measure, and *measure* is a specific observation when tracking performance. The terms *performance indicator*, *metric*, and *measure* are often used interchangeably.

policy—A rule or principle that guides or constrains the behavior of someone given decision rights. Policies provide guidelines, sometimes set limits, and sometimes enables behavior. Policies guide decision rights, which are generally conditional. For example, a first-line manager might be allowed to spend money without further approvals below a set figure, and further approvals may be required for expenditures above that amount. A hiring manager may fill a vacancy but cannot hire a relative.

process—A structured set of activities designed to accomplish a specific objective. A process takes one or more defined inputs and turns them into defined outputs (OGC[1]).

product—An input or output, whether tangible or intangible, that can be described in advance, created, and tested (OGC[1]).

program—A collection of projects with a common success criteria under integrated management. These projects consist of people, technology, and processes aimed at implementing significant business and technology change. A program is a major enterprise initiative, an element in the overall business strategy and direction.

project closeout—The last phase of a project that finalizes it and guarantees the acceptance of project, product, service, or facility. It addresses transferring the responsibility of operations, maintenance, and support to the performing organization and considers postproject evaluation, documenting the lessons learned and recommendations to support the success of future projects and communicating results.

project recovery—The effort and activities related to addressing troubled projects, followed by the decision as to whether to save it.

project start-up—The beginning of a project, a significant milestone that lays the groundwork for a successful project life cycle. However, project start-up is often overlooked as an important component of organizational change.

project termination—The action of ending a project before the delivery of its projected outcomes. Conscious project termination at the right time, based on well-communicated criteria, is one of the most serious decisions that a project manager and the board have to make.

responsibility—The authority to directly cause an action, event, or chain of events. It is a feeling of ownership. You can delegate responsibility, but you cannot delegate accountability. If someone gives you a job to do, you can get someone else to do it, but you are still accountable to produce the results. If the job is not done right, the only person to blame is you because, even though you've delegated the responsibility, you are still accountable.

stakeholder—Any individual, group, or organization that can affect, be affected by, or perceive itself to be affected by an initiative (program, project, activity, risk) (OGC[1]).

strategy—The proposed direction an organization will achieve over the long term, through the configuration of resources in a challenging environment, to meet the needs of markets and to fulfill stakeholder expectations.

value—Relative worth or importance of an effort for an organization or its key stakeholders.

Abbreviations and Acronyms

APM—Association of Project Management (United Kingdom)

CEO—chief executive officer

CFO—chief financial officer

CIO—chief information officer

CPMO—corporate project management office

CPO—chief project officer

FEED—front end engineering design

FEL—front end loading

KPI—key performance indicator

OECD—Organisation for Economic Co-operation and Development

PgMO—program management office

PMI—Project Management Institute

PMO—project management office

SOW—statement of work

VIP—value-improving practice

Index

About the Authors

Paul C. Dinsmore is president of Dinsmore Associates and a highly respected specialist in project management and organizational change. A certified project management professional (PMP), he has received the Distinguished Contributions Award and Fellow from the Project Management Institute. Paul regularly consults and speaks in North America, South America, Europe, and Africa. He is the author and/or editor of numerous articles and 18 books, including the *AMA Handbook of Project Management*. Mr. Dinsmore resides in Rio de Janeiro.

Luiz Rocha has more than 30 years of experience in project management and business consulting. Luiz worked with Andersen Consulting and Delloite in the United States and Europe when he had the opportunity to manage multi-cultural and geographically dispersed projects in Latin America, North America, and Europe. Presently he is project director with Dinsmore Associates. Luiz is an engineer by background, holding an MSc in industrial engineering from UFRJ–Brazil, a PMP certification from PMI, and an IPMA-C certification. He is also a published author of two books, *Business Metamorphosis*, in Brazil, and *Mount Athos, a Journey of Self-Discovery*, in the United States.